Student Manual

for

Generalist Practice with Organizations and Communities

Student Manual

for

Generalist Practice with Organizations and Communities
Third Edition

Karen K. Kirst-Ashman
University of Wisconsin, Whitewater
Grafton H. Hull, Jr
University of Utah
Vicki Vogel
University of Wisconsin, Whitewater

THOMSON
WADSWORTH

Australia • Brazil • Canada • Mexico • Singapore • Spain • United Kingdom • United States

Printer: Thomson West

ISBN 0-534-50630-5

Thomson Higher Education
10 Davis Drive
Belmont, CA 94002-3098
USA

For more information about our products,
contact us at:
Thomson Learning Academic Resource Center
1-800-423-0563

For permission to use material from this text or product, submit a request online at
http://www.thomsonrights.com.
Any additional questions about permissions can be submitted by email to **thomsonrights@thomson.com.**

Table of Contents

PREFACE

This Student Manual has been designed to enhance your abilities to comprehend and assimilate course content. This manual contains detailed chapter outlines intended to assist in note-taking during lectures and while reading the text. Also included is a wide range of experiential exercises and classroom discussion guidelines to allow you to apply your knowledge of the content in the book. Please also note that exercise content has been vastly expanded from the previous edition to include what was previously found in *The Macro Skills Workbook.*

The Book Companion Site at www.socialwork.wadsworth.com/ashmanhull3 provides tutorial quizzes pertaining to material and topics covered in each chapter of the book. There you will also find downloadable chapters with information on constructing résumés and finding jobs, in addition to stress and time management. This content is provided because it is vital to your success upon completion of this course.

Chapter 1
Introduction to Generalist Practice with Organizations and Communities

I. **Why Do You Need the Content in this Book?**

II. **The Generalist Intervention Model**

    A. Figure 1.1: Planned Change Steps in the Generalist Intervention Model

    B. Figure 1.2: Steps in the Planned Change Process—Initiating Macro Change

    C. A micro approach

    D. A mezzo approach

    E. A macro approach

III. **What Does Generalist Practice Mean?**

    A. The application of an eclectic knowledge base, professional values, and a wide range of skills to target any size system for change within the context of four primary processes

        1. Emphases client empowerment—the process of increasing personal, interpersonal, or political power so that individuals can take action to improve their life situations

        2. Working effectively within an organizational structure and doing so under supervision

        3. Requires the assumption of a wide range of professional roles

        4. Application of critical thinking skills to the planned change process

    B. Highlight 1.1: Dimensions in the Definition of Generalist Practice

        1. Acquisition of an eclectic knowledge base

            a. Theoretical foundation: Systems theories

            b. Human behavior and the social environment

            c. Social welfare policy and services

            d. Social work practice

            e. Research

            f. Human diversity

g. Promotion of social and economic justice

h. Populations-at-risk

2. Emphasis on client empowerment

3. Acquisition of professional values

    a. National Association of Social Workers Code of Ethics

    b. Awareness of personal values

    c. Clarification of conflicting ethical dilemmas

    d. Understanding of oppression

    e. Respect for diverse populations

4. Use of a wide range of practice skills

    a. Micro

    b. Mezzo

    c. Macro

5. Orientation to target any size system

    a. Micro

    b. Mezzo

    c. Macro

6. Effective work within an organizational structure

7. Appropriate use of supervision

8. Assumption of a wide range of professional roles

    a. Enabler

    b. Mediator

    c. Integrator/Coordinator

    d. General manager

    e. Educator

    f. Analyst/evaluator

g.   Broker

h.   Facilitator

i.   Initiator

j.   Negotiator

k.   Mobilizer

l.   Advocate

9.   Employment of critical thinking skills

10.   Use of a planned change process

    a.   Engagement

    b.   Assessment

        1)   Defining issues

        2)   Collecting and assessing data

    c.   Planning

        1)   Identifying alternative interventions

        2)   Selecting appropriate courses of action

        3)   Contracting

    d.   Implementation of appropriate courses of action

    c.   Evaluation

        1)   Using appropriate courses of action

        2)   Applying appropriate research-based knowledge and technological advances

    f.   Termination

    g.   Follow-up

C.   Figure 1.3: Definition of Generalist Practice

IV.   **Defining Generalist Practice**

IV.1. **Acquisition of an Eclectic Knowledge Base**

    A.   Systems theories

        1.   System: Set of elements that are orderly and interrelated to make a functional whole

        2.   Conceptualizing systems in macro practice

        3.   Client system—any individual, family, group, organization, or community that will ultimately benefit from generalist social work intervention

        4.   Macro Client system—involves larger numbers of clients, families, or groups of clients with similar characteristics or qualifications for receiving resources or services, or an agency or community that will be the beneficiary of the macro intervention process

        5.   The Target system—the system that social workers must change or influence in order to accomplish their goals

        6.   The Change Agent system—individual who initiates the macro change process (you assume the role of the change agent throughout the book)

        7.   The Action system—includes those people who agree and are committed to work together in order to attain the proposed macro change

    B.   Human Behavior and the Social Environment (HBSE)

        1.   Social work has a person-in-environment focus—interactions among individuals, systems, and the environment are critical

        2.   Council on Social Work Education accreditation standard

    C.   Social Welfare Policy and Services

        1.   Social policies involve the actions of government that have a direct impact on the welfare of people by providing services and income

        2.   Agency policies include those standards adopted by individual organizations and programs that provide services

        3.   Historical and analytical perspective concerning how well services meet basic human needs and support the development of human capacities

    D.   Social Work Practice

        1.   The *doing* of social work

        2.   Ability to determine what skills will be most effective in a given situation

E.   Social Work Research

    1.   Guides social workers to become more effective in practice and get better and clearer results

    2.   Empirically grounded knowledge can make a decisive difference in establishing social work as an accountable and respected profession

    3.   Four major categories of social work research:

        a.   Behavior of individual clients and their interactions with others

        b.   How services are provided, what they involve, and how successful they are

        c.   Social workers' attitudes and educational backgrounds, and what's happening in the entire profession

        d.   Organizations, communities, and social policy

F.   Human Diversity

    1.   Discrimination—the act of treating people differently based on the fact that they belong to some group rather than on their own merit

    2.   Oppression—putting extreme limitations and constraints on some person, group, or larger system

    3.   Economic deprivation—the condition of having inadequate or unjust access to financial resources

    4.   Stereotype—a fixed mental picture of members of some specified group based on some attribute or attributes that reflect an overly simplified view of that group, without consideration or appreciation of individual differences

    5.   Highlight 1.2: Empowerment of Lesbian and Gay People at the Macro Level

G.   Promotion of Social and Economic Justice

    1.   Social justice—the idea that, in a perfect world, all citizens would have the same rights, protection, opportunities, obligations, and social benefits (Barker, 1999, p. 451)

    2.   Economic justice—the idea that in a perfect world, resources would be distributed in a fair and equitable manner

H.   Populations-at-Risk

      1.   Groups of people, based on some identified characteristics, are at greater risk of social and economic deprivation than the general mainstream of society

      2.   Social workers need information about the factors that contribute to and constitute being at risk, and insight concerning these populations' special issues and needs

IV.2. Emphasis on Client Empowerment

A.   Empowerment—the process of increasing personal, interpersonal, or political power so that individuals can take action to improve their life situations

B.   Strengths perspective—focuses on client system resources, capabilities, knowledge, abilities, motivations, experience, intelligence, and other positive qualities that can be put to use to solve problems and pursue positive changes

C.   Highlight 1.3: Resiliency: Seeking Strength Amid Adversity

      1.   Resiliency—the ability of an individual, family, group, community, or organization to recover from adversity and resume functioning even when suffering serious trouble, confusion, or hardship

      2.   Two dimensions of resiliency

            a.   Risk—involves stressful life events or adverse environmental conditions that increase the vulnerability (defenseless or helplessness) of individuals or other systems

            b.   Protection—concerns those factors that buffer, moderate, and protect against those vulnerabilities

      3.   Resiliency at the organizational level

      4.   Resiliency in a community

IV.3. Assimilation of Professional Values and Ethics

A.   Values: principles, qualities, and practices that a designated group, individual, or culture deems inherently desirable (what you consider to be right or wrong)

B.   Ethics: principles based on a set of values that serve to guide one's behavior (how you behave based on values)

C.   NASW Code of Ethics

    1.   Six core values:

        a.   *Service*: The provision of help, resources, and benefits so that people may achieve their maximum potential

        b.   *Social justice*: "An ideal condition in which all members of society have the same basic rights, protection, opportunities, obligations, and social benefits" (Barker, 1999, p. 451)

        c.   *Dignity and worth of the person*: Holding in high esteem and appreciating individual value

        d.   *Importance of human relationships*: Valuing "the mutual emotional exchange; dynamic interaction; and affective, cognitive, and behavioral connection that exist between the social worker and the client to create the working and helping atmosphere" (Barker, 1999, p. 407)

        e.   *Integrity*: Maintaining trustworthiness and sound adherence to moral ideals

        f.   *Competence*: Having the necessary skills and abilities to perform work with clients effectively

D.   Awareness of Personal Values—Professionally obligated to prevent personal values that conflict with professional values from interfering with practice

E.   Clarification of Ethical Dilemmas

F.   Understanding Oppression— Recognize the injustice of putting extreme limitations and constraints on some group or institution

G.   Respect for diverse populations

IV.4. & 5. Mastery of a Wide Range of Practice Skills to Target Any Size System

A.   Historically, skills were clustered into three categories:

    1.   Casework

    2.   Group work

    3.   Community organization

B.   Highlight 1.4: Before Macro Practice: Three Models of Community Organization

     1.   Locality development—community change pursued through broad participation of a wide spectrum of people at the local community level

     2.   Social planning—a technical process of problem-solving regarding basic social problems, such as delinquency, housing, and mental health

     3.   Social action—coordinated effort to advocate for change in established laws, customs, or patterns of behavior to benefit a specific population (e.g., homeless people), solve a social problem (e.g., illicit drug use), correct unfairness (e.g., racism), or enhance people's well-being (e.g., improve access to health care)

C.   Generalist perspective assumes a multiple level approach to intervention

     1.   Micro practice—generalist social work practice focusing on planned change with and for individuals

     2.   Mezzo practice—generalist social work practice with small groups

     3.   Macro practice—generalist social work practice intending to affect change in large systems, including organizations and communities

IV.6.   Effective Work within an Organizational Structure

A.   Organizational structure—the formal and informal manner in which tasks and responsibilities, lines of authority, channels of communication, and dimensions of power are established and coordinated within an organization

B.   Agency structure

     1.   Formal—by the book and according to the rules

     2.   Informal—based on the way the agency really works

IV.7.   Use of Supervision

IV.8.   A Wide Range of Roles

A.   Role—a culturally expected behavior pattern for a person having a specified status or being involved in a designated social relationship

B.   Enabler—provides support, encouragement, and suggestions to members of a macro client system so that system may complete tasks or solve problems more easily and successfully

C.   Figure 1.4: The Enabler Role in Macro Practice

D.   Mediator—resolves arguments or disagreements among micro, mezzo, or macro systems in disagreement

E.   Figure 1.5: The Mediator Role in Macro Practice

F. Integrator/Coordinator—brings people involved in various systems together and organizes their performance

G. Figure 1.6: The Integrator/Coordinator Role in Macro Practice

H. General Manager: assumes some level of administrative responsibility for a social services agency or some other organizational system. Administrators utilize three levels of skills:

    1. Technical skills—those used to direct an agency's basic activities such as overseeing counseling techniques, developing programs, or evaluating the agency's effectiveness

    2. People skills—concern interpersonal effectiveness such as oral communication, listening, conflict management, leading, and motivating

    3. Conceptual skills—those oriented toward assessing and understanding the overall operation of the agency and how it fits into its larger macro environment

I. Figure 1.7: The General Manager Role in Macro Practice

J. Educator—conveys information and teaches skills to other systems

K. Figure 1.8: The Educator Role in Macro Practice

L. Analyst/Evaluator—ascertains the effectiveness of a program or agency

M. Figure 1.9: The Analyst/Evaluator Role in Macro Practice

N. Broker—links any size system with community resources and services

O. Figure 1.10: The Broker Role in Macro Practice

P. Facilitator: guides a group experience

Q. Figure 1.11: Facilitator Role in Macro Practice

R. Initiator—calls attention to an issue

S. Figure 1.12: The Initiator Role in Macro Practice

T. Negotiator: intermediary who acts to settle disputes and/or resolve disagreements, clearly taking the side of one of the parties involved

U. Figure 1.13: The Negotiator Role in Macro Practice

V. Mobilizer—identifies and convenes community people and resources and makes them responsive to unmet community need

W. Figure 1.14: The Mobilizer Role in Macro Practice

X.   Advocate—steps forward and speaks out on the behalf of the client system in order to promote fair and equitable treatment or gain needed resources or services

Y.   Figure 1.15: The Advocate Role in Macro Practice

IV.9. Critical Thinking Skills (Gibbs et al., 1994, 1996)

A.   Critical thinking—the ability to use intellectual and affective processes which evaluate statements, arguments, and experiences by judging the validity and/or worth of those statements, arguments, and experiences

B.   Critical thinking in social work practice involves:

1.   A predisposition to question conclusions that concern client care and welfare

2.   Asking "does it work?" and "how do you know?" when confronted with claims that a method helps clients, and also questioning generalizations about treatment methods and clients

3.   Weighing evidence for and against assertions in a logical, rational, systematic, data-based way

4.   Analyzing arguments to see what is being argued, spotting and explaining common fallacies in reasoning, and applying basic methodological principles of scientific reasoning

C.   Practice fallacies that can trick practitioners into false beliefs

1.   Charisma, charm, and possibly even glamour

2.   Newness and experience

3.   "Fact" that if something is written down, then it must be true

IV.10. The Planned Change Process

A.   Engagement

1.   Involve yourself in the situation

2.   Establish communication with everyone concerned

3.   Begin to define the parameters within which the worker and the client(s) will work

4.   Create an initial working structure

10

B.   Assessment: Identifying issues and collecting information

    1.   Identifying your client system

    2.   Assessing the client system's problems and needs from a macro perspective

    3.   Identifying client strengths

C.   Assessment and Planning in Macro Practice: The PREPARE Process

    1.   Figure 1.16: Macro Practice Planned Change

    2.   Figure 1.17: PREPARE: An Assessment of Organizational or Community Change Potential

        a.   **P**REPARE Step 1—Identify **Problems** to address

        b.   P**R**EPARE Step 2—Review your macro and personal **Reality**

        c.   PR**E**PARE Step 3—**Establish** primary goals

        d.   PRE**P**ARE Step 4—Identify relevant **People** of influence

        e.   PREP**A**RE Step 5—**Assess** potential costs and benefits to clients and agency

        f.   PREPA**RE** Step 6—Review professional and personal **Risk**

        g.   PREPAR**E** Step 7—**Evaluate** the potential success of a macro change process

D.   Implementation and Evaluation in Macro Practice: The **IMAGINE** process

    1.   Figure 1.18: IMAGINE: A Process for Initiating and Implementing Macro Change

        a.   **I**MAGINE Step 1—Start with an innovative **Idea**

        b.   I**M**AGINE Step 2—**Muster** support and formulate an action system

        c.   IM**A**GINE Step 3—Identify **Assets**

        d.   IMA**G**INE Step 4—Specify **Goals**, objectives, and action steps to attain them

        e.   IMAG**I**NE Step 5—**Implement** the plan

        f.   IMAGI**N**E Step 6—**Neutralize** opposition

        g.   IMAGIN**E** Step 7—**Evaluate** progress

E.   Termination in Macro Practice

F.   Follow-up in Macro Practice

V.   **Postscript**

A.   Highlight 1.5: The History of Generalist Practice with Organizations and Communities in the Professional Context

1.   Three major economic and social changes in United States (between the Civil War and World War I)

a.   Industrialization

b.   Urbanization

c.   Explosive immigration

2.   Two social and ideological movements that became the foundation for social work practice in the 1880s

a.   The Settlement House Movement

1)   Settlement houses—places where ministers, students, or humanitarians "settled" to interact with poor slum dwellers with the purpose of alleviating the conditions of capitalism

2)   Formed a strong partial foundation for generalist social work practice

3)   Emphasized the empowerment of people

4)   The concept of community organization and group work developed within the settlement house context

5)   Jane Addams and Ellen Gates Starr began Hull House in Chicago in 1889

b.   The Charity Organization Societies (COS)

1)   COS emphasis was not on lay communal expertise but on scientific practice and expert knowledge

2)   "Friendly visitors" tried to help people figure out how to solve their problems

3)   Focused on curing individuals rather than on empowering communities—traditional casework developed from this approach

3.   Three method tracks (casework, group work, and community organization) characterized social work through the 1950s

4. The Great Depression of the 1930s and the Social Security Act switched many aspects of service provision from the private to the public sector

5. During the 1950s social workers turned again to psychotherapy and case work

6. The 1960s produced a new focus on social change versus individual pathology

7. Accountability became a key word when talking about social service provision

8. In 1955, seven separate professional organizations came together to form the National Association of Social Workers

9. The Council on Social Work Education (CSWE), the field's accrediting body, was born in 1952 when several predecessor organizations merged

10. The prolific development of BSW programs in the late 1960s and early 1970s emphasized the need for a generalist foundation for social work practice

11. Current thinking is that the BSW is the entry-level degree and the MSW provides advanced, specialized training

---

Experiential Exercises and Classroom Simulations

Exercise 1.1: What Does Generalist Practice Mean?

A. Brief Description
   Students discuss the eight major concepts inherent in the definition of generalist practice.

B. Objectives
   Students will:
   1. Recognize the basic concepts inherent in the definition of generalist practice.
   2. Examine the significance of each concept for social work practice.

C. Procedure
   1. Review the material on the definition of generalist practice, an outline of which is provided in the box below under "Instructions for Students."
   2. Divide the class into small groups of four to six.
   3. Ask the groups to discuss the subsequent questions, select a group representative, and be prepared to report to the entire class the small group's findings.
   4. After about 20 minutes, ask the small groups to terminate their discussions and participate in a full class discussion.
   5. Ask the representative from each group to share her or his summary of the discussion. Encourage comments from all class members.

D. Instructions
   Discuss the reasons why each concept inherent in the definition of generalist practice is important in social work. The box below provides an outline of the definition.

AN OUTLINE OF THE DEFINITION OF GENERALIST PRACTICE

1. **Acquisition of an eclectic knowledge base**
   A. Theoretical foundation: Systems theories
   B. Human behavior and the social environment
   C. Social welfare policy and services
   D. Social work practice
   E. Social work research
   F. Human diversity
   G. Promotion of social and economic justice
   H. Populations-at-risk
2. **Acquisition of professional values and ethics**
   A. NASW Code of Ethics
   B. Awareness of personal values
   C. Clarification of conflicting ethical dilemmas
   D. Understanding of oppression
   E. Respect for diverse populations
3. **Use of a wide range of practice skills**
   A. Micro
   B. Mezzo
   C. Macro
4. **Orientation to target any size system**
   A. Micro
   B. Mezzo
   C. Macro
5. **Effective work within an organizational structure**
6. **Appropriate use of supervision**
7. **Assumption of a wide range of professional roles**
   A. Enabler
   B. Mediator
   C. Integrator/coordinator
   D. General manager
   E. Educator
   F. Analyst/evaluator
   G. Broker
   H. Facilitator
   I. Initiator
   J. Negotiator
   K. Mobilizer
   L. Advocate
8. **Employment of critical thinking skills**
9. **Use of a planned change process**
   A. Engagement
   B. Assessment
      1) Defining issues
      2) Collecting and assessing data
   C. Planning
      1) Identifying alternative interventions
      2) Selecting appropriate courses of action
      3) Contracting
   D. Implementation of appropriate courses of action

E.   Evaluation
    1)   Using appropriate research to monitor and evaluate outcomes
    2)   Applying appropriate research-based knowledge and technological advances
F.   Termination
G.   Follow-up

E.   Commentary
This activity may also be conducted by holding a full class discussion without breaking students down into small groups.

Exercise 1.2: Critical Thinking Skills: Finding Fallacies

A.   Brief Description
In a large group discussion students apply critical thinking skills to two scenarios occurring in a macro context.

B.   Objectives
Students will:
1.   Use critical thinking to identify fallacies.
2.   Articulate the reasons for their choices.

C.   Procedure
1.   Review the content on critical thinking, "fallacies and pitfalls" (Gibbs & Gambrill, 1996, p.71). Principles are summarized in the box below under "Instructions for Students."
2.   Read the scenarios below under "Instructions for Students."
3.   Lead a full class discussion focusing on the ensuing questions.

D.   Instructions for students
A summary of potential fallacies and pitfalls are provided in the box below.

"Fallacies and Pitfalls" for Practitioners[1]

1.   Trusting case examples instead of scientific research including surveys given to or observations made on representative samples to illustrate effective treatment approaches.
2.   Trusting individual testimonials about personal experience as absolute fact. Just because a person says and, perhaps, even thinks that a treatment has been effective, it may not be. Without scientific inquiry something entirely unrelated may have caused the improvement.
3.   Nebulous, inexact descriptions of problems, treatments, and evaluation mechanisms that make it impossible to determine what actually happened or if it did any good.
4.   Hearing only one side of an argument or approach to treatment and automatically believing it without hearing and evaluating other approaches.
5.   Depending on the idea that if the treatment approach is new and innovative, it must be good.

---

[1] Gibbs, L., & Gambrill, E. (1996). *Critical Thinking for Social Workers: A Workbook.* Thousand Oaks, CA: Sage, 71.

For each of the following two scenarios, identify which fallacies and pitfalls might characterize the scenario and explain the reasons for your choices.

Scenario A: Your mayor states that you and other citizens should trust in his good judgment about how to allocate the city's resources, although he does not as yet have a detailed plan or budget in place. He stresses that this is his second term in office and he has a sound track record for making decisions in the past. He mentions that the major newspaper in town consistently supports him and his decisions.

What fallacies and pitfalls may apply?
What are your reasons for this choice or these choices?

Scenario B: You are a social worker in a county department of social services. Your colleague Allison has just attended a seminar presented by Dr. B. S. Smock, a renowned expert in radical approaches to crisis intervention. This expert has published two books and several articles on the subject. Allison vehemently states that she thinks all the agency workers should be trained in Dr. Smock's techniques and use his suggestions. She indicates that several clients spoke at the seminar and provided testimony concerning the effectiveness of the approach. Allison is clearly a loyal and enthusiastic disciple of Dr. Smock.

What fallacies and pitfalls may apply?
What are your reasons for this choice or these choices?

E. Commentary
This exercise may also be conducted using the small group format described in Exercise 1.1.

Exercise 1.3: The Generalist Approach

The following vignettes illustrate case situations you might encounter in generalist practice. Each case could be addressed in a variety of ways, using a micro, mezzo, or macro approach. In each instance, decide how you would approach the case at each level—micro, mezzo, and macro. For each intervention level, identify the potential client, the action system, and the target system.

Vignette 1: You are a rural county social services worker for Lowater County, Iowa. Your job is to complete assessments on families needing services, make appropriate referrals, and provide short-term counseling when necessary. The Mississippi River has flooded, displacing two dozen families from their homes. After intake, a family with two preschool children has been assigned to you for assessment and referral. Other families in distress have been assigned to other workers in your department and other agencies. The family assigned to you has lost virtually everything it owns in the flood and, lacking flood insurance, has only a few hundred dollars left in savings. The mother worked as a waitress and the father as a mechanic in small, locally-owned businesses. The flood has literally wiped out their places of employment, eliminating both of their jobs. Although it was devastating for those involved, the flood was not serious enough to warrant state or national emergency assistance.

1A. What potential alternative can you pursue at the micro level to help this family?

1B. For this alternative, identify the following:

Client system _____

Action system _____

Target system _____

1C. What potential alternative might you pursue at the mezzo level?

1D. For this alternative, identify the following:

Client system _____

Action system _____

Target system _____

1E. What can you do to help at the macro level?

1F. For this alternative, identify the following:

Client system _____

Action system _____

Target system _____

Vignette 2: You are a school social worker in a large urban high school. You provide individual and group counseling to students, consultation to teachers dealing with students' behavioral and emotional issues, family assessments, short-term family counseling, assessments for individual programming, and referrals to appropriate community services. You find that teachers and administrators are referring increasing numbers of students to you because of drug use. There is currently no formal drug education program in the school.

2A. What can you do to help at the micro level?

2B. For this alternative, identify the following:

Client system _____

Action system _____

Target system _____

2C. What can you do to help at the mezzo level?

2D.   For this alternative, identify the following:

Client system _____

Action system _____

Target system _____

2E.   What can you do to help at the macro level?

2F.   For this alternative, identify the following:

Client system _____

Action system _____

Target system _____

Vignette 3: You are a county social services worker in a large urban county in the Southwest. Four Hispanic refugee families from politically turbulent Central American countries have been assigned to your caseload. Each has children ranging in age from two to fifteen. Almost no one in these families speaks English, your county's school system emphasizes an English-language-only approach (rather than bilingualism), and most of the children are not yet enrolled in public school. All four families are living in very overcrowded apartments, receive only meager public assistance, and can barely afford food and clothing. There is no readily available public housing because the waiting lists are extraordinarily long. You are familiar with many facets of Mexican-American culture, but you know little about the specific Hispanic culture from which these clients come.

3A.   What can you do to help at the micro level?

3B.   For this alternative, identify the following:

Client system _____

Action system _____

Target system _____

3C.   What can you do to help at the mezzo level?

3D.   For this alternative, identify the following:

Client system _____

Action system _____

Target system _____

3E.   What can you do to help at the macro level?

3F.   For this alternative, identify the following:

Client system _____

Action system _____

Target system _____

Working in an Organizational Structure Under Supervision

We have reviewed the *knowledge, values, wide range of skills,* and orientation to *any size system* that help to define generalist practice. The fifth and sixth components are the ability to work effectively within an *organizational structure* and the ability to do so *under supervision.* Supervision is the "administrative and educational process used extensively in social agencies to help social workers further develop and refine their skills and to provide quality assurance for the clients" (Barker, 1995, pp. 371-72). Organizational structure is the formal and informal manner in which tasks and responsibilities, lines of authority, channels of communication, and dimensions of power are established and coordinated.

Assuming a Wide Range of Roles

The seventh major element of generalist practice is the *wide range of professional roles* that generalist practitioners assume. A role is "a socially expected behavior pattern usually determined by an individual's status in a particular society" or unit of society (*Webster's Ninth Collegiate Dictionary,* 1991, p. 1021). For example, people have certain expectations of how social workers will act and of the activities they will pursue. It is helpful to conceptualize the workers' roles in terms of the target, client, change agent, and action systems.

Note that professional roles are not necessarily mutually exclusive. A worker may perform the functions of more than one role at a time. The roles include enabler, mediator, integrator/coordinator, general manager, educator, analyst/evaluator, broker, facilitator, initiator, negotiator, and mobilizer.

The *enabler* provides support, encouragement, and suggestions to members of a macro client system, thus allowing the system to operate more easily and more successfully in completing tasks and/or solving problems. In the enabler role, a worker helps a client system become capable of coping with situational or transitional stress. Specific skills used in achieving this objective include conveying hope, reducing resistance and ambivalence, recognizing and managing feelings, identifying and supporting personal strengths and social assets, breaking down problems into parts that can more readily be solved [partialization], and maintaining a focus on goals and the means of achieving them (Barker, 1991, p. 74). For example, an enabler might help a community develop a program for identifying and shutting down crack houses. Community citizens do the work, but the enabler provides enthusiastic encouragement and helps participants identify their strengths and weaknesses and work out their interpersonal conflicts while keeping on task. Enablers, then, are helpers. Practitioners can function in the role of enabler for micro, mezzo, or macro systems.[2]

The *mediator* resolves arguments or disagreements among micro, mezzo, and/or macro systems in conflict (Yessian & Broskowski, 1983, pp. 183-84). At the macro level mediators help various factions (subsystems) in a community or community systems themselves work out their differences. For example, a community (or neighborhood) and a social services organization may require mediation over the placement of a substance abuse treatment center. Perhaps the social services organization has selected a prime spot, but the community or neighborhood is balking at the establishment of such a center within its boundaries.

---

[2] Note that this definition of "enabler" is very different from that of the "enabler" as applied to cases of substance abuse. There the term refers to a family member or friend who facilitates the substance abuser in continuing to use and abuse the drug of his or her choice.

The social worker may have to improve communication among dissident individuals or groups, or help those involved arrive at a compromise. A mediator remains neutral, does not side with either party in the dispute, and understands the positions of both parties. This allows her to clarify positions, recognize miscommunications, and help all parties present their cases clearly.

Integration is "the process of bringing together components into a unified whole" (Barker, 1991, p. 116), and coordination is the organizing of elements. The *integrator/coordinator*, therefore, brings the people involved in various systems together and organizes their activities (Yessian & Broskowski, 1983, pp. 183-84). A generalist social worker can function as an integrator/coordinator "in many ways, ranging from. . .advocacy and identification of coordination opportunities, to provision of technical assistance, to direct involvement in the development and implementation of service linkages" (Yessian & Broskowski, 1983, p.184). Integrator/coordinators function in macro systems in somewhat the same way that case managers function on behalf of individual clients or families.

The *general manager* assumes a particular level of administrative responsibility for a social services agency or some other organizational system (Yessian & Broskowski, 1983, pp. 183-84). Administrators "determine organizational goals; acquire resources and allocate them to carry out programs; coordinate activities toward the achievement of selected goals; and monitor, assess, and make necessary changes in processes and structure to improve effectiveness and efficiency" (Barker, 1991, p. 5). Managers perform a number of tasks including planning programs, getting and distributing resources, developing and establishing organizational structures and processes, evaluating programs, and implementing program changes when needed (Patti, 1983).

The *educator* gives information and teaches skills to other systems (Yessian & Broskowski, 1983, pp. 183-84). An effective educator must be knowledgeable, a good communicator who can convey information clearly and be readily understood by the receivers.

Analyst/evaluators analyze or evaluate effectiveness (Yessian & Broskowski, 1983, pp. 183-84). An analyst can determine the effectiveness of a program or even of an entire agency, and he can do this in an organizational or community context. Generalist social workers with a broad knowledge base can analyze or evaluate how well programs and systems work. Likewise, they can evaluate the effectiveness of their own interventions.

The *broker* links any size system (an individual, group, organization, or community) with community resources and services. A broker also helps put "various segments of the community in touch with one another to enhance their mutual interests" (Barker, 1991, p. 27). Getting resources for client systems is the broker's mission.

A *facilitator* "serves as a leader for some group experience" (Barker, 1991, p. 80). Although the facilitator role is very useful in mezzo practice, workers also frequently assume it in macro practice. In the macro context a facilitator assumes "the responsibility to expedite the change effort by bringing together people and lines of communication, channeling their activities and resources, and providing them with access to expertise" (Barker, 1991, p. 80).

Kettner, Daley, & Nichols (1985) explain that the *initiator* calls attention to an issue. (From a systems perspective, this person is the change agent). The issue may be a community problem or need, or simply a situation that can be improved. *There need not be a problem.* In fact, preventing future problems or enhancing existing services are satisfactory reasons for initiating a change effort. Thus, a social worker may recognize that a certain policy creates problems for particular clients and bring this to the attention of her supervisor. Likewise, a client may identify ways that service could be improved and bring that to attention of his social worker. In each case, the worker is playing the role of initiator. Usually, this role requires that other roles be undertaken, because pointing out problems does not guarantee they will be solved.

A *negotiator* acts to settle disputes and/or resolve disagreements. However, unlike mediators, negotiators clearly take the side of one of the parties involved.

The *mobilizer* identifies and gathers people from the community, and makes them "responsive to unmet community need" (Halley, Kopp, & Austin, 1992, p. 256). The mobilizer's purpose is to match resources to needs in the community context. Sometimes, a mobilizer's goal is simply to make services more accessible to those in the community who need them. Other times, the goal is to initiate and develop services that will meet hitherto unmet needs. By our definition, the mobilizer operates in communities, not in organizations.

An *advocate* works "with and/or on behalf of clients (1) to obtain services or resources for clients that would not otherwise be provided; (2) to modify extant [currently operating] policies, procedures, or practices that adversely affect clients; or (3) to promote new legislation or policies that will result in the provision of needed resources or services" (Hepworth & Larsen, 1990, p. 459). In other words, the advocate speaks out on behalf of the client system in order to promote fair and equitable treatment or gain needed resources. In macro practice, of course, she would speak on behalf of some macro client system. This may be especially appropriate when a macro client system has little power to get what it needs.

Exercise 1.4: Roles in Macro Practice

Identify the Macro Practice Role(s) assumed in the following case scenarios: Roles include **enabler, mediator, integrator/coordinator, general manager, educator, analyst/evaluator, broker, facilitator, initiator, negotiator, mobilizer,** and **advocate.** Note that in some scenarios the worker may play more than one role. Explain how each role functions in the scenario.

A. A social worker employed by a neighborhood center determines that the various workers and other professionals dealing with adolescent clients are not communicating with each other. For example, school social workers have no established procedure for conveying information to protective services workers who, in turn, do not communicate readily with probation and parole workers—despite the fact that these professionals are working with many of the same clients. The neighborhood center social worker decides to bring together representatives from the various agencies that serve the center and establish more clearly defined communication channels.

Macro Practice Role(s):

Explanation:

B. A worker in a Child Protective Services Unit has developed special skills in family counseling by participating in a two-year training program. Her agency's Assistant Director asks her to provide a series of six in-service training sessions for other Child Protective Services staff.[3]

Macro Practice Role(s):

Explanation:

---

[3] In-service training is "an educational program provided by an employer and usually carried out by a supervisor or specialist to help [an employee] become more productive and effective in accomplishing a specific task or meeting the overall objectives of the organization" (Barker, 1995, p. 188).

C.   The main tasks of a Foster Care Unit are to assess potential foster parent applicants, monitor placement, manage cases as children move in and out of foster care, and train foster parents in parenting and behavior-management skills. The unit social workers hold biweekly meetings to discuss how to improve agency service provision. The workers take turns organizing the meetings and running the discussions.

Macro Practice Role(s):

Explanation:

D.   A social worker employed by a large private family services agency specializes in international adoptions, especially those involving countries from the former Soviet Union. He discovers that many of the adoptive children suffer from health problems caused by early nutritional deprivation. The worker is convinced that this is not a matter of one or two problem cases, but a disturbing pattern. No automatic referral process is in place to assess these adoptive children and direct their families to needed resources, including designated medical specialists. The worker devises a systematic process for assessment and referral.

Macro Practice Role(s):

Explanation:

E.   Agency administration asks one of three social workers in a large residential health care complex for the elderly to assess the effectiveness of its social services program.

Macro Practice Role(s):

Explanation:

F.   A social worker employed at a sheltered workshop for people with developmental disabilities[4] is assigned by her supervisor to oversee a new program that will teach behavior management skills to the adoptive parents. She will also be responsible for supervising two other social workers and training them to implement the program with their clients.

Macro Practice Role(s):

Explanation:

---

[4] Sheltered employment such as this workshop for people with developmental disabilities is "a vocational rehabilitation and training service that provides a protected and monitored work environment, additional testing, guidance, vocational training, and social rehabilitation for people who are otherwise difficult to employ" (Barker, 1995, p. 346).

G.   A group of clients inform their social worker that the community is trying to enforce a housing maintenance ordinance in a punitive and excessively picky manner. Enforcers have been sent to these clients' homes and have cited them for such minuscule matters as having pieces of siding that need repainting and rusted rain gutters. These clients are poor and have almost no access to resources for anything other than basic necessities. They implore their social worker to help them. She learns that the original intent of the ordinance was to ascertain the safety of the clients' living conditions: Were steps and railings broken? Were windows broken? Had lead paint been used? The worker, therefore, judges that both the client group and the community are trying to do the best they can, so she attempts to referee the dispute between the community client group and the community leaders imposing the ordinance.

Macro Practice Role(s):

Explanation:

H.   A social worker employed by a large public social services department increasingly hears client complaints about drug houses popping up in their residential neighborhoods. The worker identifies clients and other concerned citizens, and organizes a community meeting. He then assists community residents in formulating a plan to identify drug house locations and establish a procedure for reporting such houses to the authorities.

Macro Practice Role(s):

Explanation:

I.   A social worker at a public assistance agency is terribly troubled by the conditions in the clients' waiting room and by the tedious process of client intakes. She explores the issue, develops a proposed plan for improvement, and makes an appointment to speak with the agency's executive director about it.

Macro Practice Role(s):

Explanation:

J.   A local charitable organization cuts off its contribution to a Planned Parenthood agency[5] with a large, centrally located main clinic and three satellite clinics. The result will be a severe cutback in services and the closure of at least two satellite clinics. A huge number of clients will find it difficult if not impossible to receive adequate services. A social work counselor at one of the clinics, with the support of her supervisor, gathers facts to show the importance of the funding and arranges a meeting with the funding organization's leaders. She hopes to discuss the cuts and persuade the charitable agency to reverse its decision.

Macro Practice Role(s):

Explanation:

---

[5] Planned Parenthood agencies assist people in making decisions about pregnancy and promote birth control and contraception.

K.   A juvenile probation officer is distressed by proposed legislation that will shut down a vocational training program for juvenile offenders because of its expense. He talks to other workers and administrators in his state agency, and gathers facts and statistics that demonstrate the program's cost effectiveness. He then calls and writes to influential legislators, and meets with the chairperson of the legislative committee that recommended closing the program. He also contacts other concerned social workers and encourages them to join his effort.

Macro Practice Role(s):

Explanation:

L.   A group of community residents approaches a social worker to ask about starting a Neighborhood Watch program.[6] The worker provides them with encouragement and information.

Macro Practice Role(s):

Explanation:

Critical Thinking

Generalists must also have the ability to *think critically* in the problem-solving process. This is the eighth component in the definition of generalist practice.

Critical thinking is the ability to use intellectual and "affective processes which evaluate statements, arguments, and experiences by judging the validity and/or worth of those statements, arguments, and experiences" (Lindsay, 1995, p. 20). In other words, critical thinking entails the ability to evaluate the validity of an assumption—and even of a so-called "fact."

Gibbs et al. (1994) state that critical thinking in social work practice involves: (1) a predisposition to question conclusions that concern client care and welfare; (2) asking "Does it work?" and "How do you know?" when confronted with claims that a method helps clients, and also questioning generalizations about treatment methods and clients; (3) weighing evidence for and against assertions in a logical, rational, systematic, data-based way; and (4) analyzing arguments to see what is being argued, spotting and explaining common fallacies in reasoning, and applying basic methodological principles of scientific reasoning (pp. 11-12).

Gibbs and Gambrill (1996)[7] cite a number of "fallacies and pitfalls" that workers are likely to fall into in evaluating practice approaches (p. 71). They include the following (Gibbs & Gambrill, 1996):

1.   *Trusting case examples*—including surveys given to, or observations made on, representative samples to illustrate effective treatment approaches—*instead of scientific research.*

2.   *Trusting individual testimonials about personal experience as absolute fact.* Even though a person says and perhaps even believes that a treatment has been effective, it may not have been. Unless scientific methods have been employed, something entirely unrelated may have caused the improvement.

3.   *Accepting nebulous, inexact descriptions of problems, treatments, and evaluation mechanisms.* Such descriptions make it impossible to determine what actually happened and whether a given treatment did any good.

---

[6] Neighborhood Watch programs bring neighborhood residents together to find ways to prevent crime in their neighborhood. They devise a system for observing any suspicious behavior, especially on the part of strangers, and for alerting the proper authorities. Members also educate new people moving into the neighborhood about the program and publicize the program's existence via window decals and signs.

[7] L. Gibbs and E. Gambrill have developed an excellent student workbook entitled *Critical Thinking for Social Workers: A Workbook* (Thousand Oaks, CA: Sage, 1996) that addresses the issue of critical thinking much more extensively.

4. *Hearing only one side of an argument or approach to treatment and automatically believing it* without hearing and evaluating other approaches.
5. *Assuming that if a practice or a treatment approach is innovative, it must be good.*
6. *Assuming that if a practice or a treatment approach has been used for a long time by a lot of people, it must be good.*
7. *Believing that information cited or written down in a book, article, magazine, or newspaper must be true.*

Exercise 1.5: Critical Thinking in Macro Practice

The following statements or scenarios demonstrate fallacies that should be subjected to critical thinking and reevaluation. In each case, identify which fallacy is illustrated and explain how. (In some instances, more than one fallacy will apply.)

A. *Supervisor Talking to Supervisees:* "We've always scheduled our appointments with clients during the daytime working hours. It's always worked in the past. My motto is, 'If it ain't broke, don't fix it.'"

Which fallacy(ies) does this illustrate?

Explain

B. *Worker Complaining to a Colleague:* "I think agency administration is all wet about their programming recommendations. They don't know what they're talking about."

Which fallacy(ies) does this illustrate?

Explain

C. *Governor Talking to Reporters:* "My new welfare plan is the answer to all our problems with welfare mothers: Make them work to be eligible for their benefits and you'll solve the Temporary Assistance to Needy Families financial crisis in a hurry."

Which fallacy(ies) does this illustrate?

Explain:

D. *Worker Talking to a Colleague:* "I've had the best luck with the Gungho Intervention technique on Ollie Hopnoodle. I'm going to use it with all my clients. I think the whole agency should adopt it."

Which fallacy(ies) does this illustrate?

Explain:

E.   *Worker Giving an Informative Speech to Co-workers:* "*The Harvard Scripture of Social Work* states that doing casework with individual clients is the most important aspect of social work practice."

Which fallacy(ies) does this illustrate?

Explain:

F.   *Administrator Talking to His Staff:* "Absolute Attainment Management is the wave of the future. It beats everything about the old bureaucratic approach to running social service organizations. Every in-the-know agency is starting to use it. Let's go for it! We don't want to be left behind."

Which fallacy(ies) does this illustrate?

Explain:

G.   *Worker Talking to Agency Director:* "I heard Ernie over at Moneyplenty Mental Health Center absolutely rave about their grant-writing seminars. I've got to get myself enrolled—but the fee is about 750 big ones. Do you think the agency might pay for at least half?"

Which fallacy(ies) does this illustrate?

Explain:

The Problem-Solving Process

The ninth major element of generalist practice is application of the *problem-solving process*. Sometimes this is referred to as "planned change." It can be explained as a series of seven basic steps:

(1) Engagement. The practitioner orients herself to the problem at hand and begins to establish communication and a relationship with the individual(s) concerned.
(2) Assessment. The issues are defined and the data collected.
(3) Planning. Approaches to the problem and techniques for dealing with it are determined.
(4) Implementation (or intervention). The plans are put into effect.
(5) Evaluation. The effectiveness of the process is determined.
(6) Termination. The intervention process ends.
(7) Follow-up. The worker checks to find out whether the macro intervention process succeeded over time, or whether the same old problems resurfaced in another form.

Later chapters will discuss these steps in greater depth.

Chapter 2
Using Micro Skills in the Macro Environment

I.   **Introduction**

    A.   Assertiveness

    B.   Conflict

    C.   Working with Supervisors

II.   **Beginning Relationships in Macro Practice**

    A.   An interview in macro practice includes communicating and problem solving with groups of clients, agency administrators, your colleagues, politicians, community residents, and professionals from various other community agencies

    B.   Figure 2.1: The Worker in the Organizational, Community, and Political Macro Environments

III. **A Review of Basic Micro Skills**

IV.   **Verbal and Nonverbal Behavior**

    A.   Eye contact

        1.   Direct eye contact with an occasional glance away is most appropriate

        2.   People with different cultural backgrounds may have different expectations in terms of appropriate nonverbal behaviors

            a.   African Americans and Hispanics tend to use eye contact less frequently than whites

            b.   Native Americans and Asians tend to regard eye contact as disrespectful; they make greater use of peripheral vision

    B.   Attentive listening

        1.   Hearing is the audio perception of spoken words; listening means that you try both to hear and to understand most of what another person is saying

        2.   Three barriers to attentive listening involve three aspects of communication

            a.   Intent—some meaning he or she wishes to convey

            b.   Impact—what the receiver thinks the sender said

            c.   Environmental barriers—potential noise and distractions

        3.   Figure 2.2: Barriers to Attentive Listening

C. Facial expressions

D. Body positioning

    1. Tense/relaxed continuum

    2. Formal/informal continuum

    3. Personal space

        a. Intimate zone—from skin contact to about eighteen inches

        b. Personal zone—about eighteen inches to approximately four feet

        c. Social zone—four to twelve feet

        d. Public zone—outward from twelve feet

E. Multicultural sensitivity and nonverbal behavior

    1. Russians say yes by shaking the head from side to side and no by moving the head up and down. Most Europeans do exactly the opposite

    2. People from certain Arabic cultures prefer to be only 18 inches apart when they talk, Arabs experiencing interaction in the 4 to 8 foot zone may interpret European behavior as exceptionally cold and aloof

    3. In Japan, smiling may indicate discomfort

F. Highlight 2.1: Nonverbal Behavior, Communication, Empowerment, and People Who Have Physical Disabilities

    1. People with visual impairment

    2. People with hearing impairment

    3. People with mobility disabilities

V. Warmth, Empathy, and Genuineness

A. Warmth—Conveying a feeling of interest, concern, well-being, and liking to another individual

B. Empathy—Being in tune with how other person feels, conveying the idea that you understand how he or she feels

1. Uses of empathy

  a. Help establish an initial rapport

  b. Elicit feelings and begin talking about issues

  c. Make confrontations more palatable

2. Highlight 2.2: Practicing Empathic Responses in Macro Practice Contexts

C. Genuineness (Authenticity)—sharing of self by relating in a natural, sincere, spontaneous, open and genuine manner

VI. Communicating with Other People in Macro Contexts

A. Simple Encouragement

B. Be Sensitive to Cultural Differences

C. Paraphrasing—restating what the other person is saying, but using different words

D. Reflective Responding—translating into words what you think the other person is feeling

E. Clarification—making certain that what another person says is understood

F. Interpretation—seeking meaning beyond that of clarification

G. Providing Information

H. Emphasizing People's Strengths

I. Summarization—briefly covering the main points of a discussion or series of communications

J. Eliciting Information

  a. Closed-ended questions seek simple yes or no answers, or when there are a number of clearly defined answers to choose from

  b. Open-ended questions seek more extensive thoughts, ideas, and explanations for answers

K. The Use of "Why?"

  a. It often implies that the person to whom it's directed is at fault

  b. It can put the burden of seeking a solution on the individual to whom it is directed

L. Overlap of Techniques

VII. **Appropriate Assertiveness in the Macro Environment: Empowering Yourself and Others**

    A.   Assertiveness involves expressing yourself without hurting others or stepping on their rights

    B.   Highlight 2.3: Each of Us has Certain Assertive Rights

        1.   You have the right to express your ideas and opinions openly and honestly

        2.   You have the right to be wrong. Everyone makes mistakes

        3.   You have the right to direct and govern your own life

        4.   You have the right to stand up for yourself without unwarranted anxiety and make choices that are good for you

        5.   You have the right not to be liked by everyone

        6.   You have the right, on the one hand, to make requests and, on the other, to refuse them without feeling guilty

        7.   You have the right to ask for information if you need it

        8.   You have the right to decide not to exercise your assertive rights

VIII. **Nonassertive, Assertive, and Aggressive Communication**

    A.   Assertive communication—verbal and nonverbal behavior that permits a speaker to get points across clearly and straightforwardly, considering own rights and rights of others

    B.   Nonassertive communication—devaluing self completely, feeling that the other person and what that person thinks is much more important than one's own thoughts

    C.   Aggressive communication—bold and dominant verbal and nonverbal behavior, own view taking precedence above all others' points of view

    D.   Passive-aggressiveness—secretly or covertly aggressive

    E.   Figure 2.3: The Assertiveness Continuum

    F.   Highlight 2.4: What Would You Do?

    G.   Advantages of assertiveness

    H.   Assertiveness training

    I.   Final note on assertiveness training

IX.   Conflict and Its Resolution

A.   Interpersonal Conflict—occurs any time people involved in relationships, such as friends, family members, coworkers, or neighbors, have differing needs, wants, desires, expectations, goals, or means of achieving certain ends

B.   The Pros of Conflict (Johnson, 1997)

    1.   Can help us explore a situation more thoroughly

    2.   Can cause us to make improvements in our behavior and communication

    3.   Can generate new energy to solve a problem

    4.   Can make daily routines more exciting

    5.   Can improve the quality of problem resolution and decision-making

    6.   Can release emotional "steam"

    7.   Can enhance self-awareness

    8.   Can be fun when it is not taken too seriously

    9.   Can facilitate the development and depth of relationships

C.   The Cons of Conflict (Daft, 1998)

    1.   Takes energy

    2.   May result in winners and losers instead of compromise

    3.   Decreased collaboration and team work

D.   Personal Styles for Addressing Conflict (Johnson, 1997)

    1.   Turtle—withdraws into his or her shell to avoid conflicts

    2.   Shark—a power-hungry aggressor; will do almost anything to win

    3.   Teddy bear—values the relationship with the opponent much more than achieving his or her own goals

    4.   Fox—a compromiser; tries to reach an agreement that satisfies both parties

    5.   Owl—believes in each party making compromises, based on confrontation— much more assertive than the fox in conflictual interactions

E.   Steps in Conflict Resolution (Johnson, 1986; 1997)

    1.   Step 1: The Confrontation

        a.   Confrontation—a face-to-face encounter where people come together with opposing opinions, perspectives, or ideas in order to scrutinize or compare them

        b.   Two major issues when engaging in a confrontation

            1)   Clearly identify and examine your personal goals

            2)   Nurture your interpersonal relationship with the other person

        c.   Case Example—Step 1: Setting the Stage for a Confrontation

    2.   Step 2: Establish common ground

        a.   Most important is to keep trying to empathize with your opponent's position

        b.   Case Example—Step 2: Establish Common Ground

    3.   Step 3: Emphasize the importance of communication

        a.   Communication guidelines (Horejsi & Horejsi, 2000, p. 460)

            1)   Do not begin a confrontation when you are angry

            2)   Do not enter into a conflict unless you have a clearly established reason for doing so

            3)   If you absolutely despise your opponent or have immense difficulty reaching for any positive, empathic feeling about him, do not confront him

            4)   Include positive statements and feedback along with the negative aspects of confrontation

            5)   Be certain to explain your concerns regarding the conflict in a "descriptive and nonjudgmental" manner

            6)   Supply relevant data in support of your stance

            7)   Use "I-messages" frequently

        b.   Case Example—Step 3: Emphasize Communication

         c.   Suggestions for how to respond when someone confronts you (Nunnaly & May, 1989, pp. 135-36)

               1)   Pay very close attention to what the confronter is telling you

               2)   Explain to the confronter exactly how you will respond to his feedback

               3)   Tell your confronter that you appreciate his effort and his feedback

               4)   Approach your confronter later, and tell him how you have responded to his feedback

               5)   At the time of the confrontation, do not reproach the confronter with a criticism of your own

4.   Step 4: Emphasize your willingness to cooperate

         a.   Stress the commonalities you have with your opponent

         b.   Case Example—Step 4: Emphasize Your Willingness to Cooperate

5.   Step 5: Empathize with your opponent's perspective

         a.   Work to understand why your opponent feels the way she or he does

         b.   Case Example—Step 5: Empathize with Your Opponent's Perspective

6.   Step 6: Evaluate both your own and your opponent's motivation to address the conflict

         a.   In many situations it is possible to change the degree of motivation on your own or your opponent's part

         b.   Case Example—Step 6: Evaluate Both Your Own and Your Opponent's Motivation to Address the Conflict

7.   Step 7: Come to some mutually satisfactory agreement

         a.   Suggestions (Johnson, 1997)

               1)   Articulate exactly what your agreement entails

               2)   Indicate how you will behave toward the other person in the future as compared with the past

               3)   Specify how the other person will behave toward you

4) Agree on ways to address any future mistakes

5) Establish how and when you and the other will meet in the future to continue your cooperative behavior and minimization of conflict

  b. Case Example—Step 7: Come to Some Mutually Satisfactory Agreement

X. Working Under Supervisors

  A. Highlight 2.5: Workers' General Expectations of Supervisors: Keys to Empowerment (Halley et al., 1998; Kadushin & Harkness, 2002; Sheafor & Horejsi, 2003)

    1. Be readily available for consultation on difficult cases

    2. Make certain that workers are knowledgeable about agency policy

    3. Provide input to higher levels of administration regarding line workers' needs

    4. Facilitate cooperation among staff

    5. Nurture workers and give them support when needed

    6. Evaluate workers' job performance

    7. Facilitate workers' development of new skills

  B. Administrative Functions of Supervisors

  C. Educational Functions of Supervisors

  D. Other Functions of Supervisors

  E. Using Supervision Effectively

    1. Use your communication skills with your supervisor

    2. Keep your records up-to-date

    3. Plan your supervisory agenda ahead of time

    4. Put yourself in your supervisor's shoes

    5. Display an openness to learning and improving yourself

    6. Demonstrate a liking for your work

    7. Work cooperatively with other staff

    8. Give your supervisor feedback

9. Forewarn your supervisor about problematic situations

10. Learn your supervisor's evaluation system

F. Problems in supervision

    1. Highlight 2.6: Games Supervisors and Supervisees Sometimes Play (Kadushin, 1968)

        a. I'll be nice to you if you'll be nice to me

        b. Therapize me

        c. Good buddies don't evaluate

        d. Of course, I know much more than you do

        e. Poor, helpless, little old me

        f. Information is power

        g. Avoiding the issue

        h. Pose questions to answer questions

    2. Simple misunderstandings between supervisor and supervisee

    3. Supervisors who take credit for your work

        a. Highlight 2.7: What Would You Do?

        b. There is no perfect answer

    4. Supervisory incompetence

    5. Laziness

    6. Problems with delegation

    7. Inability to deal with conflict

    8. Postscript

Exercise 2.1: How Can You Be Assertive?

A.   Brief Description
Using a full class discussion format, students are presented with vignettes portraying uncomfortable situations and asked to suggest assertive responses.

B.   Objectives
Students will:
1.   Propose appropriate assertive responses for scenarios occurring in macro settings.
2.   Evaluate the potential benefits and costs of such responses.

C.   Procedure
1.   Review the material on appropriate assertiveness in the macro environment.
2.   Read the vignettes presented below under "instructions for students" and initiate a full class discussion for each by focusing on the subsequent questions.

D.   Instructions for Students
Read each of the following and respond to the subsequent questions.

Scenario A: You are a social worker for Heterogeneous County Department of Social Services. Paperwork recording your activities with clients is due promptly the Monday following the last day of each month. For whatever reason, you simply forget to get it in by 5:00 p.m. Monday the day it's due. Your supervisor Enrique calls you at noon the next day. He raises his voice and reprimands, "You know that reports are due promptly so that funding is not jeopardized. How many times do I have to tell you that?"

How might you respond assertively?
What are the potential benefits and costs of such a response?

Scenario B: You work with a colleague who consistently comes late to your social work unit's biweekly meetings. He typically saunters leisurely into the meeting room with a cup of decaf in hand, noisily situates himself in a chair at the rectangular meeting table, and casually interrupts whomever is speaking, asking for a brief review of what he missed. You are sick and tired of such rude, time-wasting behavior.

How might you respond assertively?
What are the potential benefits and costs of such a response?

Scenario C: You represent your social services agency at a community meeting where twelve community residents and five workers from other agencies are discussing what additional social services the community needs. Some possible grant funding has become available to develop services. The person chairing the meeting asks for input from each person present except you. Apparently, she simply overlooked that you had not gotten an opportunity to speak.

How might you respond assertively?
What are the potential benefits and costs of such a response?

E.   Commentary
This exercise may also be conducted using the small group format described in Exercise 1.1.

Exercise 2.2: Using Communication Techniques with Supervisors

A.   Brief Description
In a small group format, students formulate responses to supervisory scenarios by applying various communication techniques.

B.   Objectives
Students will:
1. Apply communication techniques to macro practice scenarios.
2. Propose appropriate responses in a supervisory context.

C.   Procedure
1.   Review the material on communicating with other people in macro contexts and working under supervisors. Communication techniques are summarized in the box below under "Instructions for Students."
2.   Divide the class into small groups of four to six.
3.   Ask the groups to formulate various responses to each of the five "Supervisor Statements" identified under "Instructions for Students" below. Instruct students to identify the kind of response each proposed reply reflects according to the nine types recognized in the box below. Indicate that some responses may reflect more than one response type. Ask each group to select a group representative who should be prepared to report to the entire class the small group's suggestions.
4.   After about 20 minutes, ask the small groups to terminate their discussions and participate in a full class discussion.
5.   Ask the representative from each group to share her or his summary of the discussion. Ask group members to explain how each of their proposed supervisee responses falls into one or more of the nine categories. Encourage comments from all class members.

D.   Instructions for Students
       Nine verbal responses used as techniques of communication are summarized in the box below.

USING VERBAL RESPONSES IN MACRO CONTEXTS

1.   **Simple Encouragement:** *Any verbal or nonverbal behavior intended to assure, comfort, or support the communication.*
2.   **Paraphrasing:** *Stating what the other person is saying, but using different words.*
3.   **Reflective Responding:** *Translating into words what you think the other person is feeling.*
4.   **Clarification:** *Choosing and using words to make certain that what another person has said is clearly understood.*
5.   **Interpretation:** *To seek meaning beyond that of clarification by helping bring a matter to a conclusion, to enlighten, or to seek a meaning of greater depth than that which has been stated.*
6.   **Providing Information:** *The communication of knowledge.*
7.   **Emphasizing People's Strengths:** *Articulating and emphasizing other people's positive characteristics and behaviors.*
8.   **Summarization:** *Covering the main points of a discussion or series of communications both briefly and concisely.*
9.   **Eliciting Information:** *Requesting knowledge you need.*

Following are a number of statements made by supervisors to their supervisees. For each, give examples of the different types of possible statements you might make or questions you might ask as a supervisee making a response. Label which verbal response or combination of responses indicated in the box above each statement reflects. Formulate as many types of the nine verbal responses as possible. Because the statements are vague, feel free to make up facts in your responses.

Supervisor Statement A: I'm concerned about the quality of your work lately. It seems you've taken a lot of sick days and your record keeping has fallen behind.

As a supervisee, how might you respond?
What type(s) of verbal response or responses does this reflect?
Explain why.
(For example:
"You sound like you're frustrated with me." *Reflective responding*
"What work are you most concerned about?" *Eliciting information*)

Supervisor Statement B: "There's an important staff meeting scheduled after work on Friday. I wouldn't make you attend if I didn't have to."

As a supervisee, how might you respond?
What type(s) of verbal response or responses does this reflect?

Supervisor Statement C: "Could you work up a one hour inservice on some aspect of your practice for the general agency staff meeting next month?"

As a supervisee, how might you respond?
What type(s) of verbal response or responses does this reflect?

> **Supervisor Statement D**: "Funding has been drastically cut. I surely wish someone around here knew more about grant writing."

As a supervisee, how might you respond?
What type(s) of verbal response or responses does this reflect?

> **Supervisor Statement E**: "There's a growing group of community residents complaining about the efficiency of our service provision."

As a supervisee, how might you respond?
What type(s) of verbal response or responses does this reflect?

E.   Commentary
This activity may also be conducted by holding a full class discussion without breaking students down into small groups.

Exercise 2.3: Practicing Empathic Responses in Macro Practice Contexts

Below are several vignettes illustrating macro situations. Formulate and write down two empathic responses for each situation. (Responses for the first vignette are provided as an example.)

Vignette #1: You are a school social worker in an urban neighborhood. Residents inform you that a vacant lot in the neighborhood—two houses away from the school—was used as a dump for dangerous chemicals between ten and twenty years ago. In the past fifteen years, a dozen children attending the school have gotten cancer.

Addressing this type of issue is not part of your job description, but you see it as your professional and ethical responsibility to help the neighborhood residents explore their options for coping with this problem. For instance, a class-action lawsuit could be brought against the companies that dumped the chemicals. If it could be proved that the companies are at fault (that is, that they acted knowingly or negligently), they could be held financially liable for their actions.

The mother of one child (Eric, 14) who has leukemia makes an appointment to see you. When she enters your office, she bursts into tears: "I am so angry! How could people do this to little children? They must have known that dumping those wastes so close to children was dangerous."

How do you respond empathically?
- "You sound really angry. I don't blame you. What are your thoughts about what to do?"
- "I'm hearing you say that you are furious about this situation. What can I do to help you?"
- "This whole situation has been a horror story for you. Where do you think we can go from here?"

Vignette #2: You are a social worker in a health care facility for the elderly. You want to start a program that will bring middle-school children to visit your elderly clients. You believe that such interactions will be mutually beneficial for both your clients and the children. You have approached Kimberly, the other social worker in the facility, with this idea, but her response was hesitant and—in your opinion— negative. You think she is worried that this proposal will create a lot more work for her, work that she is neither ready nor willing to undertake.

In fact, you have pretty much paved the way for implementing the plan: You have contacted school administrators and teachers to obtain their permission and support. You've come up with a transportation plan and a proposed form for parental permissions. Before you have the chance to approach Kimberly again, she initiates a conversation with you: She states, "I know you're trying to do the right thing with this student visitation project [this is an empathic response on Kimberly's part], *but* you're pushing me into it. I don't have enough time to do my own work, let alone get involved in some petty little program you propose."

How do you respond empathically? (Remember that you *do not have to solve the problem* right now. You simply need to let Kimberly know that you understand how she feels.)

Alternative Response #1:

Alternative Response #2:

Vignette #3:   You are a social worker at a diagnostic and treatment center for children with multiple physical disabilities. Your primary function is helping parents cope with the pressures they are under and connecting them with needed resources. The Center's staff includes a wide range of disciplines such as occupational therapy,[1] physical therapy,[2] speech therapy, psychology, and nursing. Sometimes the professionals from these other disciplines ask you to talk parents out of asking them questions, especially when a child's condition is getting worse. One day a physical therapist approaches you and asks, "Do you think you could talk to Mrs. Harris? She keeps asking me these uncomfortable questions about Sally [Mrs. Harris's daughter]. Sally's condition is deteriorating. I don't know what to say."

How do you respond empathically?

Alternative Response #1:

Alternative Response #2:

Vignette #4:   You are an intake worker at a social services agency in a rural area. Your job is to take telephone calls, assess problems, and refer clients to the most appropriate services. You identify a gap in the services available to people with developmental disabilities. You think that a social activities center would help to fill this gap by meeting some hitherto unmet needs. You talk with administrators in your agency, and they generally support the idea—but they don't know where the funding would come from. They suggest that you talk with some local politicians. You make an appointment with the President of the County Board to explain your idea and ask about possible funding. She responds, "It certainly sounds good, but who's going to pay for it and run it?"

How do you respond empathetically?

Alternative Response #1:

Alternative Response #2:

Using Verbal Responses in Macro Contexts

Communication to exchange information is the core of interpersonal interactions in macro settings. The vast array of possible communication techniques for use within agency, community, or political settings is much the same as those used in your micro and mezzo interventions with clients. There are various ways to initiate a communication, solicit information, encourage responses, and respond appropriately to another individual. Using appropriate communication techniques increases the chances that your *intent* (that is, what you want to convey) will match your *impact* (that is, what the receiver actually understands). A number of verbal responses are defined and discussed below.

---

[1] Occupational therapy is "a profession for helping physically disabled people use their bodies more effectively and mentally impaired people overcome emotional problems through specially designed work activity" (Barker, 1991, p. 160).

[2] Physical therapy is "the treatment of disease by physical and mechanical means (as massage, regulated exercise, water, light, heat, and electricity)" (*Webster's Ninth New Collegiate Dictionary*, 1991, p. 887).

Simple encouragement: Any verbal or nonverbal behavior intended to assure, comfort, or support the communication. Many times a simple one word response or nonverbal head nod combined with eye contact is enough to encourage the other person to continue. "Verbal clues such as 'mm-mm,' 'I see,' 'uh-huh' help convey that the receiver really is listening and following what the sender is saying" (Okun, 1976, p. 52).

Rephrasing: Repeating what the other person is saying by putting it into your own words. Rephrasing accomplishes several things: It communicates to the other person that you are listening to what she's saying. It notifies her that you did not understand, thus allowing her to clarify her meaning. It gives the other person time out to reflect on what she just said.

Rephrasing does not involve *interpreting* what the other person has said, only repeating her statement in different words.

Reflective responding: Translating into words what you think the other person is feeling. Such empathic responding conveys your understanding of the other person's position and of how he feels about it. It is common for a person to *talk* about his problems without really articulating how he *feels*. You can help him identify and express his feelings so that he can do something about them. Both verbal and nonverbal behavior can be used as cues for reflective responding.

Clarification: Choosing and using words to make certain that what another person has said is clearly understood. The intent of clarification is to make a communication more understandable in one of two ways (Benjamin, 1974). First, you can help another person articulate—say more clearly—what she really means by providing the words for it. This is clarification for the other person's benefit. Second, you can explain what the other person is saying for your own benefit. Many times clarification will benefit both sender and receiver. In summary, use clarification when you are uncertain about what another person means; use restatement to paraphrase exactly what the other person said, thus showing that you already understand the communication; and use reflective responding to get at the feelings and emotions behind another person's statements.

Interpretation: Seeking meaning in an effort to help bring a matter to a conclusion, to enlighten, or to seek a greater depth of meaning in what someone has said. Interpretation helps the other person look deeper into the meaning of her own words and enhances her perception of that meaning.

For instance, a colleague might say, "I like Samson, but he always seems to get the most interesting cases. It's just not fair, that's all there is to it."

You could respond by interpreting this statement: "You seem to have some conflicting feelings about Samson. On the one hand, you like him. On the other, you apparently resent the fact that he gets more challenging cases than you do."

You have gone beyond your colleague's feelings of anger and resentment and focused on the reasons for those feelings.

Providing information: Communicating knowledge. Examples are infinite. A person may ask you a specific question, or you may determine that someone needs some particular input.

Emphasizing people's strengths: Articulating and emphasizing other people's positive characteristics and behaviors. Your instructors have probably drilled into you the importance of emphasizing client strengths, but it is also important to emphasize the strengths of colleagues, administrators, and others you deal with. Each individual in the macro environment has personal strengths, weaknesses, concerns, and defenses. When you feel you must offer a constructive suggestion or criticism, a strengths perspective allows you to do so while still supporting the other person's ego. You want to convey to that person that you are on her side, and by emphasizing her strengths, you show that you are not the enemy.

Summarization: Briefly and concisely covering the main points of a discussion or series of communications. Summarization can be difficult because you must carefully select only the most important facts, issues, and themes. Exclude less essential detail. Condense so that you emphasize only the most salient points.

You can use summarization to bring a discussion to a close while focusing the main issues in others' minds. At the end of a staff meeting, you can summarize recommendations about who is to do what before the next meeting, thereby crystallizing in all participants' minds whatever plans were made.

Summarizing information periodically throughout a discussion also serves to keep the discussion on track and/or "as a transition to new topics" (Whittaker & Tracy, 1989, p.135).

Eliciting information: Requesting knowledge you need. One way to elicit information is simply to ask questions—either closed-ended or open-ended. *Closed-ended questions* seek simple, definite answers from a predetermined range of possibilities, such as "yes" or "no," or "male" or "female." Such questions do not encourage or even allow for explanation or elaboration. Open-ended questions seek more extensive presentations of thoughts, ideas, and explanations.

Overlap of Techniques

Sometimes it is difficult to label a technique specifically as "clarification" or "interpretation," but some techniques fulfill only one purpose and thus fit obviously into one category. Others combine two or more techniques because they fulfill two or more functions. The important thing is to master a variety of techniques and thereby become more flexible and more effective in communicating with others.

Exercise 2.4: Responding to Others in the Macro Environment

Look at the statements below. They might come from colleagues, supervisors, administrators, and others in the macro working environment. For each statement, give examples of the different types of possible responses. (Types of responses are listed under each statement.) The first statement is an example.

Statement #1: **(From a worker at another agency)** "I've been meaning to talk to you about your agency's policy regarding the treatment of poor clients."

Possible Responses:

Simple encouragement: "I see. Please go on."
Rephrasing: "You have some concerns about my agency's procedures for working with impoverished clients."
Reflective responding: "You're upset about the way my agency treats poor clients."
Clarification: "You're concerned about the effect of our sliding fee scale on clients who can't afford it."
Interpretation: "You have some ethical concerns about our policy on treatment of poor clients."
Providing information: "Let me give you a copy of our new policy and some data on how it affects clients."
Emphasizing people's strengths: "You always have been an exceptional advocate for the poor."
Summarization: (Since it is almost impossible to summarize one line, assume that there has been an ongoing discussion of this matter.) "Over the past few weeks, we've talked about a number of your concerns about agency policy, including treatment of staff, of people of color, and of the poor."
Eliciting information: "Can you tell me exactly which policy you are referring to?"

Statement #2: **(From a colleague at your agency)** "I'm furious with my supervisor. He never gives me credit for anything!"

Simple encouragement:

Rephrasing:

Reflective responding:

Clarification:

Interpretation:

Providing information:

Emphasizing people's strengths:

Summarization: (Since it is almost impossible to summarize one line, assume that you have had an ongoing discussion on this matter.)

Eliciting information:

Statement #3: **(From another agency's director)** "I think your agency ought to get more involved in our program."[3]

Simple encouragement:

Rephrasing:

Reflective responding:

Clarification:

Interpretation:

Providing information:

Emphasizing people's strengths:

Summarization: (Since it is almost impossible to summarize one line, assume that you have had an ongoing discussion on this matter.)

Eliciting information:

Statement #4: **(From a local politician who has significant influence over your agency's funding)** "I'd like to know why your agency's staff hasn't submitted any grants for external funding."

Simple encouragement:

Rephrasing:

Reflective responding:

Clarification:

Interpretation:

Providing information:

---

[3] Vocational rehabilitation involves training people who have physical or mental disabilities "so they can do useful work, become more self-sufficient, and be less reliant on public financial assistance" (Barker, 1995, p. 403).

Emphasizing people's strengths:

Summarization: (Since it is almost impossible to summarize one line, assume that you have had an ongoing discussion on this matter.)

Eliciting information:

The Use of "Why?"

It is easy to use the word *why* when asking questions, but be aware that "why" can sound threatening. It can "put people on the spot," and it can imply that the person to whom it's directed is at fault. Consider the question, "Why are you late?" You can rephrase it: "You're late. Is everything all right?" or "We're so glad you got here. Was traffic terrible?"

Exercise 2.5: Avoiding the Use of "Why?"

Rephrase the following "why" questions.

__Question #1:__ "We agreed at the last meeting that you'd talk to Fred—why didn't you?"

Alternative Phrasing:

__Question #2__: "Why are you always complaining about that policy?"

Alternative Phrasing:

__Question #3__: "Why did the Director reject our petition?"

Alternative Phrasing:

__Question #4__: "Why are public assistance and social security so complicated?"

Alternative Phrasing:

Appropriate Assertiveness in the Macro Environment

Most people wish they'd been more assertive on certain occasions. Yet in the midst of an interaction, they may feel uncomfortable about such behavior or find themselves caught off guard. For example, Verne and Shirley are social work practitioners in the same agency. One day Verne catches Shirley in the hall as she's rushing off to an important meeting. He asks her to finish up a report of his that is due immediately. He assures her that it won't take very long and that he will be eternally grateful. Shirley, having no time to think, agrees and hurries to the meeting. On second thought, she is disgusted with herself. She decides that Verne purposely approached her in a moment of distraction and asked a very inappropriate favor. His reports are *his* responsibility, and she curses herself for not being more assertive.

Other people actually maintain a *pattern* of nonassertiveness. Suppose a supervisor asks a worker to put in regular overtime because the supervisor knows that worker *will never say no*. The worker doesn't *want* to work overtime, and other employees are not asked to do so. Sometimes chronically nonassertive people allow their frustration to build until they can't stand being taken advantage of and simply "lose it." All their emotions explode in a burst of anger.

Nonassertive, Assertive, and Aggressive Communication

On an assertiveness continuum, communication can be rated nonassertive, assertive, or aggressive. *Assertive* communication is verbal and nonverbal behavior through which you can get your points across clearly and straightforwardly, taking into consideration both your own value and the value of whomever is receiving your message.

In *nonassertive* communication, you devalue yourself, placing the other person and his or her priorities ahead of yourself and your agenda.

Aggressiveness is at the other end of the assertiveness continuum. It is characterized by bold and dominating verbal and nonverbal behavior through which you claim precedence for your point of view over all others.

In micro, mezzo, and macro practice, appropriate assertiveness gives you a substantial advantage (Lewinsohn et al., 1978; Sundel & Sundel, 1980): more control over your work and in other interpersonal environments, the ability to avoid uncomfortable or hostile interactions with others, the sense that other people understand you better than they did before, and the enhancement of your self-concept and your interpersonal effectiveness. Appropriate assertiveness helps to reduce tension and stress.

There's no assertiveness "script" to cover every situation. You must simply consider both your own rights and the rights of the person with whom you are interacting. The following are a few examples of possible nonassertive, aggressive, and assertive responses to work situations:

Situation #1: Amorette is a social worker at a residential treatment center for adolescents with severe emotional and behavioral problems. She completes the draft of a grant application for funds to start a sex education program in the center. The proposal stipulates that experts will provide both educational programming and contraceptives. Agency policy requires that all grant proposal drafts be reviewed by the Grants Committee before they are submitted. Prunella, one of the center's teachers, is a member of the Grants Committee.

When Prunella sees the proposal, she flies through the roof. She contends that—for this population—explicit discussion of sex will only encourage experimentation. She is also appalled that the proposal includes providing contraceptives directly to the girls. "Why not show them pornographic movies too?" she mutters.

Prunella approaches Amorette and declares, "That grant proposal you wrote is totally inappropriate. Under no circumstances will I condone it!" How should Amorette reply?

Nonassertive Response: "You're probably right. I'll just forget about it."

Aggressive Response: "What's wrong with you? Are you still living in the Dark Ages or something? Maybe what you need is a little action yourself."

Assertive Response: "I understand your concerns. However, I still think this is an important issue to address. Let's talk further about it."

Situation #2: Gigette is a social worker for a public agency that provides supportive home-based services for the elderly. The agency's intent is to help people maintain their independence and reside in their own homes as long as possible. A county policy states that clients may receive a maximum of eight service hours per month from Gigette's agency or others like it. Many of Gigette's clients require more help than this. She understands that the policy was instituted to keep costs down, but she is convinced that increasing the maximum hours of service from eight to sixteen would allow many clients to remain in their own homes much longer. In the long run, this would save money, because providing or subsidizing nursing home care is monstrously expensive.

Gigette gains the support of her agency's administration and is authorized to approach Biff Bunslinger, the County Board President and explain her proposal and its rationale. His support will be crucial in changing the county's policy.

Biff listens, then says, "It's a good idea, but where will you get the money for it? What else do you want to cut? Do you have any idea what repercussions such a major policy change would have?" How can Gigette respond?

Nonassertive Response: "I don't know. I'm sorry. Let's forget it."

Aggressive Response: "You haven't heard a word I've said. Get off your butt, Biff, and start thinking about those people out there who really need help!"

Assertive Response: "I know funding is tight and that you have to balance all sort of competing financial needs. Let me show you how in the long run this plan can help your elderly constituents *and* save the county money."

Situation #3: Bo, an outreach worker for urban homeless people, is on the Board of Directors of another agency, the AIDS Support Network.[4] Eleni, another board member who is also a local lawyer, bluntly tells him, "I wish you would be more specific in your comments during meetings. I can never understand what you're talking about." What can Bo reply?

Nonassertive Response: "You're right. I'll try to speak more clearly in the future."

Aggressive Response: "I'm not nearly as unclear as you are—nor, by the way, as arrogant. If you don't understand me, maybe what I'm saying is just over your head."

Assertive Response: "I'm sorry you feel that way. Maybe you could let me know right there at the meeting when I've said something you don't understand. Also, I want you to know that I appreciate this feedback, but you might have given it with greater sensitivity to my feelings."

Exercise 2.6: Nonassertive, Aggressive, and Assertive Responses

For each of the following case vignettes, propose nonassertive, aggressive, and assertive responses that the worker involved in each case might make.

Case Vignette #1: Mohammed, a school social worker, applies for a state grant to start a summer activity program for adolescents in an urban neighborhood. Although he has already solicited support from his direct supervisor and from the school board, a principal from another school in the district objects to Mohammed's proposal: "Trying to get money for that project is inappropriate. It will result in significant differences in services between one school district and another, which is completely unfair. I think we should forget the idea."

Nonassertive Response:

Aggressive Response:

Assertive Response:

---

[4] A Board of Directors is "a group of people empowered to establish an organization's objectives and policies and to oversee the activities of the personnel responsible for day-to-day implementation of those policies" (Barker, 1991, p. 25).

Case Vignette #2: Audrey directs a group home for adults with physical disabilities. The home is run by a conservative religious organization which has publicly declared its anti-abortion stance. Her direct supervisor, the organization's director, is also strongly anti-abortion. Audrey, however, maintains a pro-choice position.

A pro-choice rally is being held this weekend, and Audrey plans to attend and participate. She even expects to carry a pro-choice banner and march in a planned procession through the main area of town. Audrey's supervisor finds out about her plans, calls her aside, and says, "I forbid you to participate in that rally. Our agency has a reputation to maintain, and I won't allow you to jeopardize it."

Nonassertive Response:

Aggressive Response:

Assertive Response:

Case Vignette #3: Hiroko is a public assistance worker for a large county bureaucracy. She is very dedicated to her job and often spends extra time with clients to make certain that they receive all possible benefits. Her colleague Bill, who has the same job title, tells Hiroko, "Either you're a fool and a drudge to work overtime like that, or you're trying to be a 'star' to feed your ego."

Nonassertive Response:

Aggressive Response:

Assertive Response:

Exercise 2.7: Assertiveness Training for You

Assertiveness training helps people analyze their own behavior and become more assertive. Alberti & Emmons (1976) developed a number of steps that will lead to the habit of assertive behavior. They form the basis for the following exercise.

1.   Recall a situation in which you could have acted more assertively. Perhaps you were too nonassertive or too aggressive. Describe the situation below.

2.   Analyze the way you reacted in this situation. Critically examine both your verbal and nonverbal behavior. Describe and explain that behavior.

3.   Choose a role model for assertive behavior in a situation similar to the one you have described. Identify the person you've chosen, then describe what happened and how she reacted assertively.

4.   Identify two or three other assertive verbal and nonverbal responses that you could have employed in the situation you described.

5.   Imagine yourself acting assertively in the situation you described. Explain what you would say and do.

6.   After you have completed these five steps, try behaving assertively in real life. Continue practicing until assertiveness becomes part of your personal interactive style. Give yourself a pat on the back when you succeed in becoming more assertive. Be patient with yourself—it's not easy to change long-standing patterns of behavior.

Conflict and Its Resolution

An *interpersonal conflict* occurs "whenever an action by one person prevents, obstructs, or interferes with the actions of another person" (Johnson, 1986, p. 199). Conflict can occur in an infinite number of ways in an unending array of contexts—micro, mezzo, and macro. This chapter focuses on conflicts between individuals in macro contexts. Chapter 3 will address specific types of conflict and conflict management guidelines for mezzo situations in macro environments.

Conflict is not always (or completely) negative (Johnson, 1986). On the positive side, it forces adversaries to examine their perspectives more thoroughly, enhances self-awareness, generates new energy for problem-solving, releases pent-up emotional steam, improves the quality of problem resolution and decision making through the infusion of new ideas, and increases excitement in otherwise humdrum daily routines. On the negative side, it requires the expenditure of considerable energy, carries with it the risk of loss (of face, position, influence, etc.), and diminishes the quality of collaboration and teamwork if hard feelings arise (Daft, 1992).

Personal Styles for Addressing Conflict

Just as each of us has a unique personality, so also does each have an individual style of conflict. Johnson (1986, pp. 208-11) describes five conflict-management styles. The categories are somewhat oversimplified, but they do illustrate broad types of behaviors people display in a conflict.

1.   *Turtles* "withdraw into their shells to avoid conflicts" (p. 208). For them, this is easier than mustering up the initiative and energy needed to address a conflict. Turtles typically have relatively poor self-concepts and are nonassertive.

2.   *Sharks,* unlike turtles, are aggressors. They move into conflict boldly, pushing aside any opponents. Sharks like power and want to win. They have very little interest in nurturing a relationship with an opponent.

3.   *Teddy bears* are essentially the opposite of sharks. They value their relationships with their opponent more than the achievement of their own goals. Teddy bears are more assertive than turtles because they do value their own ideas, but they will put those ideas aside in deference to an opponent's beliefs if they believe their relationship is threatened.

4.   *Foxes* are compromisers. Slyly, they work toward an agreement acceptable to them and to their opponent. Foxes are willing to relinquish some of their demands in order to come to a reasonable compromise. They are pretty slick at finding ways to satisfy everyone.

5.   *Owls,* like foxes, believe in compromise, but they are much more assertive in conflict. Their style can be called confrontational. Owls walk willingly, even eagerly, into conflict situations because they value *the conflict itself* as a means of brainstorming solutions, attacking problems, and enhancing relationships.

We cannot overstress the importance of getting to know yourself and your own reactions better in order to control your behavior and increase your interpersonal effectiveness. To this end, answer the following questions.

1.   What style of conflict—or combination of styles—described above comes closest to the way you usually handle a conflict?

2.   To what extent is your approach to handling conflict effective? Explain.

3.   In what ways would you like to change your approach to conflict management? (If you are satisfied with your behavior in conflictual situations, say so.)

Steps in Conflict Resolution

Johnson (1986) proposes seven steps for conflict resolution. Although it is not always possible to go through each one, it is important to keep them in mind.

Step 1: Initiate a confrontation ("the act of bringing together opposing ideas, impulses, or groups for the purpose of systematic examination or comparison" [Barker, 1991, p. 47]). First, clearly identify your goals and recognize their importance to you.

Then keep in mind the importance of nurturing your interpersonal relationship with the other person (Hooyman, 1973; Johnson, 1986; Weissman, Epstein, & Savage, 1983). You will need the support of others to achieve any macro goals you may establish. Therefore, the stronger your various relationships in the macro environment, the more likely you are to perform your job well and achieve your intervention goals.

Step 2: Agree on a definition of the problem. This definition should make neither you nor your opponent defensive or resistant to compromise. Emphasize how important the issue is to both of you.

Step 3: Recognize the importance of maintaining communication with your opponent(s) in the conflict. Many of the communication techniques already discussed can be put to excellent use in this process. Additionally, Sheafor, Horejsi, & Horejsi (1991, pp. 337-38) propose the following general communication guidelines:

- Do not begin a confrontation when you are angry. Anger makes you lose your objectivity.
- Do not enter into a conflict unless you are willing to work toward resolution. Otherwise, you are wasting your time.
- If you absolutely despise your opponent or have immense difficulty finding any positive, empathic feelings about him, do not confront him. Explore other ways of addressing the conflict (for example, through finding support from others who can deal more calmly with your opponent) or drop the matter completely.
- Include positive statements and feedback along with your negative input.
- Explain your concerns in a "descriptive and nonjudgmental" manner (Sheafor et al., 1991, p. 338). Prepare details beforehand in your head so that you can explain and clarify the issues and behaviors involved.
- Supply relevant data in support of your position. Be able to articulate your position clearly and have both your ideal solution and some potential compromises clearly established in your mind.
- Use "I-messages" frequently.   Rephrasing your thoughts in this manner emphasizes your personal caring and empathy.

Step 4: Indicate your own willingness to work with your opponent to find a mutually satisfactory solution. To minimize disagreement (or at least to develop a viable plan of action) stress whatever you and your opponent have in common.

Step 5: Empathize with your opponent. Think carefully about why she thinks, feels, or acts as she does.

Step 6: Evaluate both your own and your opponent's motivation to address the conflict. Is it worthwhile to expend the energy necessary to resolve this conflict?

Step 7: Come to some mutual agreement by following these five suggestions (Johnson, 1986). (1) Articulate exactly what your agreement entails. (2) Indicate how you will behave toward the other person in the future as compared to in the past. (3) Indicate how the other person has agreed to behave toward you. (4) Outline ways of addressing any future difficulties (such as might arise if you or the other person violates the agreement). (5) Decide how and when you and the other person will meet to continue your cooperative behavior and to minimize future conflict.

Exercise 2.9: Conflict Resolution

Recall a conflict in which you have been involved. For the purposes of this exercise, it may be work-related, school-related, or personal.

1. Describe the conflict in detail. Who was involved? What was the issue? Explain the positions taken by the opposing sides. What were the circumstances of the actual confrontation?

2. Did you follow the suggestions in Step 1 for beginning a confrontation—that is, did you identify your goals and nurture your relationship with your opponent? What, if anything, could you have done differently to improve your handling of this conflict?

3. Did you follow Step 2 by finding some common ground with your opponent? What, if anything, could you have done differently to discover some common ground?

4. Did you follow Step 3 by maintaining communication with your opponent? What, if anything, could you have done differently to improve communication?

5. Did you follow Step 4 by indicating your willingness to cooperate with your opponent? What, if anything, could you have done differently to demonstrate this willingness?

6. Did you follow Step 5 by empathizing with your opponent and trying to understand his or her perspective? What, if anything, could you have done differently to achieve this empathy and understanding?

7. Did you follow Step 6 by evaluating both your own and your opponent's motivations in this conflict? What, if anything, could you have done differently to discern and evaluate those motives?

8. Did you follow Step 7 by arriving at some mutually satisfactory agreement? What, if anything, could you have done differently to make such an agreement possible?

Working Under Supervisors

Your interpersonal relationships with agency supervisors are especially significant in the macro environment. Social work, in general, embraces the use of supervision as a professional value. Barker (1995) defines it as "an administrative and educational process used extensively in social agencies to help social workers further develop and refine their skills and to provide quality assurance for the clients" (pp. 371-72), and Shulman (1991) reinforces that the purpose of supervision is improvement of service to clients.

If you can empathize with supervisors and understand their position, you will be able to maximize the benefits of your relationships with them. On one hand, they are responsible for you and your work performance. On the other, supervisors must answer to upper levels of administration in fulfilling their other agency responsibilities.

Workers generally expect supervisors (Sheafor, Horejsi, & Horejsi, 1991; Shulman, 1991):

- To be readily available for consultation—i.e., to provide help based on professional or expert opinion
- To ascertain that workers are knowledgeable about relevant agency policies and are aware of what they should and should not do
- To inform higher levels of administration about line workers' needs
- To facilitate cooperation among staff and resolve disputes
- To nurture workers, provide support, and give positive feedback whenever possible
- To evaluate workers' job performance
- To facilitate workers' development of new and needed skills

---

Exercise 2.10: Evaluating Supervisors

Think of a supervisor you have or one you had in the past. You may choose someone you consider very good or downright terrible. In this exercise, you will evaluate that supervisor in terms of the expectations listed above, so choose someone you remember well. If you've never had a supervisor, imagine one of your instructors in that role. In this evaluation, cite pros, cons, and suggestions for improvement. It may help to mention specific interactions you had or issues you confronted with this supervisor.

1.   How readily available was this supervisor to provide help based on professional or expert opinion?

Pros:

Cons:

Suggestions for Improvement:

2.   Did this supervisor fulfill your expectations in ascertaining that you were knowledgeable about relevant agency policies so that you could do your jobs as well as possible?

Pros:

Cons:

Suggestions for Improvement:

3.   Did this supervisor fulfill your expectations in informing higher levels of administration about line workers' needs?

    Pros:

    Cons:

    Suggestions for Improvement:

4.   Did this supervisor fulfill your expectations in facilitating cooperation among staff and helping to resolve disputes?

    Pros:

    Cons:

    Suggestions for Improvement:

5.   Did this supervisor fulfill your expectations in nurturing you, providing support, and giving positive feedback?

    Pros:

    Cons:

    Suggestions for Improvement:

6.   Did this supervisor fulfill your expectations in accurately and effectively evaluating your job performance?

    Pros:

    Cons:

    Suggestions for Improvement:

7.   Did this supervisor fulfill your expectations in facilitating your development of new and needed skills?

    Pros:

    Cons:

    Suggestions for Improvement:

Using Supervision Effectively

Effective use of supervision hinges partly on your own behaviors and characteristics. Communicating clearly and regularly with your supervisor can get you the help you need in working with exceptionally difficult clients and finding resources you would not otherwise know about. The following are some helpful suggestions for maximizing your use of supervision (Austin, Kopp, & Smith, 1986; Sheafor, Horejsi, & Horejsi, 1991):

1. Use your micro communication skills with your supervisor. Check to be certain that you clearly understand the messages you hear. Ask questions. Rephrase a question if you don't think your supervisor understands what you mean. Paraphrase your supervisor's answer to ensure that you understand what was said.

2. Keep your records up-to-date. Record-keeping is essential for accountability and your supervisor is ultimately responsible for your work. If you fail to keep up with required record-keeping, it will reflect badly on your supervisor. I promise you she will not like that.

3. Plan ahead in terms of the items you include on your supervisory agenda. This gives the supervisor time to provide the information and help you need.

4. Put yourself in your supervisor's shoes. Use empathy. He is an individual with his own feelings, interests, biases, and opinions. Think about both what he needs to know and what he needs to communicate to you. It is helpful to get to know your supervisor as well as possible.

5. Display an openness to learning and improving yourself. Demonstrate a willingness to accept criticism and use it to improve your work.

6. Display a liking for your work. You can emphasize the positive aspects of your work, emphasizing those facets you especially like. Whiners get old pretty fast.

7. Work cooperatively with other staff and use teamwork. Be sensitive to the effect of your behavior on others. Show respect for the competence and talents of your peers and coworkers. Be tolerant of what you see as their shortcomings. Try to see the world from their perspective and understand why they feel and act the way they do.

8. Give your supervisor feedback. *Tactfully* let her know what you like and dislike. If you have specific needs that your supervisor can appropriately meet, express them.

9. Forewarn your supervisor about potential problems. When you don't know all the possible implications of a particular course of action or how it might affect the agency, ask your supervisor. *Don't* wait until the situation has reached crisis proportions.

10. Learn your supervisor's evaluation system so that you can adequately respond to his expectations.

Exercise 2.11: Addressing Problems in Supervision

Sometimes, for whatever reason, problems develop. They may be your own, your supervisor's, or no one's fault, but when they occur, you must address them, adjust to them, or leave for another job.

The following scenarios are taken from actual supervisory experiences. Each involves real problems that you too could confront. In each case, think about how you would use the recommendations we have just discussed to resolve the difficulties. Then answer the questions that follow.

Scenario A: Taking Your Credit

You are a social worker at a large urban diagnostic and treatment center for children with multiple developmental and physical disabilities. Your primary role includes helping parents cope with their child's disability, making referrals to appropriate resources, offering some family counseling, and interpreting the physicians' and other therapists' findings and recommendations to parents in words the parents can understand.

The city abruptly cuts off funding for transportation to the center. Many of your parents are very poor and don't own vehicles. Most of the children have such extreme physical difficulties that city buses can't accommodate them. After compiling some facts, you call various local political leaders and share with them your serious concerns. Because of your efforts, the local City Council Chairperson convenes a meeting to address and remedy this transportation problem. You are very proud of yourself because you feel you are primarily responsible for this solution.

You share the news with your supervisor and indicate enthusiastically that you are planning to attend the meeting. She says, "I don't think you need to attend the meeting. I'll go instead." You emphasize how hard you've worked on this project and make clear that you would really like to attend. You suggest that, perhaps, you could both go.

She responds, "No, I don't think so. I'll go." You are devastated.

1.	Try to empathize with this supervisor by discerning what her reasons might be for reacting like this.

2.	In this situation, how could you use the suggestions for assertiveness and confrontation described earlier in this chapter?

3.	Consider the suggestions for using supervision effectively. Which of them could help you in this case?

4.	If you were the supervisee portrayed here, how important would it be to you to receive credit for your accomplishment? Would you feel that it was the goal that mattered rather than *who* achieved it?

5.	If you are the supervisee portrayed here and you *do* care about receiving credit for your work, what will you do if all the suggestions you have proposed thus far fail? (For example, will you go to an administrator above your supervisor for help and risk your supervisor's wrath? Will you learn a lesson from the experience and keep your successes to yourself in the future? Will you try to put it out of your mind and go on with your daily business? Will you start looking for another job?) There is no "correct" answer. You must identify various options, weight the pros and cons of each, and decide what to do.

Scenario B: The Communication Gap

You are a newly hired social worker for a unit of boys, ages 11 to 13, at a residential treatment center for youths with serious behavioral and emotional problems. Your responsibilities include counseling, group work, case management, some family counseling, and consultation with child-care staff on matters of behavioral programming. Two of the twelve boys in the unit have been causing you particular trouble. They are late for their weekly counseling sessions and sometimes skip them altogether. When you do talk to them, they don't respond to your questions. Instead, they walk around the room, tell you that you don't know what you're doing, poke holes in the furniture with their pencils, and call you vulgar names.

You are at a loss regarding what to do with these two clients. In your weekly one-hour session with your supervisor, you explain the situation. He makes several vague suggestions about videotaping some of your sessions, making home visits, and talking about the boys' behavior with them. At the end of the session, you feel you've gotten nowhere, and you still don't understand what you should do. You have difficulty following what your supervisor is saying. You can't "read" him. Sometimes you think he's joking, but you can't be sure.

1.	Try to empathize with this supervisor by discerning what his reasons might be for reacting like this.

2.	In this situation, how could you use the suggestions for assertiveness and confrontation described earlier in this chapter?

3. Consider the suggestions for using supervision effectively. Which of them could help you in this case?

4. Consider the possibility that you tried a range of approaches and none worked. If you decided that your supervisor was incompetent and really unable to help you, what would you do? Might you consider turning to other people in the agency for help? If so, how would you do so?

Scenario C: The Angry Response

You are a social worker at a health care center (nursing home) who has a variety of clients diagnosed as "mentally ill." Every six months, a staffing is held at which social workers, nurses, therapists (speech, occupational, physical), physicians, psychologists, and psychiatrists summarize clients' progress and make recommendations. It is your job to run the staffing and write a summary of what is said.

You are new at your job and unfamiliar with this agency. During the staffing, the psychiatrist is very verbal—in fact, you would describe him as "pushy." You feel intimidated and are uncomfortable asserting your own opinions when they are different from, or even opposed to, his. Because of his advanced education, his professional status, and his self-confident demeanor, you feel that his views are probably more important and valid than yours. After the staffing, your supervisor calls you aside. His face is red and his voice has a deadly, steel-like calm. He reams you out for letting the psychiatrist take over the staffing. This surprises and upsets you so much that you do not hear many of the specific things he says. You just know that he is furious with you and has implied—or even stated—that you are an incompetent wimp. He walks off in a huff.

1. Try to empathize with this supervisor by discerning what his reasons might be for reacting like this.

2. In this situation, how could you use the suggestions for assertiveness and confrontation described earlier in this chapter?

3. Consider the suggestions for using supervision effectively. Which of them could help you in this case?

Scenario D: Problems with Delegation[5]

You are a caseworker for a social services agency in a rural county. Your job includes a wide range of social work practice, from investigating child abuse cases to working with families of truants to providing supplementary services to the elderly who want to remain in their own homes. You have a heavy caseload, but feel very useful. In general, you really like your job.

The problem is that your supervisor insists on reading every letter and report you write before it goes out. You think this is a terribly time-consuming waste of effort. In many instances, it also delays your provision of service, and you feel that it's condescending and implies a lack of confidence in your professional abilities.

1. Try to empathize with this supervisor by discerning what her reasons might be for reacting like this.

2. In this situation, how could you use the suggestions for assertiveness and confrontation described earlier in this chapter?

---

[5] A primary administrative task for supervisors is mastering the art of delegation. Delegation is "assigning responsibility or authority to others" (*Webster's Ninth New Collegiate Dictionary*, 1991, p. 336).

3.	Consider the suggestions for using supervision effectively. Which of them could help you in this case?

4.	In the event that your efforts to improve this situation fail, what would you do?

Scenario E: No Action

You are a social worker in a large urban community center serving multiple community needs. Services include counseling for emotional and behavior problems, provision of contraception, recreational activities for adults and youth, day care for working parents, meals for elderly citizens, some health care, and a variety of other services. Your job focuses primarily on counseling the center's clients referred for this purpose. You enjoy your job and are proud of being a professional social worker.

The problem is another social worker whose office is next to yours. He has a similar job but is assigned a different caseload and a slightly different range of responsibilities. The bottom line is that you seriously question his professional competence. You've observed him using what you'd describe as "comic book therapy" with the children and adolescents on his caseload. In other words, his clients come in and select comic books from his vast collection instead of receiving any real counseling. He has boasted on several occasions that he only went into social work because he was eligible for a scholarship.

One day you approach one of your clients, a fairly bright and articulate boy of 13. You are surprised to see him reading something in the center's waiting room, and you are disturbed when he obtrusively places his hand over a portion of a picture in the book. It strikes you as odd that his hand is placed over the rear half of a horse. He looks surprised to see you and he comments on the horse's long white mane. The mane is indeed remarkable: it reaches to the ground and extends another foot. When you ask your client what the book is about, he sheepishly shows you the picture, which depicts a castrated horse (hence, the mane and tail elongated due to hormonal changes). The book's title is *Washington Death Trips*. Among other items pictured in the book are dead babies in caskets, people who have butchered over 500 chickens by hand for no reason, and various infamous murderers. The boy tells you that your colleague lent him this book.

You are furious. Not only does this colleague offend your professionalism and your professional ethics, he even has the gall to interfere with your clients. You immediately go to your supervisor, who is also his supervisor, and complain about the incident.

Your supervisor—a well-liked, easy-going, but knowledgeable and helpful person—hems and haws. He implies that methods of counseling are each professional's own business, but you believe that your supervisor is afraid to confront your colleague.

1.	Try to empathize with this supervisor by discerning what his reasons might be for reacting like this.

2.	In this situation, how could you use the suggestions for assertiveness and confrontation described earlier in this chapter?

3.	Consider the suggestions for using supervision effectively. Which of them could help you in this case?

4.	If your efforts to improve this situation fail, what will you do? Can you ignore this issue?

Postscript

In summary, life with supervisors will not always be ideal. When a problem occurs, all you can do is use your communication skills to your best advantage, identify your alternatives, weigh the pros and cons of each, and choose your course of action.

Fortunately, you will probably also have supervisors who will serve as primary mentors. A mentor is someone who encourages you to do your best, exposes you to new knowledge and ideas, and provides you with opportunities to develop your skills and competence.

Exercise 2.12: A Role Play in Supervision

For this exercise students pair off, with one person playing a supervisee and the other a supervisor. You and your partner choose who will play which role. The supervisee should use the suggestions provided in this chapter to confront the supervisor assertively and use supervision effectively. Allow five to ten minutes for the role play, then answer the questions.

Supervisee: *You are a generalist practitioner in a foster care placement unit in a large county social services agency. You received your annual performance review report from your supervisor. The format requires a summary statement by the supervisor. Yours reads, "This worker does a pretty good job of completing her work on time." You feel this is a very negative statement, substantially detracting from a positive evaluation. You believe that you work exceptionally hard, often volunteer to accept difficult cases, and take pride in your performance.*

Supervisor: *You have two dozen supervisees. You don't like to give radically different performance reviews to your workers because these can make for hard feelings and jealousy among staff. You don't think the review is really relevant anyway since salaries are based solely on seniority, not on merit. In your view, your significant communication with workers is carried on during your biweekly individual supervisory conferences, and you think this particular supervisee is doing a good job.*

1.   What communication, confrontation, assertiveness, and supervisory techniques did the supervisee use during the role play?

2.   How effective were these techniques in resolving the issue?

3.   What other techniques, if any, might the supervisee have used to improve her effectiveness?

I.   **Introduction**

II.   **Networking**

    A.   Networks—a number of individuals or organizations that are interconnected to accomplish a goal that each feels is worthwhile

    B.   Highlight 3.1: Networking in Action

    C.   Importance of Networking

        1.   Clients benefit from informal helping networks

        2.   Networks reach out to clients

            a.   Cross cultural situations

            b.   Networking roles played by churches

            c.   Networking is critical in rural areas

        3.   Networks augment formal resources

        4.   Networks help navigate formal systems

            a.   Networking to fill a service gap

            b.   Highlight 3.2: Networking for Latchkey Kids

            c.   Service fairs

        5.   Networks help workers cope

        6.   Networks: Mutual Aid

    D.   Types of Networks

        1.   Classified into categories based on:

            a.   Type of relationship among members

            b.   Degree of intimacy members share

            c.   Difficulty level of the help needed

            d.   Size of network

E.   Problems with Networks

1.   When professionals do not value the contributions of informal networks

2.   When a worker takes such an active leadership role with a client's informal network that the client feels incompetent or left out

3.   Within formal networks when negative or dysfunctional relationships reduce the network's effectiveness

4.   Failure to share information with other network members

5.   Lack of support from all agencies involved in network activities

6.   If some professionals question whether the informal network can maintain an adequate level of confidentiality about the client's situation

7.   Methods for overcoming difficulties in networking

   a.   Recognize and acknowledge mutual interests of different agencies and resources

   b.   Provide various avenues of communication to bridge the gaps

F.   Worker Roles in Networking

1.   Highlight 3.3: Worker Roles with Self-Help Groups (Maguire, 1991)

   a.   Providing a place to meet

   b.   Contributing or arranging for funds

   c.   Providing information to members

   d.   Training members as leaders

   e.   Referring people to the group

   f.   Publicizing group activities

   g.   Accepting referrals from the group

   h.   Providing credibility in the larger community

   i.   Providing credibility in the professional community

   j.   Serving as a buffer between the group and other agencies/organizations

   k.   Providing social and emotional support for group leaders

   l.   Consulting with group leaders

III. **Working In and With Teams**

    A.   Characteristics of Effective Teams (Larson & LaFasto, 1989; Fatout & Rose, 1995)

        1.   Clear goals

        2.&3.   Structure and membership tied to goals

            a.   Problem-solving teams

            b.   Creative teams

            c.   Tactical teams

        4.   Commitment of all members

        5.   Collaborative climate

            a.   Groupthink—occurs when too much emphasis rests on collaboration and conformity and not enough attention is given to thinking critically about alternative

            b.   Critical thinking—challenging assumptions, verifying facts, questioning opinions not supported by data, and being willing to consider ideas that others have rejected

        6.   Standards of excellence—measures of the value and worth of actions

        7.   Information-based decision making

        8.   External support and recognition

        9.   Principled leadership

IV. **Planning and Conducting Meetings**

    A.   Plan ahead

    B.   Clarify purpose and establish objectives

    C.   Select participants

    D.   Select a time and place

        1.   Set meeting times weeks in advance if possible

        2.   Don't hold meeting and eat simultaneously

        3.   Hold meetings in meeting rooms—not in your office

        4.   Choose locations that simplify accomplishment of group business

5.   Meeting location needs to be accessible to those with disabilities

6.   Purpose of meeting should determine seating arrangements and overall room layout

E.   Prepare an agenda

     1.   Agenda—a list of topics to be addressed at a meeting in some sort of prioritized order

     2.   Agenda items

           a.   Announcements

           b.   Decision items

           c.   Discussion items

     3.   Highlight 3.4: Example of an Agenda

F.   Start meetings on time

G.   State the ending time at the start

H.   Let people know how much of your time they can have

I.   Keep the group on target

     1.   Focus on goals and operating within time constraints

     2.   Promote harmony but not at the expense of thinking critically about options

     3.   Test for agreement whenever apparent compromises appear to be achieved

     4.   Use humor to relax the group or to break the tension

     5.   Avoid personal attacks and don't let others engage in them

     6.   May need to interrupt a participant who talks too much

     7.   Structure the process

           a.   Identify items on which there is already unanimity and approve them together. Sometimes called a consent agenda

           b.   Approval of a lengthy document might best be done *ad seriatim* (item by item)

           c.   Periodically summarize the areas of agreement and sum up when decisions have been made

           d.   Avoid discussing irrelevant topics or rehashing previous decisions

        e.   If new topics are brought up, it is often better to place them on future agendas

        f.   If appropriate, a new business item can be referred to a committee

        g.   Keep necessary reports brief

        h.   When oral reports are needed, ask for succinctness and place a time limit on each report

    J. End the meeting on time

        1. Highlight 3.5: Ending Meetings

            a. Meetings should be ended whenever any of the following is evident (Jay, 1984)

                1) More facts are required

                2) The group needs the input of people not present

                3) Members need more time to talk to others

                4) Events may change the direction in the immediate future

                5) There is not enough time to deal with the topic adequately

                6) A subgroup can handle this more easily than the entire group can

                7) A decision has been reached

    K. Plan for follow-up meetings

        1. Minutes—official record of actions taken by the group

        2. Highlight 3.6: Minutes of a Meeting

V. **Parliamentary Procedure**

    A. Parliamentary procedure—a highly structured technique used by groups of various sizes to make decisions and conduct business

    B. *Robert's Rules of Order* (Robert, 1970)—first published in 1876, and the most commonly used set of procedures

    C. Advantages and disadvantages of parliamentary procedure

D.   Basic parliamentary concepts

1.   Motions—proposed actions that the group is asked to support

2.   Privileged motions—deal with the agenda itself but not with any particular business before the group. They have the highest priority of the four categories

     a.   Motion to recess

     b.   Motion to adjourn

3.   Incidental motions—relate to the business under discussion

     a.   Point of order—used when a participant is concerned about some aspect of the way business is being transacted

     b.   Point of information—used when a participant is not clear about something occurring in the meeting

4.   Subsidiary motions—help deal with motions that are currently on the floor

     a.   Table or Postpone—delays action on the proposed motion

     b.   Amend—used to change the proposed motion in some way

5.   Highlight 3.7: Common Parliamentary Definitions

     a.   Ad hoc committee—a special committee assigned one primary responsibility and then terminated

     b.   Adjourn—to end a meeting officially

     c.   Agenda—an official list of business to be discussed or decided at a meeting

     d.   Amend—to add, delete, or substitute words or portions of a motion

     e.   Bylaws—the major rules of an organization, usually more detailed than the constitution

     f.   Call the question—a motion to stop debate and immediately vote on the matter before a group

     g.   Committee—any portion of the total group assigned a specific task

     h.   Constitution—a document that describes the basic laws and governing procedures of an organization

     i.   Debate—discussion of topics a group is addressing

     j.   Executive committee—a subgroup composed of the chief officers of an organization, often including one or more elected members

k.   Filibuster—speaking for the primary purpose of taking up time and preventing a group from voting on a topic

l.   Majority vote—greater than one half of the total of persons voting or ballots cast

m.   Minutes—the official record of decisions reached by a group

n.   Motion—a proposal, requiring action, submitted to a group

o.   Nomination—a formal proposal for some office

p.   Plurality—the receipt of more votes than any other person, but less than a majority

q.   Point of order—a statement to the presiding officer of a group that a mistake has occurred or a rule should be enforced

r.   Proxy—a signed statement giving another person the right to vote in one's place

s.   Quorum—the minimum number or proportion of members needed to legally transact business

t.   Recess—a short break in a meeting

u.   Refer to committee—a motion to delegate work on some specific matter to a smaller group

v.   Second—an indication of approval of a proposed motion

w.   Seriatim—a method of discussing and voting on a document by section

x.   Standing committee—committee that continually exists and handles certain types of business

y.   Table—a motion to indefinitely postpone action on a motion already on the floor

z.   Unanimous—any vote on which there is no dissent

E.   Main motions

1.   Introduce the primary issue before the group

2.   Most motions need a second

3. Highlight 3.8: Classes of Motions

    a. Privileged motions

    b. Incidental motions

    c. Subsidiary motions

    d. Main motions

4. Motions that require a two-thirds majority to pass

    a. Object to consideration of a motion

    b. Call to suspend the rules

    c. Call for an immediate vote

    d. Limit or extend debate

    e. Rescind a motion under consideration

5. Voting on motions

F. Other parliamentary rules

1. Quorum—minimum number of members who must be present to conduct business and make decisions

2. Officers

3. Committees

    a. Standing—permanent

    b. Ad hoc—temporary committees established to address some specific issue

    c. Steering—sometimes created to help run an organization that does not want to become too formal

4. Filibustering—endlessly speaking on a matter, thereby preventing a group from conducting its business

VI. Managing Conflict

A. Conflict is normal; can be positive or negative; fear and discomfort with conflict is common

B. Highlight 3.9: Conflict in the Hospital

C.   Forms of Conflict

      1.   Interpersonal—occurs when disagreement over a concrete issue escalates to include personal attacks

      2.   Scarce Resources—occurs over the use of, or access to money, time, attention, or power

      3.   Representational—occurs when one person represents a group whose interests differ from those of other groups

      4.   Intercessional—when you must intercede between two or more individuals or groups in conflict

D.   Types of Conflict (Bisno, 1988; Strom-Gottfried, 1998)

      1.   Interest/commitment conflict—characterized by basic genuine clashes of opposing interests, values, or commitments

      2.   Induced conflict—created to reach goals that could otherwise not be attained directly

      3.   Misattributed conflict—based on an honest mistake

      4.   Data conflict—occurs when two sides have either inconsistent or inadequate data upon which to make decisions

      5.   Structural conflict—dispute arising from differences in such factors as power, time, or physical or other environmental barriers

      6.   Illusionary conflict—similar to misattributed conflict, but based on something that was blamed on the wrong person or group

      7.   Displaced conflict—directed at people or concerns other than the real source of conflict

      8.   Expressive conflict—rests primarily on a wish to express hostility, aggression, or other strong feelings

E.   Highlight 3.10: Steps in Managing Conflict

F.   Advanced Conflict Management: Guidelines and Strategies

      1.   Focusing on power

            a.   Always assess both your power and that of your adversary

            b.   Avoid full disclosure of your power

            c.   Always use power sparingly

      2.   Forestalling or sidestepping conflict

3. Generating conflict

4. Conflict management by covert means

    a. Passive resistance—simply drag your feet in ways that create problems for the opponent

    b. Concealment—do not let the other party know what you are doing

    c. Manipulation—influence others without their being aware of it

    d. More specific tactics

        1) Negativism and noncompliance with rules

        2) Stonewalling—refusing to act on a matter

        3) Deceit or deception

        4) Seduction—offering of inducements to convince neutral parties to join you or to convert opponents to your side

        5) Emotional extortion—withholding something valued by the other

        6) Divide and conquer—reduces the influence of the adversary and neutralizes opposing players

5. Conflict management by emergent agreement—one side convinces the other to change

6. Conflict management by coactive disputation—both parties are willing to consider joint problem solving, using facts to settle disputes, and remain open to persuasion

7. Conflict management by negotiated agreement

8. Conflict management by indirect means or procedural measures

    a. When both sides cannot or will not negotiate

    b. When other management approaches are unpalatable

9. Conflict management by exercise of authority/power

Exercise 3.1: Identifying Your Own Networks

A. Brief Description
    Students will identify and categorize their own networks.

B. Objectives
    Students will:
    1. Recognize their own personal and professional networks.
    2. Understand the ways in which networks can help fill basic human needs.

C. Procedure
    1. Ask each student, working alone, to identify the networks of which they are a part. Then ask them to categorize each of them into those which are professional networks and those which are personal.
    2. Ask students to identify which of their networks (if any) might be helpful in situations listed in the box below.
    3. After about 10-15 minutes ask students to identify their networks and to indicate which, if any, of the boxed situations could be helped by their network.

D. Instructions for Students
    Identify the networks of which you are a part. Categorize each of them into those which are professional networks and those which are personal. Which network (if any) would be helpful in the following situations.

Which of Your Networks Might be Helpful in These Situations?

1. You need advice about a personal problem.

2. You want to know how to register to vote in your community.

3. You need to refer a client to a substance abuse program.

E. Commentary
    This exercise can be done in groups of 4-6 students with a recorder reporting back to the larger group.

Exercise 3.2: Teamwork

A. Brief Description
    Students discuss groups and teams of which they are a part and compare these to characteristics of effective teams.

B. Objectives
    Students will:
    1. Recognize the many groups and teams of which they are a part.
    2. Learn to evaluate groups and teams using a measure of effectiveness.

C.   Procedure
    1.   Review the characteristics of effective teams as described in the chapter.
    2.   Ask students to list 3 groups or teams of which they are a member.
    3.   Ask them to compare each of these groups/teams on the basis of the characteristics shown in the box below.
    4.   Allow about 15 minutes for this exercise.
    5.   Ask class members to report on groups/teams which they believe were especially effective or especially ineffective. Encourage class members to discuss why a particular group was effective or ineffective.

D.   Instructions for Students
List 3 groups or teams of which you are a member. These can be from your work, class, or personal life. Using the characteristics of effective teams noted in the box below, identify which (if any) of these groups/teams were particularly effective.

Characteristics of Effective Teams

1.   Clear goals
2.   Structure and membership tied to goals
3.   Commitment of members (team spirit)
4.   A climate of collaboration
5.   Commitment to excellence
6.   External recognition and support
7.   Principled leadership

E.   Commentary
This exercise can also be done with students working in small groups.

Exercise 3.3: Conflict

A.   Brief Description
Students learn to identify and appropriately categorize types of conflicts.

B.   Objectives
Students will:
    1.   Appropriately identify types of conflicts in their own lives.
    2.   Develop skill in articulating their opinions.

C.   Procedure
    1.   Discuss in class the various forms of conflict encountered in social work practice.
    2.   Ask students, working alone, to identify two conflicts in their own lives and to categorize these using the categories interpersonal, resource, representational and intercessional.
    3.   Allow about 10-15 minutes for this process.
    4.   Ask students to identify a conflict and to give their reasons why they believe the conflict fits into one of the categories shown below.
    5.   Invite other students to ask questions or offer their opinion as to an appropriate category.

D.   Instructions for Students
Identify two conflicts in which you have been involved in your school, work, or personal life and indicate whether each conflict was an interpersonal, resource, representational, or intercessional conflict. Be prepared to explain why you chose a particular type of conflict.

E.   Commentary

This exercise can be done in small groups with students presenting their categorization to other group members.

Exercise 3.4: Networking

List at least four reasons why networking is important in social work.

Recommendations for Developing Networks

Developing effective networks is an important skill for social workers working in the community. The suggestions below can help you achieve this.

Identify Significant Informal Networks

Learn the names of the service clubs, fraternal organizations, and neighborhood associations in your community. Find out what special interests or focuses these groups may have. Identify all the major churches in your community and learn the names of their pastors. Find out whether these churches offer support groups or other services targeted at specific problems. In rural communities, try to learn the names of most community leaders, professionals in the health care and human services fields, and elected officials. If you are new to a community, ask established friends and colleagues to introduce you to those on your "need to know" list.

In addition, learn the names, functions, and services offered by all formal social service providers in your community. Keep a file, Rolodex, or database of these organizations, with the names of your contact people. Make a point of visiting each agency or organization and participating in any activities— such as Christmas open houses, anniversary celebrations, and similar activities—that further your learning.

Strengthen your ties to other networks by learning names, responding promptly to requests for information or assistance, and thanking people for their help. When the time comes that you need assistance for your clients, it will be much easier if you have laid the groundwork first. Recognize that networks change over time and that there is a mutuality at work: those who give help reasonably expect to be able to ask for it themselves later.

Exercise 3.5: Your Personal Network

You have learned about the importance of personal networks in helping social workers cope with their own stresses and frustrations. List at least five individuals you would include in your support network.

Recognize Different Types of Networks

Networks differ in a variety of ways. For example, some networks provide help with very complex problems. Others offer only minor or modest assistance. Formal networks tend to have greater resources available for dealing with major problems. Informal networks generally lack either the resources or the scope of formal networks. Some networks, such as church groups, are characterized by a high degree of intimacy between members. Again, more formal networks often lack this degree of intimacy since relationships are based upon professional contact. From time to time, a network may come into existence and then disappear. Sometimes a community is confronted with a particular problem. Those with mutual interests come together, respond to the problem, and then go their separate ways. This tends to happen when tragedy—a flood, a major fire, an outbreak of illness—strikes a community or organization or when another transient stressor appears.

Consider each of the following situations. Then identify a resource from your network that you could rely on to help you. These resources may or may not be on the list you made in exercise 3.5.

1. Your car breaks down on the way to your first day at your field placement. You need a ride to work for the next two days. Who would help?

2. Payday is still a week away and you need another $50 to get a wart removed from your nose. Who would lend you $50?

3. Your computer and printer just quit, you have a paper due tomorrow morning at 8:00 A.M., and the campus computer labs are closed. Whose computer and printer could you use?

4. You have decided to come out of the closet and acknowledge that you are gay (or lesbian). Who is the first person you could depend on for support?

Exercise 3.7: Professional Networking

As you can see, networks come in handy in personal situations. They are equally important in your professional roles. Respond to the situation below:

Your new client is a woman with chronic mental illness who can function as long as she takes her medication. However, because of her illness she often forgets and decompensates. Who would you go to help her develop (or redevelop) a network that she could rely on? List at least five possible individuals or groups that might be of assistance.

Team Work in Macro Practice

Social workers often work in teams composed of other social workers, various professionals, or citizens. Teams composed of members from several disciplines are referred to as interdisciplinary or multidisciplinary teams. Their membership might include social workers, psychologists, psychiatrists, nurses, and others with needed expertise. Other opportunities to work on teams arise when you participate as a member of an agency board of directors, an advisory committee, or a task force.

The most effective teams have a number of things in common (Larson & LaFasto, 1989). Those commonalities are enumerated below:

1. Clear Goals: As might be expected, lack of clarity about a team's purpose can be devastating. Ideally, the goals should be clear to all members and represent ends that members believe in.

2. Team Structure and Membership Tied to Goals: Both the people on a team and the way the team organizes its work are important variables. Problem-solving teams require different skills than do teams trying to create a new agency or program. Similarly, those who are skilled at planning are helpful in the latter situations but they may not function well when the task is to carry out day-to-day operations.

3. Membership Commitment: The best teams show an *esprit de corps* (team spirit). They enjoy working together and look forward to achieving the team's goals.

4. A Climate of Collaboration: Collaboration is more likely to exist when members know and trust each other. The more team members can come to rely on each other, the greater the potential for collaboration. In a true collaborative environment, members value one another's contributions and trust one another.

5. Commitment to Excellence: A team committed to excellence measures its individual and corporate actions and achievements against some benchmark. All members of the team—or at least most of them—commit themselves to meet this standard and may pressure other members to do the same. Poor quality work is not acceptable.

6. External Recognition and Support: Teams benefit from the recognition and support of outside individuals or groups. This recognition helps insure a "we" feeling and cements the members' connections to the team.

7. Principled Leadership: The best team leaders are clear and consistent in what they say to and about the team. Members need to know that the leader trusts and respects their abilities. Principled leadership shows itself through praise for the contributions of individual members and the ability to shed or control one's own tendency to "showboat."

Whether you're a member or a team leader, be aware of what makes a team effective. That awareness will help ensure both the achievement of team goals and the satisfaction of team members. You must be sensitive to the presence or absence of these characteristics, work to strengthen the team, and contribute your talents to achieving your team's goals.

Exercise 3.8: Practicing Team Work

Social workers participate as members of teams on a fairly routine basis. Respond to each of the situations below.

A. It is your first week of work at a residential treatment center for adolescents with emotional problems. At 10:00 AM you have your first meeting with the "M" team, which consists of you (the social worker), a Ph.D. psychologist, a psychiatrist, a nurse, and the cottage parents from cottage B (your cottage). Just prior to the meeting your supervisor asks you to list the professional knowledge and skills each of these people will bring to the meeting. This isn't "busy work." She wants you to appreciate the value of all the professionals on this team. List the professional contributions each might bring to this meeting based upon their professions and positions.

Psychiatrist

Psychologist

Nurse

Cottage Parents

B. You have been assigned to work with a team of community citizens seeking to "improve the quality of life in the Tanktown." The team has been floundering for several months. Read the information provided about the team and review the characteristics of effective teams. Then identify what you see as the possible problems that may be causing this group's inability to get things done.

The Quality of Life Team (or Q-Team as they like to call themselves) has been meeting for the past four months. They were appointed by the mayor to "improve the quality of life in Tanktown." Members include residents of the community, business owners, students, and several ministers. The mayor chose people who worked in his last election campaign. Meetings have been spent arguing about what the team should focus on. Discussions center around members' very different opinions about what Tanktown's most important problems are. Several members have missed at least five meetings, and the others tend to push ideas that are supported by a majority of the team. The mayor told the group he'd check back in a year to see how they were doing. List the characteristics of effective teams that this group appears to lack. Explain each item.

How to Plan and Conduct Meetings

"Meetings, meetings, meetings! I don't have time for all these meetings." This is a lament that you are likely to hear from time to time in your practice. Meetings can be an important means of getting work done, but often they seem to waste precious time. Social workers spend time in all kinds of meetings—staff meetings, team meetings, community meetings—so it is important that this time be used efficiently. When meetings waste people's time, they typically react negatively. So how do you increase the likelihood that a meeting will be productive? Several recommendations are in order.

A. *Establish Purpose and Objective of Meeting*

Everyone invited to a meeting should know why it's being held. Without clarity about the basic agenda, the meeting is likely to evolve into a confused mess.

B. *Choose Meeting Participants*

Whenever possible, select those who will come to the meeting. Depending upon the meeting's purpose, you may need people who are critical thinkers, who possess certain expertise, and who work well together. You also want people who are committed to the meeting's purpose and who will actually show up, so take into account any possible barriers to participation.

C. *Choose a Time and Place*

Where will you meet? When will you meet? These are not insignificant decisions. The time of day may encourage or discourage attendance. The location must be accessible to all participants and conducive to doing business. Take into account such things as room size in relation to size of group, ventilation, and availability of aids such as blackboards. Give clear directions to the meeting site and to parking areas. Don't expect people who use public transportation to make a meeting at the county seat fifteen miles away. Ideally, schedule your meeting far enough in advance so that people can put it on their calendars. Be sure to remind them as the day of the meeting approaches. Don't assume that everyone will come to a meeting that was scheduled two months ago. Consider possible seating arrangements. Do you need a table and chairs? Should the room be set up theater-style? The purpose of the meeting helps determine room layout.

D. *Send Out an Agenda*

The agenda is simply a list of the things you expect to cover at the meeting. It includes the date, time, and place of the meeting, and alerts participants to what they will be doing and when. The list of items to be addressed should be brief and requires no details. Bring extra copies of the agenda to the meeting. Someone will forget his agenda—count on it.

Background material should accompany the agenda. It's a waste of time to have people read documents at the meeting itself. Be aware that the difficulty level of the decisions to be made at the meeting will probably dictate how much you can get done in the time allotted. Usually the agenda is arranged so that housekeeping items such as approval of minutes, brief reports, and announcements are covered at the very beginning. The most important and difficult items should appear in the middle of the agenda after people warm up. Save the end of the agenda (and meeting) for routine items or those which can be put off until later. Remember, you have only so much time to work with.

E.   *Manage the Time*

Start the meeting on time. Ignore the stragglers, and reward those who come on time. Introduce people if they don't already know one another. Announce the purpose of the meeting, and begin to move through the agenda. Remind people when the meeting will end and end it sooner if you get your business done ahead of time. If time expires and you have not covered everything, bring the last item to closure and adjourn. When you promise people the meeting will end at 5:00 p.m., stick to it. This encourages participants to stay on the topic and get the work done in a timely fashion. If the meeting is mired in muck and a decision can't be reached, don't be afraid to end the meeting. Sometimes a decision *can't* be reached because additional facts are required, important participants are absent, more time is needed for discussion, or the matter should be dealt with by another group (such as a subcommittee) (Jay, 1984).

Plan for any follow-up meetings, scheduling these as soon as possible. Make sure that decisions made at the meeting are carried out and identify the person(s) responsible for this. Ensure that minutes are prepared and distributed to participants prior to the next meeting.

F.   *Manage the Discussion*

Whether you are a leader or a member in a meeting, you have a role to play in keeping the group on target. Test whether items under discussion are related to the agenda. If not, you've gotten off the subject. Contribute your ideas, but make sure they're always on target. Encourage everyone to speak, allowing and encouraging dissent and differences of opinion. Critical thinking demands that opposing ideas be considered. Test for real acceptance of compromises rather than accepting a false sense of harmony.

Don't let the discussion become personal. Some meetings get a bit hot, and so do the participants. Poke fun at yourself, but not at others. Reframe comments that seem to attack people rather than challenge ideas. Model fairness, impartiality, and concern for all participants.

Encourage or arrange for *brief* reports. There is nothing more boring than listening to long reports that should have been reduced to writing and distributed before the meeting.

Exercise 3.9: Planning and Conducting Meetings

Doing a meeting right takes careful planning and attention to detail. The exercise below is designed to help you identify and plan for some of the most important considerations in setting and conducting a meeting.

The agency director has asked you to handle the details for a forthcoming meeting. The participants are community representatives interested in services for people with disabilities. Your director wants to impress upon her guests the agency's commitment to serving this population, and she tells you to set the meeting for either August 1st or September 1st at your option. All of the other details are also up to you.

A.   Identify below the decisions you will have to make (for example, setting the meeting date and time).

B.   Now identify specifically what you decided about each item above (for example, set meeting for September 1st).

C.   What further information, if any, do you need from the Director?

You are invited to observe a meeting of a community coalition created to reduce street violence. Below is a summary of the minutes of the meeting. Read it, and identify any improvements you think are warranted in the conducting of this group's meetings.

> The meeting began at 1:20 p.m. after a short delay to locate the light switches for the meeting room and to accommodate late-comers who were confused about the meeting location. Since agendas were not mailed ahead of time, Chairperson Reno opened the meeting by reading the agenda aloud. The agenda included (1) action on the curfew ordinance, (2) planning for next week's community forum, and (3) discussion of adding to the coalition a representative from the Parents-Teachers Association at the high school. There being no objections, the agenda was adopted as read.
>
> The secretary reminded the group that we had decided at the last meeting to talk about proposing changes to the curfew ordinance. The group discussed this matter and voted to talk to the City Council about changing the curfew. It was agreed that the coalition would meet again later this month to review progress on this matter. The meeting adjourned at 3:00 p.m.

List the actual or potential problems you noted in this brief record. Discuss briefly what should have been done.

Actual or Potential Problems   What Should Have Been Done

Understanding Parliamentary Procedure

It's almost impossible for a group to accomplish anything without first agreeing on a set of rules and procedures. Imagine, for instance, a group of 10 social workers all shouting out ideas and expecting that anyone who could yell loud enough would get his way. Suppose one person said, "I propose the rest of you give all your money to me for my vacation. You have to because I said it first." Without a method for handling routine business, dispatching harebrained ideas without too much fuss, and ensuring that everyone gets a chance to participate in decision making, anarchy would reign.

Robert's Rules of Order (Robert, 1970) provides a systematic and fair way of transacting business. Because they were originally used in British legislative sessions during the nineteenth century, these rules are generally referred to as "parliamentary procedure." Most groups—legislative bodies, committees, task forces, etc.—use parliamentary procedure to conduct their business. Often the group's official documents such as their constitution or bylaws state that business is to be conducted in accordance with *Robert's Rules of Order*.

Like any set of rules, parliamentary procedure has strengths and limitations. It is an effective means of dealing with proposals from group members, making formal decisions, and ensuring that all members have the right to be heard. It is also a much quicker way of reaching a decision. Imagine having to talk everyone into agreeing to something rather than relying on a decision by the majority. Unfortunately, parliamentary procedure can be misused by group members—for example, there are tactics they can use to stall. Even under normal circumstances, debate and voting on a proposal usually produce clear winners and losers, which can lead to hard feelings and impede the ability of members to compromise on other issues. Finally, anyone who doesn't understand parliamentary procedure will feel left out of the discussion or afraid to share her ideas for fear of making some mistake.

What Must I Know?

A variety of terms are routinely used in parliamentary procedure. They include:

Motions: Motions are the primary means of conducting business under parliamentary procedure. They fall into four primary categories: privileged, incidental, subsidiary, and main motions. Motions are usually stated in this form: "I move approval of the budget for 1998," or "I move we refer this matter to the finance committee." Some categories of motions, however, are stated differently.

- *Privileged motions* influence or impact on the formal agenda. For example, a motion to adjourn and a motion to recess—both of which mean the group will cease deliberation for a period of time—are privileged. As their name implies, these are motions of the greatest importance.
- *Incidental motions* concern procedures. A body's failure to follow proper procedure might be met with a motion expressed in the words, "Point of order!" This motion and its sibling "Point of information" must be addressed immediately. When a member raises one of these motions, the presider (group leader) is required to let that person speak. This, in turn, is known as "recognizing" the person who has raised the motion. A point of information might be raised when something in the discussion is unclear, which is why it takes precedence over other motions. After all, you don't want to vote on something you don't understand (unless you're practicing for a future job in the U.S. Congress).
- *Subsidiary motions* include moving to table, postpone, or amend a motion already being discussed. We refer to motions being discussed as "on the floor." Thus, you might say "I move to amend the proposed budget to add 5% salary increases for the staff for next year."

  A motion to table a motion already on the floor is an attempt to postpone any discussion or decision on the proposal indefinitely. Tabling motions are raised when it becomes clear that no decision is going to be reached or that debate is going in circles. A motion to "refer to committee" is used when a matter is best left in the hands of a smaller group for study and recommendation.
- The last category is *main motions*, which accomplish most of a group's business. Although these are of the lowest priority among motions, they are nevertheless important. Without a main motion on the floor, group discussion can wander all over the place because it has no clear focal point. Moving to approve the purchase of new furniture or the proposed budget is a typical example of a main motion. Essentially, main motions bring matters to the floor for discussion and decision. When you make such a motion you are usually accorded the right to speak first. Others may follow until all have had an opportunity to present their ideas.

Seconds: Most motions require a second before discussion is permitted. A second is simply a statement ("I second the motion") indicating support for a motion. Usually, without a second, a motion dies.

Debate: Debate is almost always required on a motion, but there are exceptions. Point of order and point of information motions require no second and are not debatable. Debate is not allowed on motions to table, to "call the question" (that is, to end debate and vote on the motion), or to remove an item previously tabled.

Amendments: An amendment is a proposal to modify a motion on the floor. Each proposed amendment must be voted on before the original motion. Amendments are a way of modifying a motion to gain support from other members. Each proposed amendment is voted on until no further amendments are suggested. At that point a vote is taken on the motion as amended.

Voting: Generally speaking, most motions must be voted on by the group. Voting is usually done by voice vote or a show of hands. The presider will say, "All those in favor of the motion, say aye." Following the ayes there will be a similar call for no votes and sometimes for abstentions (those who choose not to vote). Paper ballots are used in some groups for elections of officers and similar votes. In some groups the presiding officer may also vote. This is specified in the bylaws of the organization under most circumstances. A simple majority (over 50 percent) of those present supporting a motion is needed for passage. Amendments to the group's constitution or bylaws usually require a two-thirds vote to pass. The presider is responsible for announcing the results of the vote. The secretary (official recorder of actions of the group) will enter this decision in the minutes of the body. The minutes are the official record of actions taken by the group.

Other Important Concepts: Almost every group has subgroups (usually called committees) responsible for handling certain types of business. Committees do some of the business of the group between meetings and prepare materials for consideration by the larger group. For example, the board of directors of a group I serve on has committees dealing with personnel, finance, the annual dinner, buildings and grounds, and membership. Each committee has a specific area of responsibility. Any time a matter that falls into one of those areas comes before the board of directors, it is referred to the appropriate committee for a recommendation or decision. Often, after discussing a matter, the committee makes a report and a recommendation to the entire board.

Committees fall into three general categories. *Standing committees* (such as personnel and finance) exist all of the time. Their existence is spelled out in the organization's constitution or bylaws. The constitution is the primary set of rules for an organization, establishing its purpose and outlining its operational system—such as membership, elections, and officers. Bylaws are the guiding rules for the organization's conduct and rank just below the constitution in importance.

From time to time the board I mentioned above finds it necessary to establish other committees to handle specific, one-time issues. For example, an *ad hoc committee* was established to plan a retirement party for the executive director. Since we do not anticipate having such parties on a regular basis, it makes sense to create a temporary committee.

An *executive committee* is responsible for making decisions for the board between meetings. The executive committee is usually empowered to expend funds for emergencies and to handle any other decisions needing immediate action. Most executive committees are composed of the officers of the board (president, vice president, secretary, treasurer) and a few other members chosen at large. The president of the organization usually presides over both the executive committee and the organization as a whole. The treasurer handles financial affairs, and the secretary is the official record-keeper of the organization. Duties of the vice-president vary from organization to organization.

Other rules that govern most organizations and groups include:

- A quorum—a minimum number of members, usually specified in the bylaws—is needed to transact business.
- Rules may specify the categories of members eligible to vote on certain issues.

Skill in using parliamentary procedure is very helpful for a social worker working with groups, committees, and other decision-making bodies. A knowledgeable worker can assist the group to conduct its business efficiently and effectively.

Without peeking back at the chapter, quickly match the terms on the left with the definitions on the right.

_____	1.	Robert's Rules of Order	A. Official recorder of group decisions
_____	2.	Secretary	B. Accomplish primary business of group
_____	3.	Point of Order	C. Guidelines used in parliamentary procedure
_____	4.	Minutes	D. Minimum number of members needed to transact business
_____	5.	Second	
_____	6.	Amendment	E. Motion indicating proper procedure is not being followed
_____	7.	Debate	
_____	8.	Executive Committee	F. Committee that exists continuously
_____	9.	Standing Committee	G. Proposed modification to a motion
_____	10.	Constitution and by-laws	H. Discussion about a motion
_____	11.	Main Motions	I. Governing rules of an organization
_____	12.	Quorum	J. Composed of officers of organization and charged with acting for the body between meetings
			K. An indication of support for a motion which has just been proposed
			L. Official record of actions taken by a group

Conflict Management

You may wonder why we talk about managing conflict instead of preventing or stopping it. The fact is that conflict is a normal characteristic of society. Conflict occurs over ideas, philosophies, resources, personalities, goals, and objectives. Ideally, conflict should be kept on a substantive level rather than on a personal or emotional level. Conflict on substantive matters can generate new ideas, open up alternatives, and allow for a clear airing of positions. Conflict on affective or emotional matters can be personally hurtful, is usually unproductive, and may preclude reaching a mutually satisfactory conclusion.

Few of us look forward to dealing with conflict. In fact, some people will do anything to avoid it, but it is nearly impossible to be effective in a group if you are unwilling or unable to handle conflictual situations. This is certainly true at the macro level. If you are trying to get approval of a law prohibiting discrimination against people on the basis of their sexual orientation, you will most certainly engender conflict. Similarly, if you attempt to get a landlord to fix up his rundown slum buildings, you can expect resistance and/or conflict because your goal and his are on a collision course. Conflict is also a normal developmental phase in most groups. Thus, as a group leader you must anticipate this and be prepared to manage it. To do so requires that you be able to identify different types of conflict. Each type is described briefly below in figure 3.1.

Figure 3.1: Types of Conflict

Type of Conflict	Characteristics	Example
Interpersonal Conflict	Involves at least 2 individuals and strong disagreement over which to support	Two neighborhood social workers arguing over antidrug program positions

Resource Conflict	Differences arise when resources are insufficient to satisfy all parties	Residents demand that the city council provide a police substation in their neighborhood
Representational Conflict	Occurs when one attempts to represent one's group	Worker representing local group creates conflict by advocating for better drug law enforcement
Intercessional Conflict	Occurs when one attempts to intercede between or among warring factions	Worker intervening between groups with drastically different goals is embroiled in conflict

We can help groups and individuals by enabling them to recognize when they are in conflict and to carefully identify their differing perspectives. We must do this in a way that validates people's rights to have different opinions and needs while at the same time making it clear that differences can be discussed, negotiated, and resolved. Helping differing parties present their perspectives, using good listening skills, and searching for common ground between them is a service for which each social worker should be prepared. This is an appropriate place to use one's critical thinking skills—especially those that challenge assumptions—and to recognize emotional as opposed to rational arguments.

Exercise 3.12: Recognizing Types of Conflict

It is important to be able to recognize the type of conflict existing in a group or organization. Identify the type of conflict displayed in each of the following vignettes, and explain your reasons for that choice.

A.   "As chair of the homeless coalition, I can't sit here and let this city council tear down the old courthouse without a fight. We have 50 homeless families in this city and the city owns a building that would make a wonderful shelter. Mayor Jones, why can't you see the benefits that using this structure for a shelter would bring to the community?"

"The city council has to be concerned about more than just homeless people, Ed. We need the space occupied by the old courthouse for downtown parking. We're losing business to the mall outside of town because we have no place for people to park downtown. The city council asked me to work with you to find some other solution for this homeless problem."

Type of Conflict:

Explain:

B. "If we add money to the budget so we can hire another building inspector, we won't be able to put another police officer on the force. What with the increase in gang activity here, I believe we need more cops, not more building inspectors."

"Figuring out what makes the most sense within the budget is important, Mary. We have only $75,000 left in the personnel budget. I think the money will produce better benefits for the community if we add the inspector. There are too many substandard homes and apartments in the community, some of which are being used as drug houses. An inspector could help us cope with this at least as well as another police officer."

Type of Conflict:

Explain:

C. "Constanza, I am tired of hearing of the so-called benefits of the DARE program. Show me an ounce of research that proves this program actually keeps school kids from using drugs. The whole thing is just a big public relations program. I think we should concentrate our efforts on something we *know* works—like the Police Dog Sniffer program. We know the dogs can sniff out drugs in school lockers."

"José, police dogs are fine after the fact, but they do nothing to prevent drug use. We should spend our money on prevention, not intervention."

Type of Conflict:

Explain:

D. "You're on their side! Why don't you ever see our perspective? All you ever do is agree with the Razers."

"Oh, right. Man, if he's on our side we're in big trouble. He can't understand anything 'cause he's not a home boy."

"Washington, Alonzo, I'm not on anyone's side. I'm supposed to find a way to keep you from stomping each other and keep you out of jail besides. My point is that I think the Guns proposal to keep the downtown area off limits to gang activity makes sense. It lets both your groups use the downtown as individuals, *and* it keeps the police off your butts. The minute you start something downtown, you've got the mayor, the council, and business owners turning up the heat. Both of your gangs get fried whenever that happens. Just because Alonzo suggested it, doesn't make it automatically a bad idea. Now get out of my face unless you have a better idea."

Type of Conflict:

Explain:

81

Conflict Management Strategies

Strategies for managing conflict fall into two general categories: There are some we use when we try to mediate a conflict in order to reduce its impact. Mediational conflict resolution aims at getting the opposing sides to work out a compromise. This approach is discussed by Johnson (1992) and outlined below:

Figure 3.2: Mediational Conflict Resolution Strategies

1.   Anticipate conflict and be alert to its signs.
2.   Reframe individual conflict as a matter for the entire group.
3.   Seek and listen to all viewpoints, identifying similar and dissimilar positions.
4.   Avoid situations and solutions that produce clear winners and losers.
5.   Ask groups to cooperate and compromise rather than compete with one another.

Sometimes we do not wish to reduce conflict, but to use it to achieve goals for our clients. Maybe we are trying to force a change in some situation. Unfortunately, one side is not budging, so mediational strategies are inappropriate. Figure 3.4 describes the use of conflict as a specific strategy.

Figure 3.3: Conflict Strategy

Conflict Strategy	Rationale for Use
Assess your power and your adversary's power	Knowing whether you have the power (money, time, votes, etc.) to overcome your opponent is critical
Never disclose all your power	This keeps your opponents off balance and leaves them wondering if you have more influence than they can observe
Use power sparingly	This keeps your real strength a secret and keeps you from wasting a precious resource
Avoid unnecessary conflict	Conflict should not be the chosen approach when other less polarizing methods will achieve the same end
Generate conflict when other non-conflictual approaches have failed	Conflict can force others to see how something will affect them, challenge weak agreements, and encourage differences of opinion
Use covert methods to avoid direct conflict	Useful when the risk of direct conflict is too high—get others to fight for you, or employ passive resistance

Of course conflict can also be managed by other methods. One side can change its mind when confronted with evidence. The two sides may negotiate their differences. Both might agree to abide by the decision of an outside party (perhaps an arbitrator). In other situations the use of authority by either side or by an outside party may end the conflict. For example, the federal government has periodically ordered railroad workers and their employers back to work, thus forcing an agreement because the nation would be badly hurt by a railroad strike.

Exercise 3.13: Managing Conflict

In the following case example, a conflict is brewing within the staff of a hospital social work department. Assume you are a new worker in this unit and that you are concerned about the apparent split developing over the best way to handle a hospital-proposed reduction in patient services.

Miguel, the most senior social worker in the unit, is speaking angrily about the situation: "We have always been a department that offered help to anyone we felt was at high risk. That risk could be financial, emotional, social, or medical. We've never set some group aside and said, 'We won't help you.' That's not what social work is all about."

"Micky, I know you're upset. But we don't own the hospital—we just work here. If the hospital director says we have to focus our services rather than take all comers, I don't see what we can do" says Betty, the acting department director.

"You can't fight city hall" says Mel, another worker.

"Baloney," Todd chimes in. "This hospital has built a fine reputation and we're not going to let it get destroyed without a fight."

Discuss what you might say to the group members to build cooperation, encourage compromise, hear their various viewpoints, find a common ground among members, and produce an environment of respect for everyone's ideas. In short, how would you keep the conflict from escalating?

Exercise 3.14: Using Conflict as a Strategy

Refer back to the case scenario described in exercise 3.13. Assume that you are successful in getting your colleagues to form a united front against the proposed changes in hospital rules. Identify and list some strategies or guidelines mentioned in the book that you might find useful for getting the hospital administrator to change her mind.

Chapter 4
Understanding Organizations

I. **Introduction**

II. **Defining Organizations, Social Services, and Social Agencies**

    A. Organizations (definition) (Daft, 2004)

        1. Social entities

        2. Goal-directed

        3. Deliberately structured and coordinated activity systems

        4. Linked to the external environment

    B. Social services

        1. Institutional—those provided by major public service systems that administer such benefits as financial assistance, housing programs, health care, or education

        2. Personal social services—address more individualized needs involving interpersonal relationships and people's ability to function within their immediate environments

        3. Human services, social services and sometimes, social welfare are often used interchangeably

        4. Human services—programs and activities designed to enhance people's development and well-being

        5. Social welfare—the nation's system of programs, benefits, and services that help people meet those social, economic, educational, and health needs that are fundamental to the maintenance of society

    C. Social agencies—organizations providing social services that are usually staffed by human services personnel (including professional social workers, members of other professions, paraprofessionals, clerical personnel, and sometimes volunteers)

        1. Public—run by a designated unit of government and are usually regulated by laws that directly affect policy

        2. Private—privately owned and run by people not employed by a government

            a. Nonprofit—run to accomplish some service provision goal, not to make financial profit for private owners

            b. Proprietary or for-profit—provide designated social services, often quite similar to those provided by private social agencies; a major purpose is to make money

III. Organizational Theories

A. Systems Theories—emphasize how all parts of the organization (subsystems) are interrelated and function together to produce output

B. Classic Scientific Management Theories—emphasize that specifically designed, formal structure and a consistent, rigid organizational network of employees are most important for an organization to run well and achieve its goals

C. Human Relations Theories—emphasize the role of the informal social interaction, group formation, and communication processes in an organization's functioning

   1. Theory X and Theory Y

      a. Theory X

         1) Managers view employees as incapable of much growth, and believe they must control, direct, force, or threaten employees to make them work

         2) Employees are perceived as inherently disliking work and having relatively little ambition

         3) Inconsistent with what behavioral scientists assert are effective principles for directing, influencing, and motivating people

      b. Theory Y

         1) Managers view employees as wanting to grow and develop by exerting physical and mental effort to accomplish work objectives

         2) Believe that the promise of internal rewards are stronger motivations than external rewards and punishments

         3) Most employees are assumed to have considerable ingenuity, creativity, and imagination

         4) Mistakes and errors are viewed as necessary to the learning process

   2. Theory Z—based on five assumptions initiated in Japanese industry

      a. Views workers as lifetime employees instead of people having a series of short-term jobs in different organizations over a career's time

      b. Presumes that employees undergo long periods of evaluation and are not promoted quickly

      c. Assumes workers progress down career paths that aren't specialized

    d. Collective decision making—workers collectively address issues and arrive at some consensus regarding how to proceed

    e. Collective responsibility—emphasizes the importance of all workers being responsible for the successful functioning of the organization

  D. Cultural Perspective

    1. Organizational culture—the set of key values, beliefs, understandings, and norms that members of an organization share

    2. Advantage—performance becomes predictable, thus requiring less effort to develop new approaches

    3. Disadvantage—may squelch innovative ideas with pressure to retain the old way of thought

  E. Economics Perspective—emphasizes that organizations proceed in whatever way necessary to maximize profits or outputs

    1. Poses difficulties for social workers who maintain professional values and ethics

    2. Places primary emphasis on profit and productivity

  F. Contingency Perspective—maintains that each element involved in an organization depends on other elements; therefore, there is no one generally best way to accomplish tasks or goals

    1. Strength—flexibility

    2. Potential weakness—lack of direction

  G. Which organizational theory is best?

IV. Social Agencies as Systems

  A. Systems theories involve concepts that emphasize interactions among various systems including individuals, families, groups, organizations, and communities

  B. Systems theories definition of terms:

    1. System—a set of orderly and interrelated elements that form a functional whole

    2. Boundaries—repeatedly occurring patterns that characterize the relationships within a system and give that system a particular identity, setting it apart from other systems

    3. Subsystem—a secondary or subordinate system, a smaller system within a larger system

    4. Homeostasis—the tendency for a system to maintain a relatively stable, constant state of balance

5. Role—a culturally determined pattern of behavior expected of an individual in a specified social relationship

6. Relationship—the mutual emotional exchange; dynamic interaction; and affective, cognitive, and behavioral connection that exists between two or more persons or systems

7. Input—the energy, information, or communication flow received from other systems

8. Output—what happens to input after it has been processed by some system

9. Feedback—a special form of input that involves a system receiving information about that system's own performance

10. Interface—the contact point between various systems, including individuals and organizations, where interaction and communication may take place

11. Differentiation—a system's tendency to move from a more simplified to a more complex existence

12. Entropy—the natural tendency of a system to progress toward disorganization, depletion, disintegration, and, in essence, chaos

13. Negative entropy—the progress of a system toward organization, growth, and development

14. Equifinality—there are many different means to the same end

V. Viewing Organizations from a Systems Perspective

A. Figure 4.1: Fastbuck and WINK—Similar Processes

B. Resource input

C. Process through organizational technology

D. Output

E. Outcomes

VI. The Nature of Organizations

A. Agency settings

1. Predominantly social work settings

2. Host settings—the main service provided by the agency is not social services

B.   Organizational goals

1.   Organizational goal—a desired state of affairs which the organization attempts to realize

2.   Organizational goals serve at least three major purposes:

   a.   Provide guidelines for the kinds of functions and activities organizational workers are supposed to pursue

   b.   Constitute a source of legitimacy which justifies the activities of an organization and, indeed, its very existence

   c.   Serve as standards by which members of an organization and outsiders can assess the success of the organization—that is, its effectiveness and efficiency

3.   Official goals—the general purposes of the organization as put forth in the charter (mission statement), annual reports, public statements by key officials and other authoritative pronouncements

4.   Operative goals—designate the ends sought through the actual operating policies of the organization

5.   Multiple goals—social service organizations are often complex entities that aim to accomplish multiple goals

6.   Goal displacement—often occurs when the means to a goal becomes the goal itself

   a.   Occurs when organization continues to function but no longer achieves the goals it's supposed to

   b.   Highlight 4.1: Goal Displacement—Process Superseding Progress

7.   Systems theories, organizations, and goal displacement

   a.   Goal attainment—refers to what is supposed to happen through the intervention process

   b.   Figure 4.2: The Process of Goal Displacement

C.   Organizational culture

1.   Organizational culture—the set of key values, beliefs, understandings, and norms that members of an organization share

   a.   What kind of attire is considered appropriate within the organization's cultural environment

   b.   Each agency has its own personality

D. Organizational structure

    1.   Organizational structure—the manner in which an organization divides its labor into specific tasks and achieves coordination among these tasks

    2.   All large agencies and some smaller ones have a formal structure

    3.   Agencies develop informal structures and lines of communication

    4.   Lines of authority—the specific administrative and supervisory responsibilities of supervisors to their supervisees

        a.   Figure 4.3: Multihelp—An Example of a Formal Organizational Chart

        b.   Agencies also develop informal channels of communication

    5.   Channels of communication

    6.   Dimensions of power

        a.   Highlight 4.2 Power and Politics in Organizations

            1)   Types of power in organizations

                a)   Legitimate power—based on an individual's job position within the organization

                b)   Reward power—based on one's ability to provide positive outcomes and prevent negative outcomes

                c)   Coercive power—resulting from the use of punishment and threat

                d)   Referent power—derived from being well-liked by others

                e)   Expert power—based on having special information or expertise that is valued by an organization

            2)   Enhancing your power within organizations

    7.   Informal structure: Multihelp—An example

        a.   Figure 4.4: Contrasting Formal and Informal Structures in Agencies

E. Centralized versus decentralized organizations

VII. The Macro Context of Organizations

A. The shifting macro environment and shrinking resources

    1. Downsizing—decreasing programs and/or staff when funding support shrinks

    2. Temporary Assistance to Needy Families (TANF)

    3. Highlight 4.3: Managed Care and Service Provision: Problems and Ethical Issues

        a. Ethical issues in managed care

        b. Managed care and advocacy in social work practice

B. Necessary resource inputs

C. Legitimation—appropriate status or authorization to perform agency functions and pursue agency goals that is granted by external entities

D. Client sources

    1. Highlight 4.4: Organizations in a Global Context: Helping People of Other National Origin

        a. National origin—involves individuals', their parents', or their ancestors' country of birth

        b. Refugees—people who have crossed national boundaries in search of refuge

        c. Immigrants—those individuals who have been granted legal permanent residence in a country not their own

        d. Global network—includes international, national, and local agencies, both public and private and professionals and paraprofessionals from a variety of disciplines

    2. International organizations

        a. Intergovernmental organizations

        b. Premigration services—include helping migrants get their documents in order, understand and follow required procedures, obtain necessary medical evaluations, and cope with cultural changes and conditions

    3. National organizations

    4. Local organizations

    5. Social services for immigrants and refugees

E.   Relationship with other organizations

    1.   Uninvolved relationships among organizations

    2.   Complementary relationships among organizations

    3.   Competitive relationships among organizations

VIII.   Social Work Organizations in National and International Contexts

A.   ACOSA (Association for Community Organization & Social Administration)—provides a forum for enhancing macro practice theory, research, and skills

B.   IASSW (International Association of Schools of Social Work)—committed to promoting peace, human rights, and social justice through social work education

C.   IFSW (International Federation of Social Workers)—an international organization of national professional social work organizations in 78 countries

IX.   Methods of Management

X.   Working in a Bureaucracy

A.   Value discrepancies between workers and "the system"

    1.   Highlight 4.5: Orientation Conflicts Between Helping Professionals and Bureaucracies

        a.   Orientation of helping professionals

        b.   Orientation of bureaucratic systems

B.   How to survive in a bureaucracy

    1.   Whenever your needs or the needs of your clients are not met by the bureaucracy, use the following problem-solving approach:

        a.   Precisely identify the need

        b.   Generate a list of possible solutions

        c.   Evaluate merits and shortcomings of the possible solutions

        d.   Select a solution

        e.   Implement the solution

        f.   Evaluate the solution

    2.   Learn how your bureaucracy is structured and how it functions

    3.   Remember that bureaucrats are people with feelings

4. If you are at war with the bureaucracy, declare a truce or the system will find a way to eliminate you

5. Know your work contract and job expectations

6. Continue to develop your knowledge and awareness of specific helping skills

7. Identify your professional strengths and limitations

8. Be aware that you can't change everything, so stop trying

9. Learn how to control your emotions in your interactions with the bureaucracy

10. Develop and use a sense of humor

11. Learn to accept your mistakes and perhaps even to laugh at some of them

12. Take time to enjoy and develop a support system with your colleagues

13. Give in sometimes on minor matters

14. Keep yourself physically fit and mentally alert

15. Leave your work at the office

16. Occasionally, take your supervisor and other administrators to lunch

17. Do not seek self-actualization or ego satisfaction from the bureaucracy

18. Make speeches to community groups that accentuate the positives about your agency

19. No matter how high you rise in a hierarchy, maintain some direct service contact

20. Do not try to change everything in the system at once

21. Identify your career goals and determine whether they can be met in this system

XI. A Total Quality Approach to Management

A. Defining total quality management ("a management approach that focuses on managing the total organization to deliver quality to customers")

B. Clients as customers

C. Customer feedback

D.   Quality as the primary goal

    1.   Lutheran Social Services of Wisconsin and Upper Michigan's six components of quality (1993, p. 8)

        a.   Accuracy measures the extent to which actual service provision matches customers' expectations

        b.   Consistency is "service accuracy over time"

        c.   Responsiveness refers to timeliness of service provision

        d.   Availability is the ease with which customers can obtain services

        e.   Perceived value concerns the extent to which customers feel satisfied with the service

        f.   Service experience sums up the total service event

    2.   Highlight 4.6: The Seven Sins of Service

        a.   Apathy (DILLIGAD—Do I Look Like I Give a Damn?) syndrome

        b.   Brush-off—getting rid of the customer as soon as possible and doing the least work necessary

        c.   Coldness—chilly hostility, curtness, or impatience intended to convey to the customer they are a nuisance and please go away

        d.   Condescension—treating customers with a disdainful patronizing attitude that implies you as the worker are more knowledgeable and better than the customer

        e.   Robotism—treat each customer identically, without changes in facial or verbal expression

        f.   Rule book—if you want to think as little as possible, use the rule book to give the organization's rules and regulations absolute precedence

        g.   Run around—stalling customers by using as little of your own time as possible, while wasting vast amounts of the customer's time

    3.   Mission statement—summarizes an agency's mission, that is, its official goals

E.   Employee empowerment

    1.   Highlight 4.7: Empowerment on a Macro Level

        a.   Obstacles

            1)   Expectations of funding sources

            2)   Social environment

            3)   Intrapersonal issues

            4)   Interpersonal issues

        b.   Supports

            1)   Staff development

            2)   Enhanced collaborative approach

            3)   Administrative leadership and support

F.   Use of teams and teamwork: Melding mezzo and macro practice

    1.   Teams—task-oriented groups of five to fifteen employees who are responsible for planning and producing an entire product or process

    2.   Groups as opposed to teams—groups do not necessarily work cooperatively, individual roles may be unclear, participation of individual members may be hampered or discouraged, and frequently individual group members are seen as stars instead of cooperative co-participations

G.   A total quality approach to leadership

H.   Establishing a culture of quality

    1.   Leaders are responsible for changing the organizational culture from one that dwells on status quo to one that gets excited about change

    2.   A long-term perspective

I.   TQM tools

    1.   Charts

    2.   Benchmarking—a process whereby agencies find out how others do something better than they do and then try to imitate or improve on it

J.   Beyond quality: The learning organization

1.   Learning organization—one in which everyone is engaged in identifying and solving problems, enabling the organization to continuously experiment, improve, and increase its capability

2.   Five primary concepts that characterize the learning organization

a.   Shared leadership—concerns how responsibility for making decisions, directing operations, and achieving organizational goals is shared among all employees

b.   Culture of innovation—searching for new ideas, creative problem solving, and suggestions for improvements are encouraged and expected

c.   Customer-focused strategy—the organization seeks to serve customers effectively by identifying needs, in some instances, even before customers have done so, and then developing ways to satisfy those needs

d.   Use of multidisciplinary teams—encourages the free flow of ideas

e.   Intensive use of information—involves aggressively scanning both the external and internal environments for information

XII.   **Common Problems Encountered in Organizations**

A.   Impersonal behavior

B.   Rewards and recognition

C.   Agency policy and worker discretion

D.   Traditions and unwritten rules

Experiential Exercises and Classroom Simulations

Exercise 4.1: Comparing and Contrasting Organizational Theories

A.   Brief Description
Students compare and contrast five theoretical perspectives on organizations.

B.   Objectives
Students will:
1.   Recognize the basic concepts inherent in six theoretical perspectives on organizations.
2.   Examine the similarities and differences among the six approaches.

C. Procedure
1. Review the material on theoretical perspectives of organizations.
2. Divide the class into small groups of four to six.
3. Ask the groups to discuss the subsequent discussion questions, select a group representative, and be prepared to report to the entire class the small group's findings.
4. After about 20 minutes, ask the small groups to terminate their discussions and participate in a full class discussion.
5. Ask the representative from each group to share her or his summary of the discussion. Encourage comments from all class members.

D. Instructions for Students
1. What are the primary concepts involved in each of the following theoretical perspectives on organizations?

> a. Systems theories;
> b. Classical scientific management theories;
> c. Human relations theories;
> d. Cultural perspective;
> e. Economics perspective;
> f. Contingency perspective.

2. What are the similarities and differences among the six perspectives?
3. Which theoretical perspective(s) is(are) best? Explain why.

E. Commentary
This activity may also be conducted by holding a full class discussion without breaking students down into small groups.

Exercise 4.2: Identifying and Evaluating Management Concepts

A. Brief Description
In a large group discussion students respond to brief descriptions of management approaches. They are asked to identify whether each description reflects a traditional bureaucratic or Total Quality Management style and to explain the reasons for their answers.

B. Objectives
Students will:
1. Identify basic concepts in two opposing management styles.
2. Assess the pros and cons of principles involved.

C. Procedure
1. Review the content on working in a bureaucracy and a total quality approach to management.
2. Read the brief descriptions of management approaches below under "Instructions for Students."
3. Lead a full class discussion focusing on the ensuing questions. Note that each description of a management approach may reflect concepts inherent in both traditional bureaucracies and total quality management.

D.   Instructions for Students
For each of the following brief descriptions of a management approach, answer the subsequent questions.

> Description A: Agency management emphasizes that workers should be consistent in their service provision, responsive to clients, and readily available when needed.

1.   To what extent does this management approach reflect that of a traditional bureaucracy or total quality management?
2.   What more specific concepts inherent in traditional bureaucracy or total quality management are reflected and why?
3.   What are the pros and cons of this management approach?

> Description B: Agency leaders should serve as watchdogs to make certain that the agency functions smoothly.

1.   To what extent does this management approach reflect that of a traditional bureaucracy or total quality management?
2.   What more specific concepts inherent in traditional bureaucracy or total quality management are reflected and why?
3.   What are the pros and cons of this management approach?

> Description C: The agency frequently solicits feedback from clients and other community residents regarding the effectiveness and efficiency of its service provision.

1.   To what extent does this management approach reflect that of a traditional bureaucracy or total quality management?
2.   What more specific concepts inherent in traditional bureaucracy or total quality management are reflected and why?
3.   What are the pros and cons of this management approach?

> Description D: The agency is made up of numerous highly specialized units assigned to perform specific job tasks. The intent is to have the service provision process run smoothly and get things done. The rules are there to help practitioners accomplish their tasks in designated and consistent ways. Allowing practitioners much of their own decision-making initiative only paves the way for mistakes.

1.   To what extent does this management approach reflect that of a traditional bureaucracy or total quality management?
2.   What more specific concepts inherent in traditional bureaucracy or total quality management are reflected and why?
3.   What are the pros and cons of this management approach?

E.   Commentary
This exercise may also be conducted using the small group format described in exercise 1.1.

Exercise 4.3: Defining Types of Agencies

Match the following terms with their respective definitions:

a. Social services
b. Institutional services
c. Personal social services
d. Social agency

e. Public social agency
f. Private social agency
g. Nonprofit social agency
h. Proprietary agency

_____: A social agency that provides some designated social services, often quite similar to those provided by private social agencies, but with the additional aim of making a profit for its owners.

_____: An agency "usually staffed by human services personnel (including professional social workers, members of other professions, subprofessional specialists); clerical personnel"; and sometimes volunteers (Barker, 1991, p. 217.)

_____: An agency run by designated units of government and usually regulated by laws that affect its policies.

_____: A social agency—usually providing some type of personal social services—that is funded by churches, charitable organizations, foundations, etc. It is run by a board of directors, and it does not make a financial profit for private owners (Barker, 1995).

_____: Services "with a basic purpose to enhance the relationships between people, and between people and their environments, and to provide opportunities for social fulfillment" (Barker, 1995, p. 279).

_____: Services including income maintenance, health care, education, employment, and housing (Barker, 1995, p. 279).

_____: An agency that is privately owned and run by people not employed by government.

_____: The functions that social work practitioners and other helping professionals perform for: improving people's health; enhancing their quality of life; "helping people become more self-sufficient; preventing dependency; strengthening family relationships; and restoring individuals, families, groups, or communities to successful social functioning" (Barker, 1995, p. 221).

Organizational Theories

There are several major theoretical perspectives on how organizations are or should be run—for example, "classical scientific management theories," "human relations theories," and "systems theories" (Sarri, 1987, pp. 30-32).

Classical scientific management theories emphasize a specifically designed, formal structure and a consistent, rigid organizational network of employees (Holland & Petchers, 1987; Sarri, 1987). Each employee has a clearly defined task calling for minimal independent functioning. Supervisors closely scrutinize the workers' activities. Efficiency is paramount and performance is quantified (that is, made very explicit regarding what is expected), regulated, and measured. Worker morale is relatively insignificant. Administration discourages employee input regarding how organizational goals can best be reached. Employees are required to do their jobs as instructed and as quietly and efficiently as possible. Traditional bureaucracies operate according to classical scientific management theories.

Human relations theories emphasize "the role of the informal, psychosocial components of organizational functioning" (Holland & Petchers, 1987, p. 206), on the grounds that satisfied, happy employees will be most productive. These theories are concerned with "employee morale and productivity; . . . satisfaction, motivation, and leadership; and . . . the dynamics of small-group behavior" (Sarri, 1987, p. 31). Administrators are responsible for enhancing workers' morale, so effective, capable administrators are vital. The immediate work group (a mezzo system) is also crucial in human relations theories. Employees are encouraged to work cooperatively together and to participate in group decision making. Employers encourage employee input concerning organizational policies and practices.

Systems theories construe "the organization as a social system with interrelated parts, or subsystems, functioning in interaction and equilibrium with one another. It perceives the organization as an adaptive whole rather than as a structure that is solely rational-legal" (Holland & Petchers, 1987, p. 207). Systems theories emphasize the interactions of the various subsystems involved. Additionally, the importance of the environment and the impacts of other systems upon the organization are stressed. In some ways, systems theories might be considered more flexible than many other theories. Irrational, spontaneous interactions are expected rather than ignored. Systems theories emphasize constant assessment and adjustment.

Exercise 4.4: Relating Concepts to Theory

Each concept listed below characterizes one of the organizational theories. Identify the organizational theory it characterizes and explain the concept's significance to that theory.

1. *Concept: Importance of the environment*

   Organizational theory it characterizes:

   Explain the concept's significance:

2. *Concept: Clearly defined, structured job descriptions*

   Organizational theory it characterizes:

   Explain the concept's significance:

3. *Concept: Quantified job performance*

   Organizational theory it characterizes:

   Explain the concept's significance:

4. *Concept: Employee satisfaction*

   Organizational theory it characterizes:

   Explain the concept's significance:

5. *Concept: Work group cooperation*

   Organizational theory it characterizes:

   Explain the concept's significance:

Social Agencies as Systems

Systems theory is one theoretical or conceptual perspective on the world of organizations. It stresses the relationships among various systems including "individuals, groups, organizations, or communities" (Barker, 1991, p. 233), so it is an exceptionally useful way for social work practitioners to conceptualize service provision to clients. The following concepts are especially significant in understanding the macro environment.

A *system* is a set of orderly and interrelated elements that form a functional whole. A nation, a public social services department, and a newly married couple are all *social systems*—that is, they are composed of people and affect people.

Boundaries are the repeatedly occurring patterns that characterize the relationships within a system and give that system a particular identity. A boundary is like the membrane surrounding and enclosing a living cell (Barker, 1991, p. 26). For example, a boundary may exist between the protective service workers in a large county social service agency and those who work in the financial assistance department of the same agency. The two departments are set apart by boundaries that specify workers' designated job responsibilities and the clients they serve. Yet each group is part of the larger agency.

A *subsystem* is a secondary or subordinate system within a larger system. The protective services workers and the financial assistance workers form two subsystems of the same agency.

Homeostasis is the tendency for a system to maintain a relatively stable, constant state of balance. If something disturbs the system, it will strive "to adapt" and "restore the stability previously achieved" (Barker, 1991, p. 103). Homeostasis, then, is the status quo—whether that condition is positive or negative.

A *role* is "a culturally determined pattern of behavior that is prescribed for an individual who occupies a specific status" (Barker, 1991, p. 203).

A *relationship* is "the mutual emotional exchange; dynamic interaction; and affective, cognitive, and behavioral connection that exists" between two or more persons or systems (Barker, 1991, p. 199).

Input is the energy, information, or communication flow received from other systems. For example, a public agency may receive input from the state in the form of funding.

Output is the result after input has been processed by the system: "The status of a client's problem at the time of case termination" or the progress made after treatment are forms of output (Chess & Norlin, 1988, p. 27).

Feedback is a special form of input whereby a system receives information about its own performance.

Negative feedback is input about negative aspects of functioning. It enables the system to correct any deviations or mistakes and return to a more homeostatic state.

Positive feedback is input about a system's positive functioning that enables the system to emphasize and reinforce positive elements of functioning.

An *interface* is "the point of contact or communication between different systems, organizations, or individuals" (Barker, 1991, p. 117). For example, an interface may be a meeting between a worker and an administrator. *Differentiation* is a system's tendency to move from a more simplified to a more complex existence. A social services agency is likely to develop more detailed policies and programs over its lifetime.

Entropy is the natural tendency of a system to progress toward disorganization, depletion, and, in essence, death. Nothing lasts forever.

Negative entropy is the process of a system toward growth and development—the opposite of entropy. Individuals develop physically, intellectually, and emotionally as they grow. Social service agencies grow and develop new programs and clientele.

Equifinality is the idea that there are many different means to the same end.

Select a social services agency in your area and make an appointment to speak with a social worker or administrator. You may conduct the interview over the phone if necessary. Your goal is to better understand organizational functioning by applying a systems perspective. Ask the interviewee the following questions and record her responses. Note that the questions are rephrased in systems terms in parentheses.

1.   How is the agency structured—that is, what professional departments or units does it comprise *(what are its various subsystems)*? How many departments or units are there?

2.   How are professional departments or units defined *(what are their boundaries)*? Are they divided according to the problems they address—for example, all staff serving abused children under one umbrella? Or according to function—e.g., intake, assessment, referral, counseling? Or according to some combination of the two?

3.   Do you consider the agency relatively stable *(maintaining homeostasis)*? Are funding sources *(input)* stable? What are the primary funding sources for service provision?

4.   How is the effectiveness of service provision *(output)* measured?

5.   What types of feedback are solicited from consumers, such as clients or other agencies purchasing services?

6.   Has the agency recently received any positive or negative feedback about its effectiveness? If so, what was this feedback?

7.   Over time, has the agency become more complex—for example, added new services, served new client groups, or added new staff *(differentiation)*? If so, in what ways?

8.   Is the agency generally improving its ability to function and provide effective services *(negative entropy)*? Is it encountering increasing problems—for example, funding, regulations, or changing client needs *(entropy)*? In either case, in what ways?

Exercise 4.6: Comparing Social Service Agencies

Social workers have a professional responsibility to continuously assess the effectiveness of their organizational contexts and work to improve service provision. The functioning of social service organizations, however, can differ widely. That is why we use systems terminology to compare their basic processes.

An industrial factory takes raw materials *(input)* and submits them to a manufacturing *process* in which those materials are gradually reshaped, blended, and/or recombined to produce the desired product *(output)*. Along with the raw material, the financial resources to maintain the manufacturing process are considered input. In terms of social service organizations, the raw material is clients (Holland & Petchers, 1987) and the financial input is funding support, such as public funding, fees, donations, or grants. Social services organizations apply their funding to the helping *process* to produce some effective service—*output*—for clients.

Select two social service organizations and contact workers or administrators. Try to choose two dissimilar agencies—for example, one public and one private, one that serves children and one that serves the elderly, one that addresses problems of poverty and one that addresses problems of mental illness. This will allow you to make broader, more striking comparisons. For each agency, find the following information: (1) forms of input, both client and financial support; (2) treatment or service provision process; and (3) output, or how service effectiveness is determined and measured.

Agency A

1a. What sources comprise Agency A's financial input?

1b. What are the characteristics of Agency A's clientele input (for example, problem type, age range, needs, strengths)?

2. Describe the treatment or service provision process that Agency A employs.

3. How does Agency A determine or measure its service effectiveness or output?

Agency B

1a. What sources comprise Agency B's financial input?

1b. What are the characteristics of Agency B's clientele input (for example, problem type, age range, needs, strengths)?

2. Describe the treatment or service provision process that Agency B employs.

3. How does Agency B determine or measure its service effectiveness or output?

Use the information above to answer the following questions:

1. How are Agencies A and B similar or different in terms of their financial input?

2. How are Agencies A and B similar or different concerning their clientele input?

3. How are Agencies A and B similar or different concerning their process of service provision?

4. How are Agencies A and B similar or different concerning their determination and measurement of service effectiveness?

The Nature of Organizations

Organizations are particularly important to you for three basic reasons. First, you will most likely be employed by one. Second, the organization itself can create problems for you. Third, Hasenfeld (1984) stresses that you need to understand organizations in order to plan the implementation of macro changes. The ensuing discussion stresses the following concepts: agency settings; organizational goals; the macro context of organizations; and organizational structure.

Agency Settings—Primary or Secondary

Social workers usually work in either primary or secondary organizational settings. Each setting has particular implications for effective practice.

Primary settings are agencies where social work is the main or primary profession employed. Most public social service agencies are primary settings. Administrators, supervisors, and most employees are social workers with social work titles, though the agency may also employ homemakers, psychologists, or other professionals.

Social workers tend to share similar professional values and perspectives because they've had similar education and training. In such an agency, therefore, everyone understands the social work role.

Secondary settings usually employ a variety of professional staff and social services are not their main business. Consider hospitals and schools. Medical care of patients is the primary service of the hospital. Medical personnel (including nurses and physicians) comprise the largest segment of the professional staff. Most administrative staff and supervisors have medical backgrounds. Social work is just one of several ancillary professions—including dietitians, pharmacists, and chaplains—contributing to the overall goal of providing medical care.

Such an environment can prove challenging for social workers. Typically social workers must learn the language (for instance, medical terminology or relevant abbreviations) used by the other professions. Unlike many primary settings, the hospital is likely to operate on the basis of a definite pecking order with physicians at the top. Sometimes social work values and perspectives will clash with those of the physicians and other medical personnel.

Exercise 4.7: Primary and Secondary Social Agency Settings

1.   Name two primary social agency settings. Describe the professional role of social workers in each setting.

2.   Name two secondary social agency settings other than hospitals and schools. Describe the professional role of social workers in each setting.

Organizational Structure

Each agency has its own personality. That is, it is more formal or informal, structured or unstructured, innovative or traditional than other agencies. When you begin working at an agency, you must try to understand its character. How much freedom will you have in your daily professional activities? What tasks are most important (for example, documentation of treatment effectiveness, other record-keeping, administrative conferences, or number of hours spent with clients)? What are the agency's expectations regarding services to clients? Are workers expected to provide services to clients directly or to serve as case managers for other service providers?

All large agencies (and many smaller ones as well) have a *formal* structure. Sometimes it is explicated in an organizational chart showing who reports to whom. Such charts depict lines of authority and communication, and many agencies operate according to this chart.

Equally often, however, agencies develop *informal* structures and lines of communication. Many structure their units so that all workers in the unit report to one supervisor. Consider the Brack County Foster Care Unit, comprising five workers and a supervisor. When workers have questions or problems, they often discuss their cases with other workers in the unit or with the senior worker in another unit instead of taking the problem to the Foster Care Unit Supervisor. As a result, this supervisor lacks information that might be important in doing her job.

This may seem like a bad arrangement, but it has some beneficial aspects. Workers are sometimes uncomfortable talking with their supervisors, but they are willing to seek help from other more experienced workers. Sharing of ideas and problems fosters camaraderie among the workers, which decreases their stress levels and can lead to better job performance. Human relations theories stress the importance of such interpersonal communication and support in organizations.

We neither praise nor criticize the existence of informal structures and communication channels. We simply acknowledge that they do exist and must be dealt with. Being aware of both formal and informal avenues within your agency can strengthen your ability to do your job. Once you know all your options and alternatives, you can make more informed choices.

Keep three concepts in mind when you appraise an agency's formal and informal structures. These are *lines of authority, channels of communication,* and *dimensions of power.*

Lines of Authority

An agency's formal structure depends on *lines of authority* (Daft, 1992). For our purposes, authority is the specific administrative and supervisory responsibilities of supervisors for their supervisees. Agency policy usually specifies these lines of authority in writing.

Often, an agency's formal structure is outlined in an organizational chart (Lauffer, Nybell, and Overberger, 1977). Individual staff positions are indicated by labeled squares or circles. The "hierarchy of authority" in an organizational chart is depicted by vertical lines leading from supervisors down to supervisees (Daft, 1992, p. 13). Generally, positions higher on the chart have greater authority than those placed lower. In essence, these lines represent "who is responsible for whom" (Lauffer et al., 1977, p. 31).

The chart in figure 4.1 reflects the hierarchy of authority for Multihelp, an agency providing assessment and therapeutic treatment to children with multiple developmental and physical disabilities.

Rectangles in figure 4.1 designate positions with some degree of administrative responsibility. The bolder the rectangle, the more authority and responsibility the position entails.

The Executive Director has the most authority and is responsible for the overall performance of Multihelp. Below him are five agency directors—the Medical Director (a physician), and the directors of accounting, maintenance engineering, food services for clients and staff, and transportation services for clients. Each director (except the Director of Accounting) is, in turn, responsible for the supervision of other staff further down the hierarchy of authority. The Medical Director oversees the entire clinical program—occupational therapy, physical therapy, speech therapy, psychology, and social work—including the work of the various departmental supervisors. Circles at the bottom of the chart represent line staff who work directly with clients.

Does the chart make clear how this agency is run? Look at the Social Work Department: two direct service workers report directly to their Social Work Supervisor. They serve their clients, look to their own supervisor for direction, and live happily ever after—right?

The "catch" is that formal organizational charts depict lines of *formal* authority within agencies. An agency's actual chain of command may follow the formal chart fairly closely, but an agency is equally likely to develop *informal* channels of communication and power.

Channels of Communication

All agencies have "multiple networks of communication by which members relay and receive information" (Resnick & Patti, 1980, p.51). Communication, of course, is "a process by which information is exchanged between individuals through a common system of symbols, signs, or behavior" (*Webster's Ninth New Collegiate Dictionary*, p. 266).

Formal lines of authority suggest that such communication flows harmoniously and synchronously along these designated channels. Supervisees are *supposed* to communicate primarily with their identified supervisors for direction and feedback. Supervisors are *supposed* to communicate directly with their supervisees and the managers who supervise them. But Multihelp does not work this way.

Dimensions of Power

Power is "the possession of resources that enables an individual to do something independently or to exercise influence and control over others" (Barker, 1991, p. 177). Like channels of communication, dimensions of power are supposed to follow the lines of authority. That is, those in supervisory positions are supposed to have actual power (that is, clear-cut influence and control) over their employees. In a real-life agency, this may or may not be the case.

Informal Structure: The Multihelp Example

Look at Multihelp's Social Work and Psychology Departments, illustrated in figure 4.4. This subsection of the organizational chart contrasts the formal and informal structures for these two agency departments. The *real* channels of communication and dimensions of power among supervisors and direct service staff are very different from those depicted in the formal organizational chart. The real relationships reflect the personalities and interactions among people with unique perspectives and identities, strengths and weaknesses, and problems and needs.

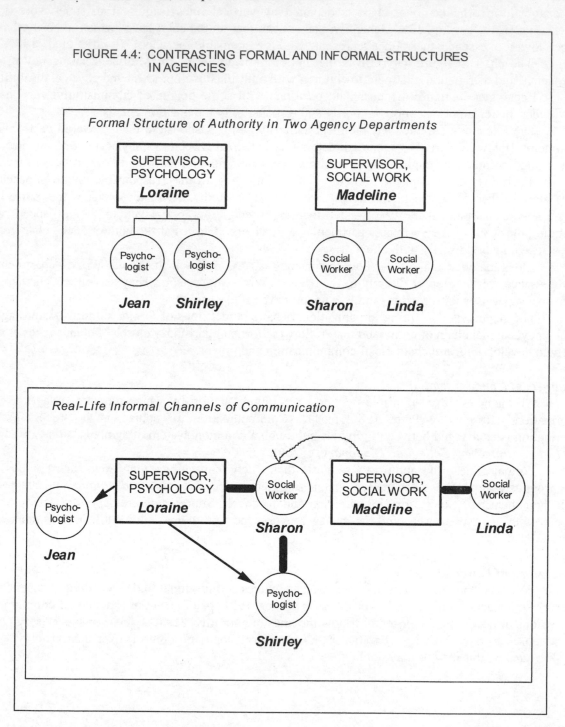

FIGURE 4.4: CONTRASTING FORMAL AND INFORMAL STRUCTURES IN AGENCIES

Formal Structure of Authority in Two Agency Departments

SUPERVISOR, PSYCHOLOGY
Loraine

SUPERVISOR, SOCIAL WORK
Madeline

Psycho-logist
Jean

Psycho-logist
Shirley

Social Worker
Sharon

Social Worker
Linda

Real-Life Informal Channels of Communication

SUPERVISOR, PSYCHOLOGY
Loraine

Social Worker
Sharon

SUPERVISOR, SOCIAL WORK
Madeline

Social Worker
Linda

Psycho-logist
Jean

Psycho-logist
Shirley

The formal structure shows that Loraine, the Psychology Department's Supervisor, is responsible for the administration and supervision of both Jean's and Shirley's job performances. Both these workers have master's degrees in psychology. Likewise, the formal structure reveals that Madeline, the Social Work Department's Supervisor, has direct supervisory authority over both Sharon and Linda, each of whom has a master's degree in social work.

The lower box portrays the real-life informal structure of these departments. Sharon, one of the social workers, is a good friend of Loraine's. They are both single, so they frequently socialize and even vacation together. (See the bold line connecting them in figure 4.4.)

Sharon, on the other hand, does not get along with Madeline, her Supervisor. It is fair to say that they have a personality conflict—though the term is difficult to define. For whatever reason, they do not like each other. Sharon considers Madeline incompetent, lazy, and interested in doing as little work as possible. Madeline perceives Sharon as an overly energetic, impulsive "go-getter"—"a bull in a china shop." They interact as little as possible, and most of their communication is in the form of memos—usually direct commands from Madeline to Sharon. (Note the arrow that swoops up from Madeline and down again to Sharon. Communication and power consistently flow downward from Madeline to Sharon in a dictatorial, hierarchical fashion.)

Madeline, however, has much in common with Linda, the other social worker. They meet socially and frequently eat lunch together. Madeline views Linda as a calm, competent worker who communicates well and as an enjoyable social companion. She treats Linda as a friend and an equal. (The thick linear bond linking Madeline and Linda horizontally illustrates this relationship.)

Psychology Department Supervisor Loraine sees Jean as a competent professional colleague. (Note that Jean appears slightly below Loraine in figure 4.4. The connecting arrow flows from Loraine down to Jean because Loraine maintains her supervisory and administrative status.) They like each other on a professional basis, but they do not have a personal friendship.

Loraine perceives Shirley in a much different light. She regrets hiring her and has begun to document Shirley's difficulties in performance in preparation for "letting her go"—dismissing her from the agency. (Thus, Shirley is positioned significantly below Loraine, the arrow connecting them running from Loraine down to Shirley. The chain of communication and power clearly positions Loraine in the more powerful, communication-controlling position, and Shirley in an inferior, less powerful, communication-receiving status.

However, the plot is even more complicated. Sharon is substantially younger than Loraine and about the same age as Shirley, who is also single. Sharon and Shirley have much in common and are close friends. (See the bold vertical line connecting them. This indicates that they consider each other equals, friends, and colleagues.)

Sharon is in an uncomfortable and tenuous position. On the one hand, she values her friendship with Loraine and sees Loraine as a professional ally in the agency, someone who can provide her with some leverage against Madeline. On the other hand, Sharon also likes Shirley, and understands that Loraine is not perfect. Sharon can listen to Shirley's complaints against Loraine and provide some sympathy, but she must be extremely careful not to speak against either Loraine or Shirley to the other person. It is not easy to maintain such a balancing act.

We neither praise nor criticize informal structures of communication and authority. We simply acknowledge that they do exist in almost every agency—including yours. In practice, being aware of both formal and informal agency structures may strengthen your ability to do your job.

What eventually happened at Multihelp? Shirley left to take a position in another state, and she and Sharon soon lost contact. Six months later, Sharon also left the agency for another social work position better suited to her energetic, enthusiastic style. She became a counselor for teens with serious behavioral and family problems. Sharon and Loraine maintained their personal friendship for many years after Sharon left the agency. No one knows what happened to Madeline, Linda, or Jean.

Exercise 4.8: Analyzing Formal and Informal Organizational Structure

Choose an organization, preferably some type of social services agency. For the purposes of this assignment, however, any agency—including your university or some segment of the university—will do. Contact an employee, a supervisor, or an administrator in the agency you selected, and ask for a copy of the organizational chart. Explain to your contact person that you want to study the formal *lines of authority,* the *channels of communication,* and the *dimensions of power* illustrated in the chart. Define the terms for your contact, then ask the following questions and record his or her answers:

1.   A.   To what extent do the channels of communication in the agency follow the formal lines of authority depicted in the organizational chart?

        B.   If there are specific differences between the chart and the reality, describe them.

        C.   What are the positive and negative effects of these differences?

2.   A.   How closely do the dimensions of power in the agency match the formal lines of authority depicted in the organizational chart?

        B.   If there are specific differences between the chart and the reality, describe them.

        C.   What are the positive and negative effects of these differences?

Management Style and Organizational Culture

Organizations also differ in their management styles—that is, in how employees are thought of and treated. These styles often reflect some combination of organizational theories.

We will explore two somewhat extreme examples of such styles. First, the traditional bureaucratic management style: Bureaucracies, by definition, emphasize a hierarchical power structure with little, if any, input from lower-level staff or clients. Second, we will examine an alternative type— total quality management—which prioritizes clients and their input first, staff who work directly with clients second, and so on. Upper levels of administration—including the agency director—are in a sense considered less consequential in the service delivery process.

Organizational culture is "the set of values, guiding beliefs, understandings, and ways of thinking that is shared by members of an organization and is taught to new members as correct" (Daft, 1992, p. 317). Such culture varies dramatically from one organization to another in terms of strictness of structure and extent of worker flexibility.

A bureaucracy, for instance, is "a system of administration marked by officialism (lack of flexibility and initiative combined with excessive adherence to regulations in the behavior of usually government officials), red tape (official routine or procedure marked by excessive complexity which results in delay or inaction), and proliferations (rapid growth by production of new parts, cells, buds, or offspring)" (*Webster's Ninth New Collegiate Dictionary*, 1991, pp. 188, 820, 941, 988). We have already discussed bureaucratic management style. It reflects concepts emphasized in scientific management organizational theories, emphasizes how specifically designed, formal structure and a consistent, rigid organizational network of employees are most important if an organization is to run well and achieve its goals (Holland & Petchers, 1987; Sarri, 1987). Each employee holds a clearly defined job and is told straightforwardly and exactly how that job should be accomplished. This school of thought calls for minimal independent functioning on the part of employees. Supervisors closely scrutinize the latter's work. Efficiency is of utmost importance. How people feel about their jobs is insignificant. Administration avoids allowing employees to have any input regarding how organizational goals can best be reached. Rather, employees are expected to do their jobs as instructed—and as quietly and efficiently as possible.

Its polar opposite is *Total Quality Management (TQM)*, a style currently employed by many social service organizations.[1] This management perspective emphasizes organizational process, attainment of excellent quality service, and empowerment of employees. Barker (1995) defines TQM as "an orientation to management of organizations, including social services agencies, in which quality, as defined by clients and consumers, is the overriding goal, and client satisfaction, employee empowerment, and long-term relationships determine procedures" (pp. 383-84).

Bedwell (1993) provides a more straightforward description of TQM: "The essence of total quality is simple: Ask your customers what they want; then give it to them!" (p. 29).

Essentially, TQM considers clients, other agencies that purchase services from the TQM-oriented agency, and the agency's staff very important. Agency staff most directly involved with clients are significant because their interactions with clients directly affect client (customer) satisfaction. TQM maintains that quality of service provision is also critical. Each social services agency must specify its own definition of quality in the context of its own purpose. Dimensions may include accuracy, consistency, responsiveness, availability, perceived value (by clients), and service experience—the entirety of the service event as perceived by clients (Lutheran Social Services of Wisconsin and Upper Michigan, 1993, p. 8). In contrast to traditional bureaucracies, TQM empowers employees to perform their jobs as effectively and efficiently as possible. It emphasizes participative management that places the major responsibility for effective service provision on direct service workers. Teamwork and shared responsibility among workers are top priorities. TQM encourages teams to stress the importance of open communication, identify problems and issues, discuss potential alternatives, make decisions about how to proceed, set goals, and evaluate progress. Employees are consistently encouraged to assess processes and procedures and make improvements. Essentially, supervisors and administrators should "serve as integrators and facilitators, not as watchdogs and interventionists" (Kanter, 1989, p. 89). Agencies adapting TQM eagerly solicit feedback from clients about service effectiveness.

Exercise 4.9: Organizational Culture Investigation

The two questionnaires below contain questions you can ask to evaluate organizational culture. They compare two organizational cultures—a traditional bureaucracy and a client/employee centered agency employing TQM. This exercise will sensitize you to differences in organizational culture and to how those differences may affect you professionally.

Select a social services agency—large or small, public or private—in your area. You may interview a worker, a supervisor or agency administrator, or both a worker *and* an administrator. (If you choose this last option, you can compare their impressions of the organizational culture. Frequently, workers—who are in direct contact with clients and their views—perceives an organization very differently than do administrators—who are exposed to political, funding, and regulatory pressures from the external macro environment.) This questionnaire will not yield a specific score to precisely define organizational culture, but it will provide you with some thought-provoking information about agency life.

Instruct the interviewee(s) to answer both questionnaires to the best of her ability, using this scale: (1) never; (2) infrequently; (3) sometimes; (4) frequently; and (5) always. Record her responses below.

Add up the scores for each questionnaire separately and divide each by ten. The two average scores will range from 1—low organizational commitment to that management style—to 5—very high commitment to that management style. You may find an inverse relationship between scores on the Bureaucratic and Customer/Employee Orientation questionnaires, reflecting the extreme differences between the two.

---

[1] The concepts involved in Total Quality Management were developed by W. Edward Deming (1982, 1986) and others (Crosby, 1980; Feigenbaum, 1983; Juran, 1989).

Bureaucratic Orientation Questionnaire[2]

1. Most professional employees in this organization hold a clearly defined job with clearly designated responsibilities.

Never	Infrequently	Sometimes	Frequently	Always
1	2	3	4	5

2. Most professional employees in this organization are told straightforwardly and specifically how their jobs should be accomplished.

Never	Infrequently	Sometimes	Frequently	Always
1	2	3	4	5

3. Supervisors closely scrutinize employees' work.

Never	Infrequently	Sometimes	Frequently	Always
1	2	3	4	5

4. The administration considers efficiency to be of the utmost importance.

Never	Infrequently	Sometimes	Frequently	Always
1	2	3	4	5

5. Decisions about agency policy and practice tend to be made by higher administration and flow from the top down.

Never	Infrequently	Sometimes	Frequently	Always
1	2	3	4	5

6. Power in the agency is held primarily by top executives.

Never	Infrequently	Sometimes	Frequently	Always
1	2	3	4	5

7. Communication in the organization flows from the top down.

Never	Infrequently	Sometimes	Frequently	Always
1	2	3	4	5

---

[2]Many of the questions listed below are derived from the conflicts posed by Knopf (1979) that occur between the orientations of helping professionals and bureaucratic systems.

8. There is little communication among horizontal units—that is, units of approximately equal status that perform different functions.

Never	Infrequently	Sometimes	Frequently	Always
1	2	3	4	5

9. The organization emphasizes a rigid structure of power and authority that works to maintain stability and the status quo.

Never	Infrequently	Sometimes	Frequently	Always
1	2	3	4	5

10. The organization and its administration place great importance on specified rules and policies and expect employees to adhere to them.

Never	Infrequently	Sometimes	Frequently	Always
1	2	3	4	5

TOTAL: = _____ ÷ 10 = _____ (AVERAGE SCORE)

Customer/Employee Orientation Questionnaire

1. The organization places primary importance on the client (customer) and on effective service to clients.

Never	Infrequently	Sometimes	Frequently	Always
1	2	3	4	5

2. The organization holds in high regard practitioners who provide services directly to clients.

Never	Infrequently	Sometimes	Frequently	Always
1	2	3	4	5

3. The organization's administrative structure is viewed primarily as a support system for clients and direct service workers.

Never	Infrequently	Sometimes	Frequently	Always
1	2	3	4	5

4. The organization's administration considers quality of service—consistency of service provision, responsiveness to clients' needs, and service availability—its major goal.

Never	Infrequently	Sometimes	Frequently	Always
1	2	3	4	5

5. Organizational leadership seeks to empower agency practitioners so that they can do their jobs as effectively as possible.

Never	Infrequently	Sometimes	Frequently	Always
1	2	3	4	5

6. Professional employees are encouraged to provide input into how the organization is run.

Never	Infrequently	Sometimes	Frequently	Always
1	2	3	4	5

7. The organization values client feedback and incorporates it into improving service provision.

Never	Infrequently	Sometimes	Frequently	Always
1	2	3	4	5

8. Professional employees are encouraged to work together to improve service provision.

Never	Infrequently	Sometimes	Frequently	Always
1	2	3	4	5

9. Communication flow is open and frequent among most agency units.

Never	Infrequently	Sometimes	Frequently	Always
1	2	3	4	5

10. Professional employees feel that their input to upper levels of administration is valued and put to use.

Never	Infrequently	Sometimes	Frequently	Always
1	2	3	4	5

TOTAL	=	_____	÷	10	=	_____	(AVERAGE SCORE)

After calculating scores, explain to the interviewee(s) which organizational culture his agency reflects. Give brief examples of traditional bureaucracy and of TQM. Then ask the following questions about the organization's culture and effectiveness.

1. How would you describe the organization's culture?

2. To what extent do you feel the organization's culture enhances or detracts from practitioners' ability to do their work effectively?

3. What are the strengths of the organization's culture?

4. What are the weaknesses of the organization's culture?

5. Ideally, what changes, if any, would you make in the organizational culture?

I.   **Introduction**

II. **Change in Organizations**

    A.   Highlight 5.1 A word about innovations

    B.   Undertaking specific projects

        1.   Service projects—address needs or issues requiring some new, innovative, or untried approach

        2.   Support projects—involve short-term endeavors aimed at specific ends that support some other agency activity

    C.   Initiating and developing programs

        1.   Programs—relatively permanent structures designed to meet ongoing client needs; they carry out policies that are intended to meet community or organizational goals

        2.   Gaps in service delivery system

    D.   Changing agency policies

        1.   Informal agency policies

            a.   Highlight 5.2 Case Example: "Hidden" Informal Policies

            b.   Informal policies on practice procedures (practice procedures—refer to the way organizations or individuals within them go about doing their business)

            c.   Informal agency goals—often replace formally stated goals and thus become the real goals the agency strives to reach (goal displacement)

            d.   Informal personnel practices

III. **Beginning the Change Process**

    A.   Change agent—the person who feels some change within the agency is needed

    B.   Action system—the people and resources you will organize and employ to work toward the needed change

    C.   Innovation proposal—the idea you want to implement

    D.   Action plan—a detailed blueprint for how to go about achieving the desired change

E.   Two major tasks

1.   Identify the action system's potential goal

2.   Think about the opposition you anticipate

IV.   The Process of Organizational Change

A.   The planned change process

1.   Engagement (of client systems in appropriate working relationships)

2.   Assessment (including identifying issues, problems, needs, resources, and assets, collecting and assessing information, and focusing on strengths)

3.   Planning (for service delivery by using empirically based interventions designed to achieve client system goals and by developing, analyzing, advocating, and providing leadership for policies and services to promote social and economic justice)

4.   Implementation (selecting and undertaking appropriate courses of action, and applying empirical knowledge and technological advances)

5.   Evaluation (of both program outcomes and practice effectiveness)

6.   Termination

7.   Follow-up

B.   Figure 5.1: PREPARE: An Assessment of Organizational or Community Change Potential

C.   Case Example—Deciding to go macro

D.   Step 1: **P**REPARE—Identify **problems** to address

1.   Substep 1: Decide to seriously evaluate the potential for macro level intervention

a.   Case Example—Substep 1

2.   Substep 2: Define and prioritize problems

a.   Case Example—Substep 2

b.   Figure 5.2 Identify Problems to Address—Substep 2

3.   Substep 3: Translate problems into needs

a.   Problems—any sources of perplexity or distress

b.   Needs—physical, psychological, economic, cultural, and social requirements for survival, well-being, and fulfillment

114

        c.   Figure 5.3: Identify Problems to Address—Substep 3

        d.   Five phases for clarifying and substantiating an unmet need in order to prepare for program development within your agency (Hasenfeld, 1987)

                1)   Get background data and _____ ion to clarify exactly what the need is

                2)   Recognize and specify other agencies or programs in the community that already address the need

                3)   Talk to other professionals serving similar clients

                4)   Get clients involved

                5)   Consider the value of a more formal needs assessment (needs assessment—formal evaluations of client needs within the organizational context and of resident needs within the community context)

        e.   Case Example—Substep 3

    4.   Substep 4: Determine which need or needs you will address

        a.   Focus on one at a time

        b.   Case Example—Substep 4

E.   Step 2: P**REP**ARE—Review your macro and personal **Reality**

    1.   Macro reality—the macro environment in which you work

    2.   Personal reality—the personal strengths and weaknesses that might affect your ability to effect a macro intervention in the macro environment

    3.   Substep 1: Evaluate macro variables working for or against you in the macro change process

        a.   Figure 5.4: Assess Your Macro and Personal **Reality**—Substep 1

        b.   Resources

        c.   Constraining regulations

        d.   Internal political climate

                1)   Factors against change

                      a)   An organization that has undergone a number of major external alterations and upheavals in recent months will probably be more resistant to change

     b)   An agency that is wedded to a specific philosophy or treatment modality

     c)   Age of the agency and longevity of its staff

    2)   Highlight 5.3 Bureaucratic Succession: Opportunity for Positive Change

  e. External political climate

  f. Other factors

  g. Case Example—Substep 1

 4. Substep 2: Review your personal reality—strengths and weaknesses that may act for or against successful change efforts

  a. Figure 5.5: Evaluating Personal Characteristics for Macro Practice: Macro Practice Builds on Macro Practice Skills

  b. Case Example—Substep 2

F. Step 3: PR**E**PARE—<u>Establish</u> primary goals

 1. Characteristics of goals

  a. Goals are derived from some identified problem

  b. The problem can be translated into some specific need

 2. Three concepts relevant to goal selection

  a. Potential for permanence

  b. Greater influence

  c. Acceptance

 3. Case Example—**Establish** Primary Goals

G. Step 4: PRE**P**ARE—Identify relevant **People** of influence

 1. Highlight 5.4 Leadership Styles of Decision-Makers

  a. Climber—tends to closely control subordinates to ensure nobody else is seen as a rising star

  b. Conserver—toils to preserve the homeostatic status quo

  c. Zealot—a go-getter who exudes energy and loves creative innovation

        d.   Advocate—a person who has exceptionally high commitment to the goals of the organization or unit of which she or he is a member, or to a client population serviced by the agency

        e.   Statesperson—is more concerned with the welfare of society as a whole than with the agency or a particular client population

  2.   Figure 5.6: PREPARE—Identify Relevant **People** of Influence

  3.   Case Example—PREPARE: Identify Relevant **People** of Influence

  4.   Rationales for internal advocacy

H.   Step 5: PREP<u>A</u>RE—<u>**Assess**</u> potential costs and benefits to clients and agency

  1.   Opportunity cost—how you might miss out on other good opportunities where your time would be better spent

  2.   Three questions to ask before pursuing a new project

        a.   Will the results be worth the effort?

        b.   Might alternative solutions produce more benefits at less cost?

        c.   Who gets the benefits and who pays the costs?

  3.   Case Example—PREPARE: **Assess** Potential Costs and Benefits to Clients and Agency

I.   Step 6: PREPA<u>RE</u>—Review professional and personal **<u>Risk</u>**

  1.   Figure 5.7: PREPARE—Evaluate Professional and Personal **Risk**

  2.   Three questions to ask yourself before seriously undertaking macro change in an organization

        a.   Could I lose my job?

        b.   Will my career path be affected?

        c.   Will I strain interpersonal relationship at work?

  3.   Highlight 5.5 Consider "Covert Operations"

  4.   A strengths perspective on risk

  5.   Case Example—PREPARE: Review Your Professional and Personal **Risk**

J.   Step 7: PREPAR**E**—**Evaluate** the potential success of a macro change process

    1.   Substep 1: Review the PREPARE process and weigh pros and cons of proceeding

        a.   Three possible conclusions

            1)   You might make a definite commitment to continue the change process

            2)   You might determine that the time is not right

            3)   You might decide that the potential for effective organizational change is too poor to continue your efforts

        b.   Figure 5.8: PREPARE—**Evaluate** the Potential Success of a Macro Change Process

        c.   Case Example—Substep 1

    2.   Substep 2: Identify possible macro approaches to use, estimate their effectiveness, and select the most appropriate one

        a.   The transitional stage between deciding to pursue a macro change effort and actually doing it

        b.   Case Example—Substep 2

        c.   Highlight 5.6: Summary Outline of the PREPARE Process

            1)   **P**: Identify **Problems** to address

                a)   Substep 1: Decide to seriously evaluate the potential for macro level intervention

                b)   Substep 2: Define and prioritize problems

                c)   Substep 3: Translate problems into needs

                d)   Substep 4: Determine which need or needs you will address

            2)   **R**: Review your macro and personal **Reality**

                a)   Substep 1: Evaluate macro variables working for or against you in the macro change process. These variables include:

                    (1)   Resources

                    (2)   Constraining regulations

          (3)   Internal political climate

          (4)   External political climate

          (5)   Other factors

    b)   Substep 2: Review your personal reality—strengths and weaknesses that may act for or against successful change efforts

3)   **E**: **Establish** primary goals

4)   **P**: Identify relevant **People** of influence

5)   **A**: **Assess** potential benefits to clients and agency

6)   **R**: Review professional and personal **Risk**. Questions you might ask include:

    a)   Could I lose my job?

    b)   Will my career path be affected?

    c)   Will I strain interpersonal relationships at work?

7)   **E**: **Evaluate** the potential success of a macro change process

    a)   Substep 1: Review the PREPARE process and weigh the pros and cons of proceeding

    b)   Substep 2: Identify possible macro approaches to use, estimate their effectiveness, and select the most appropriate one

---

Experiential Exercises and Classroom Simulations

Exercise 5.1: Understanding Change in Organizations

A.   Brief Description
Using a small group format, students investigate the meanings of project implementation, program development, and agency policy change by exploring the major concepts involved, their similarities and differences, and examples of each.

B.   Objectives
Students will:
1.   Recognize the basic concepts inherent in the three types of organizational change.
2.   Examine how the types of organizational change compare and differ.
3.   Identify examples of each.

C. Procedure
    1. Review the material on change in organizations provided in the text including a word about innovations, undertaking specific projects, initiating and developing programs, and changing agency policies.
    2. Divide the class into small groups of four to six.
    3. Ask the groups to discuss the subsequent questions, select a group representative, and be prepared to report to the entire class the small group's findings.
    4. After about 20 minutes, ask the small groups to terminate their discussions and participate in a full class discussion.
    5. Ask the representative from each group to share her or his summary of the discussion. Encourage comments from all class members.

D. Instructions for Students
Address the following issues:
    1. Describe the major concepts involved in project implementation, program development, and agency policy change.
    2. In what ways are the three types of organizational change similar?
    3. In what ways are the three types of change different?
    4. Provide some examples of each type of change.

E. Commentary
This activity may also be conducted by holding a full class discussion without breaking students down into small groups.

Exercise 5.2: Identifying Leadership Styles of Decision-Makers

A. Brief Description
Using a small group format, students identify the leadership style reflected in each of several leader descriptions.

B. Objectives
Students will:
    1. Identify which leadership style characterizes examples of leaders.
    2. Compare and contrast the dimensions of leadership styles.
    3. Describe an ideal leadership style and explain why.

C. Procedure
    1. Review the material on leadership styles of decision-makers provided in the text.
    2. Provide students with copies of the matching exercise under "Instructions for Students."
    3. After allowing students a few minutes to complete the exercise, initiate a full class discussion regarding the following questions and issues:
        a. What leadership style characterizes each leader description and why?
        b. In what ways are these five leadership styles different?
        c. In what ways are these five leadership styles similar?
        d. What is the ideal leadership style? How does it differ from any or all of these?

D.   Instructions for Students

Match the following leadership styles with the descriptions cited below. Note that some descriptions may apply to more than one leadership style.

    A. Climber
    B. Conserver
    C. Zealot
    D. Advocate
    E. Statesperson

1.   A leader who is more concerned with the welfare of society as a whole than with the agency or a particular client population.

    a.   What leadership style(s) characterize(s) this leader?
    b.   Explain why.

2.   A leader who is very concerned with and interested in him/herself and his/her own work.

    a.   What leadership style(s) characterize(s) this leader?
    b.   Explain why.

3.   A leader who likes to closely control subordinates to ensure nobody else is seen as a rising star.

    a.   What leadership style(s) characterize(s) this leader?
    b.   Explain why.

4.   A leader who has exceptionally high commitment to the goals of the organization or unit of which she or he is a member.

    a.   What leadership style(s) characterize(s) this leader?
    b.   Explain why.

5.   A leader who is a superduper go-getter, exudes energy, and loves creative innovation.

    a.   What leadership style(s) characterize(s) this leader?
    b.   Explain why.

6.   A leader who is a skilled administrator and is exceptionally committed to the agency and its clients.

    a.   What leadership style(s) characterize(s) this leader?
    b.   Explain why.

7.   A leader who will probably not support subordinates' ideas for change, but might just confiscate them and take them as her/his own.

    a.   What leadership style(s) characterize(s) this leader?
    b.   Explain why.

8.   A leader who is not so much concerned about quality of service provision as following the rules to the letter.

   a.   What leadership style(s) characterize(s) this leader?
   b.   Explain why.

9.   A leader who has excellent public relations skills but is not very good at attending to detail or carrying through with long-term proposals.

   a.   What leadership style(s) characterize(s) this leader?
   b.   Explain why.

10.   A leader who will probably not spend much time listening to your ideas.

   a.   What leadership style(s) characterize(s) this leader?
   b.   Explain why.

E.   Commentary
This activity may also be conducted by holding a full class discussion without breaking students down into small groups.

Exercise 5.3: Evaluating Personal Characteristics for Macro Practice

   Evaluating your own characteristics, strengths, and weaknesses is as important in macro practice as in micro or mezzo practice. Indeed, macro practice skills are built upon micro and mezzo practice skills, and you will use the same interpersonal skills in macro practice as you do at the other levels.

   Picture yourself working with staff, administrators, and clients in an agency. Answer the questions and follow the instructions below:

1.   Complete the following four "Who are you?" statements, using adjectives, nouns, or phrases. If you had to summarize who you are, what would you say?

   I am

   I am

   I am

   I am

2. What adjectives would you use to describe yourself? Underline all that apply.

Happy	Sad	Honest	Dishonest	Sensitive
Insensitive	Trustworthy	Untrustworthy	Caring	Uncaring
Outgoing	Shy	Withdrawn	Friendly	Unfriendly
Religious	Not-very-religious	Nervous	Calm	Formal
Informal	Aggressive	Assertive	Timid	Confident
Not-very-confident	Careful	Careless	Capable	Incapable
Independent	Dependent	Affectionate	Cool	Wary
Bold	Cheerful	Witty	Unassuming	Thorough
Easy-going	Determined	Clever	Responsive	Strong-minded
Leisurely	Industrious	Weak-willed (at least sometimes)	Controlled	Spontaneous
Serious	Funny	Tough	Pleasant	Daring
Eager	Efficient	Not-so-efficient	Artistic	Tactful
Intolerant	Vulnerable	Likable	Smart	Understanding
Impatient	Patient	Imaginative	Wordy	Concise
Open-minded	Funny	Organized	Somewhat-disorganized	Conscientious
Late	Emotional	Unemotional	Controlled	Open
Creative	Curious	Sincere	Precise	A-little-haphazard
Cooperative	Ethical	Brave	Mature	Spunky

3. Cite your four greatest strengths—personal qualities, talents, or accomplishments.

Strength   A

Strength   B

Strength   C

Strength   D

4. Several weakness are listed below. To what extent do you suffer from each? Rate yourself on each one by placing the appropriate number beside it.

1. Very serious   2. Moderately serious   3. Mildly serious   4. Not at all serious

Lack of understanding of community service system _____
Personal stress _____
Exhaustion and fatigue _____
Over-involvement with job _____
Insufficient time _____
Lack of self-confidence _____

5. Cite your four greatest weaknesses.

Weakness   A

Weakness   B

Weakness C

Weakness D

6.   How do you think your personal strengths will help you work with other staff, administrators, and clients in macro practice situations?

7.   What weaknesses, if any, do you think you need to address to improve your ability to work with staff, administrators, and clients in macro practice situations?

8.   ***Step 3: PREPARE***—**Establish** ***Primary Goals***
     What is required to fulfill your identified needs? What goals do you think you might be able to accomplish in your own macro environment? It is too early to establish detailed, specific objectives, but identifying a primary goal will give you a sense of direction.
     Examples of goals may range from the establishment of regular meeting times for physicians, social workers, and nurses in a hospital to discuss cases, to the shifting of the program focus of a social work unit from individual services to group or community service. A goal may be as minute as designing a new face sheet on a case record or as major as establishing a workshop to improve administration-staff relationships (Resnick, 1980c, p. 212).

9.   ***Step 4: PREPARE***—***Identify Relevant*** **People** *of Influence*
     Who might be available to help you make the changes you've identified? There might be specific individuals or groups in the organization or the community, people or groups with access to influence or power—such as agency supervisors, administrators, or community leaders. Subjectively consider to what extent you can anticipate support from each person or group identified.

10. ***Step 5: PREPARE***—**Assess** ***Potential Financial Costs and Potential Benefits to Clients and Agency***
     Any macro change requires some new input. Such input can take the form of actual money spent or of staff time—another expensive resource (Rubin & Rubin, 1992).
     It may be difficult to estimate actual costs, but you do need to think about costs in a general way. Does your macro change require $500,000 for new staff and office space expansion when your agency is strapped for funds? Or does your macro proposal require a few hours per week of several staff members' time, plus the cost of supplies and funding for publicity to advertise a new service?
     Rubin and Rubin (1992, p. 391) suggest asking three basic questions before pursuing a new project. First, "Will the results be worth the effort?" Second, "Might alternative solutions produce more benefits at less cost?" Third, "Who gets the benefits and who pays the costs?"

11. ***Step 6: PREPARE***—***Review Professional and Personal*** **Risk**
     There are three more questions to ask yourself before you undertake macro change in an organization (Resnick & Patti, 1980). Evaluate the potential risk of each.
     •   First, to what extent are you in danger of losing your job if you seek to make this change? Do you perceive no, some, moderate, or serious danger?
     •   Second, to what extent will such macro change efforts decrease your potential for upward mobility in the agency? Might you make enemies who could stand in the way of your future promotions?

124

- Third, to what extent would your efforts for macro change seriously strain your interpersonal relationships at work? Risk factors include the need to pressure administrators who do not want to be pressured and may seek to punish you; the chance that you will be viewed as a troublemaker or will annoy your colleagues by asking them to contribute their time and effort.

Of course, sometimes involvement in macro activity will *enhance* your standing in an agency. It can demonstrate initiative and a sense of responsibility that others might highly respect.

12. ***Step 7: PREPARE*—Evaluate *the Potential Success of a Macro Change Process***

The last step in the PREPARE process determines whether you should continue your change efforts or stop right here. It consists, essentially, of the following two substeps.

Substep 1: Review the prior PREPARE process, and weigh the pros and cons of proceeding with the change process. Specifically, appraise client need (as established in Step 1), positive organizational variables in your macro reality and your personal assets (Step 2), potential support from people of influence (Step 4), and potential financial benefits (Step 5). Then weigh these variables against negative organizational variables in your macro reality and your personal deficiencies (Step 2), potential resistance from people of influence (Step 4), potential financial costs (Step 5), and your own potential risk (Step 6). Figure 5.2 illustrates Step 7 in the PREPARE process.

At the end of this decision-making process, you will be left with one of three decisions: to make a definite commitment to the change process, to accept that the time is not right and postpone your plans, or to forget the idea altogether.

Substep 2: Assuming that you are committed to the macro change, identify possible approaches, roughly estimate their potential effectiveness, and select the most appropriate one. Approaches may be directed at changing agency policy, at developing a new program, or at undertaking some more limited project. Chapter 6 will continue where this chapter leaves off in the macro change process.

Figure 5.8: PREPARE-- **Evaluate** the Potential Success of a
Macro Change Process

Evaluate the *PROS* that include:

	Established in Step
Client Need	1
Positive Organizational and Other Macro Variables	2
Your Own Strengths	2
Potential Support	4
Financial Benefits	5

Weigh the pros against the *CONS* that include:

	Established in Step
Negative Organizational and Other Macro Variables	2
Your Own Weaknesses	2
Potential Resistance	4
Financial costs	5
Your Risks	6

**CONTINUE
WITH
MACRO CHANGE
PROCESS**

**POSTPONE
CHANGE
PROCESS**

**TERMINATE
CHANGE
PROCESS**

Read the following case vignette and answer the subsequent questions using each step of the PREPARE process. Feel free to add creative ideas and solutions to each phase of the decision-making process.

You are a social worker for Shatterproof County Department of Social Services in the Public Assistance Division.[1] Shatterproof is a huge urban county populated primarily by people of color. Following the demise of Aid to Families with Dependent Children (AFDC),[2] your agency is struggling to adapt to new policies, regulations, and requirements concerning the distribution of clients' needed resources. You and your colleagues are working to adjust and conform to new expectations. However, that is not the immediate focus of your concern.

In working for the county these past three years, you have become increasingly disturbed about the way many workers treat clients, most of whom are women of color. You feel that workers are pressured to process clients through the problem-solving process as quickly as possible and that too little emphasis is placed on client empowerment. Empowerment is the "process of increasing personal, interpersonal, or political power so that individuals can take action to improve their life situations" (Gutierrez, 1995, p. 205).[3] You feel strongly that if workers assumed an empowerment-oriented approach, more clients would be able to gain control of the solutions to their own problems. Such an approach might involve teaching workers how to focus on empowerment approaches and techniques, including "accepting the client's definition of the problem," "identifying and building upon existing strengths," engaging in a realistic assessment of the client's power in her personal situation, "teaching specific skills" (such as "skills for community or organizational change; life skills," such as parenting, job seeking, and self-defense; and interpersonal skills, such as assertiveness, social competency, and self-advocacy"), and "mobilizing resources and advocating for clients" (Gutierrez, 1995, pp. 208-10).

So you begin to wonder what you might be able to do about this situation. Clients ought to be allowed more input into the definition and solution of their problems, but workers are not as receptive to clients as they should be. Adopting an empowerment approach could greatly help in successfully implementing the new public assistance programs. Of course, this is not the agency's only problem. Workers are overly burdened with paperwork, and computers and programs are already outdated. Nevertheless, in your mind empowerment remains the dominant issue. You think social workers, supervisors, and administrators should be educated about empowerment issues and trained to implement empowerment approaches in practice. Emphasis should be placed on both empowerment values and skills. How can you increase awareness and implementation of a philosophy of empowerment in your huge agency? Upper-level administrators seem to inhabit some unreachable plane. There are only so many hours in your workday. What are your options? Can you start small by trying to reach workers in your own unit? (There are seven of you who report to one supervisor.) Can you initiate training for yourself and the other six workers in your unit?

Will the unit and the agency accept an empowerment approach? What factors will help you and what will hinder you? What will training the unit staff cost? The agency may have some funding available to provide in-service training for workers,[4] because it does require every worker to complete

---

[1] Public assistance is "a government's provision of minimum financial aid to people who have no other means of supporting themselves" (Barker, 1995, p. 305).

[2] AFDC was "a public assistance program, originating in the Social Security Act as Aid to Dependent Children, funded by the federal and state governments to provide financial aid for needy children who are deprived of parental support because of death, incapacitation, or absence" (Barker, 1995, p. 14).

[3] Many of the concepts presented here are taken from L. M. Gutierrez (1995). "Working with women of color: An empowerment perspective." In J. Rothman, J. L. Erlich, & J.E. Tropman (eds.), *Strategies of Community Intervention* (pp. 204-220). Itasca, IL: F. E. Peacock.

[4] In-service training is "an educational program provided by an employer and usually carried out by a supervisor or specialist to help an employee become more productive and effective in accomplishing a specific task or meeting the

continuing education units (CEUs)[5] on a regular basis. As a matter of fact, you have a flier announcing an empowerment training seminar led by an expert in the field. You also know of a social work professor in the local university who might be able to do some training or to refer you to someone who can. What would that cost? Is there any possibility of getting volunteers to do the training on a limited basis?

Are there other potential barriers to training besides cost? Certainly the agency's CEU requirements are in your favor. Although the agency is in some turmoil due to new programs and requirements, it seems there has always been some degree of hubbub. That's really nothing new. Training a single unit is a relatively small task. Ideally, you'd like to include the entire agency, but that's something to think about in the future. You can think of no one outside the agency who would actively oppose your plan.

Do you think you can "pull off" such a project, even though training programs aren't in your job description? What personal characteristics will work to your advantage in the process? For example, are you capable, responsible, and/or assertive? Do you have exceptionally strong communication or negotiation skills? On the other hand, what weaknesses do you have that might act against a successful change process? For example, is it difficult for you to ask for things? Do you consider yourself shy or lacking in confidence?

The bottom line is that you really want other workers to work with clients more effectively by adopting an empowerment approach. Your goal, then, is to figure out how to provide training to help them do just that. You've discussed the idea with colleagues who seemed mildly positive about it. You don't think they'd be willing to take on primary responsibilities for the project, but it would be worthwhile speaking with some of them further.

Your colleague and friend Ortrude has some difficulties organizing and following through on details, but she usually speaks up for anything she believes in. Maybe you can win her support. There is also Virgilia, a hard, responsible worker who usually keeps her opinions to herself. You don't feel you know her very well, but she might be in favor of your idea. On the downside, there's your colleague and non-friend Bentley who typically "pooh-poohs" any innovative idea.

The agency's voluntary In-service Training Committee suggests and plans training for various agency units, so you will have to approach its members, and they might be supportive—even though their funding is limited and fluctuating. Since you don't personally know any committee members, you have no natural "in."

As to people in the community, you've already established that at least one expert is available (though you don't know what her fee would be) and that the professor at the university is another possibility.

What about your own position and how initiating such a project might affect you both professionally and personally. Your supervisor Astral is a "laid-back" type who generally gets her work done in a leisurely fashion. (Actually, you think she's kind of "spacey.") She is not someone to depend upon for high-powered consultations or for strong support for this initiative. On the other hand, if you're willing to do the work yourself, she will probably approve the project and send it up for higher level authorization. All agency in-service training must be approved by the agency's Assistant Director, Harvey. You think Harvey, a scrooge-like accountant at heart, is more likely to approve such a plan if it isn't extremely costly.

---

overall objectives of the organization" (Barker, 1995, p. 188).

[5] Acquiring CEUs often involves successful completion of "qualified academic or professional courses" (Barker, 1995, p. 79). One intent is to keep professionals in a range of professions updated with current knowledge relevant to their fields.

Exercise 5.4 (1):

<u>Step 1: Identify Problems to Address</u>
　　　　Substep 1.1: Evaluate the potential for macro level intervention. Discuss the seriousness of the identified problem situation in the case example above. In your own words, describe what you see as the core issue(s).

　　　　Substep 1.2: Define and prioritize the problems you've identified in the case example.

　　　　Substep 1.3: Translate problems into needs.

　　　　Substep 1.4:   Determine which need or needs you will address if you are in this worker's situation.

Exercise 5.4 (2):

<u>Step 2: Review Your Macro and Personal Reality</u>
　　　　Substep 2.1: Evaluate the organizational and other macro variables potentially working for or against you in the macro change process as portrayed in the above case example. Fill out figure 5.3, then explain the reasons for your responses below.

Figure 5.3: PREPARE--Evaluate Your Professional and Personal Risk

To what extent are you in danger of:	No danger	Some danger	Moderate danger	Serious danger
1. losing your job?				
2. decreasing your potential for upward mobility?				
3. seriously straining work relationships?				

Explain the reasons for your responses.

　　　　Substep 2.2: Assess your personal reality—that is, the strengths and weaknesses that may act for or against a successful change effort. Exercise 5.1 may help you with this question.

Exercise 5.4 (3):

<u>Step 3: Establish Primary Goals</u>
　　　　List the goals you would pursue if you were in the position described above.

Exercise 5.4 (4):

<u>**Step 4: Identify Relevant People of Influence**</u>

In the following figure, list individuals and groups both inside and outside of the agency.

Figure 5.4: PREPARE--Identify Relevant **People** of Influence

Potential _Action Systems_	_Name_	Potential Support			
		Very good	Mildly good	Mildly bad	Very bad
Individuals in the Organization					
Groups in the Organization					
Individuals in the Community					
Groups in the the Community					
Others					

Give a brief explanation of your choices.

Exercise 5.4 (5):

Step 5: Assess Potential Financial Costs and Potential Benefits to Clients and Agency
        Use the case example in your response.

Exercise 5.4 (6):

Step 6: Review Professional and Personal Risk
        Could you lose your job, decrease your potential for upward mobility, and/or seriously strain your work relationships?

Exercise 5.4 (7):

Step 7: Evaluate the Potential Success of a Macro Change Process
        Substep 7.1: Review (and summarize) **the prior PREPARE process, and weigh the pros and cons of proceeding with the macro change process.**

PROS

        Client need (see Step 1):

        Positive organizational and other macro variables (see Step 2):

        Your own strengths (see Step 2):

        Potential support (see Step 4):

        Financial benefits (see Step 5):

CONS

        Negative organizational and other macro variables (see Step 2):

        Your own weaknesses (see Step 2):

        Potential resistance (see Step 4):

        Financial costs (see Step 5):

        Your risks (see Step 6):

        Substep 7.2: Identify possible macro approaches to use in the case example and determine how you would proceed (that is, continue the macro change process, postpone it, or drop the whole idea).

Exercise 5.5: Creative Macro Change

Below are three case scenarios that might involve project implementation, program development, or policy change. For each, determine what type of change should be pursued, provide a rationale for your answer, and discuss potential benefits and problems of this change.

Case Scenario A: You are the social worker at an elementary school. You notice that an increasing number of children come from turbulent homes. With each passing year these children present more problems with truancy. Their grades deteriorate and their illicit drug use soars. They need help. But what kind? Your job is to intervene individually with children suffering the most severe crises. You do some individual counseling, make some family visits, run a few support and treatment groups, and attend numerous assessment and planning meetings.

In a social work journal, you read about a new type of alternative approach for children at risk for the very problems you're seeing. One idea in particular catches your eye: A school in Illinois developed a "Friendship System" for children-at-risk. Volunteers solicited from among social work students at a nearby university attended a dozen training sessions, learning how to deal with these children. Each volunteer was then paired with a child and became the child's "special friend." The required commitment period was one year. Volunteers' responsibilities included spending time with the child at least once a week, being available when the child needed to talk, and generally being a positive role model for the child.

The program seems similar to Big Brothers/Big Sisters in which volunteers "work under professional supervision, usually by social workers, providing individual guidance and companionship to boys and girls deprived of a parent" (Barker, 1995, p. 35). But children in the Friendship System might or might not be from single-parent homes. The Friendship System's only prerequisite for the children is that school staff designate them as at-risk of problems including truancy, deteriorating school performance, and drug use, and school staff have substantial latitude in determining a child's eligibility for the program. Typical criteria include a recent divorce in the family, extreme shyness and withdrawal, academic problems, or other social problems. You think, "Wouldn't it be great if my school system had something like that in operation?"

What type of change would you consider pursuing—implementing a project, developing a program, or changing a school policy? Provide a rationale for the proposed change and discuss its potential benefits and problems.

    A.   What type of change should be pursued?
    B.   Explain your reasons for choosing this change.
    C.   What are the potential benefits and problems of this change?

Case Scenario B: Your agency requires clients to fill out a 27-page admissions form before they can receive services. A large percentage of the agency's clients are Hispanic, and they speak very little English so the admissions form effectively prohibits Hispanic clients from receiving service. Because of the language difference, the agency blocks clients from receiving service.

What type of change would you consider pursuing—implementing a project, developing a program, or changing an agency policy? Provide a rationale for the proposed change and discuss its potential benefits and problems.

    A.   What type of change should be pursued?
    B.   Explain your reasons for choosing this change.
    C.   What are the potential benefits and problems of this change?

Case Scenario C: You are a social worker in a rural county social services agency. The towns in the county range in size from 1500 to 10,000 people, and the area has become increasingly impoverished as a number of small cheese and leather factories have left the area. Many people are struggling to survive in old shacks with little clothing and food. You know you can't overhaul the entire public assistance system, but you would like to initiate a food drive or collection to temporarily relieve people's suffering.

What type of change would you consider pursuing—implementing a project, developing a program, or changing an agency policy? Provide a rationale for the proposed change and discuss its potential benefits and problems.

    A.   What type of change should be pursued?
    B.   Explain your reasons for choosing this change.
    C.   What are the potential benefits and problems of this change?

Chapter 6
IMAGINE How to Implement Macro Intervention: Changing Agency Policy

I.   **Introduction**

II.   **The Planned Change Process and Organizational Change**

    A.   Figure 6.1: Macro Practice Planned Change

    B.   Highlight 6.1: A Word About Engagement

III.   **IMAGINE: A Process for Organizational Change**

    A.   Figure 6.2: IMAGINE—A Process for Initiating and Implementing Macro Change

    B.   **I**MAGINE: Develop an innovative **Idea**

        1.   Case Example: Start with an Innovative Idea

    C.   I**M**AGINE: **Muster** support and formulate an action system

        1.   Conceptualizing the macro practice environment

            a.   The macro client system—includes those people who will ultimately benefit from the change process

            b.   Figure 6.3: The Macro Client System in Macro Practice

            c.   The change agent system—the individual who initiates the macro change process

            d.   A note about the agency as a change agent system—we will generally refer to the agency as the agency system instead of the change agent system

            e.   The target system—the system that social workers must change or influence in order to accomplish their goals

            f.   Figure 6.3: The Target System

            g.   The action system—includes those people who agree and are committed to work together to attain the proposed macro change

            h.   Figure 6.5: The Change Agent, Action, Target, and Macro Client Systems

            i.   Case Example: Conceptualizing Relevant Systems in the Macro Environment

        2.   Formulate an action system: The application of mezzo concepts to macro practice

3.   Composition of the action system

      a.   Understanding of and commitment to purpose

      b.   Group leadership and participation skills

      c.   Case Example: **Muster** Support and Formulate an Action System

D.   IM**A**GINE: Identify <u>**Assets**</u>

1.   Assets are resources and advantages that will help you to undertake and complete your proposed change process

2.   Case Example: Identify **Assets**

E.   IMA<u>**G**</u>INE: Specify <u>**Goals**</u>, objectives, and action steps to attain them

1.   Primary goals do not usually specify how they will be achieved

2.   Objectives—smaller, behaviorally specific subgoals that serve as stepping stones on the way to accomplishing the primary goal

3.   Writing clear action steps—the tasks one must complete (in the correct order and within the designated time frame) to achieve the desired objective [who, what, when]

4.   Case Example—Specify **Goals**, Objectives, and Action Steps to Attain Them

F.   IMAG<u>**I**</u>NE: <u>**Implement**</u> the plan

1.   The plan will need to be monitored carefully to keep the change process on course

2.   Case Example: **Implement** the Plan

G.   IMAGI<u>**N**</u>E: <u>**Neutralize**</u> opposition

1.   Communicating with decision-makers

2.   Logical administrative reactions

3.   Phases of resistance

      a.   Monumental negativism

      b.   Mulled over issues and thought about possibilities

      c.   Conflict

      d.   Covert resistance possible after proposal is implemented

4. Collaborative and adversarial strategies

    a. Continuum from collaborative to adversarial strategies

    b. Collaboration and persuasion

    c. Four basic steps in persuading

        1) Initiate persuasion by:

            a) Establishing something in common

            b) Sharing honest feelings

            c) Blunt assault—takes sharing honest feelings much farther

        2) Allow time to discuss and answer questions

        3) State proposal clearly and straightforwardly

        4) Summarize progress with the decision makers and any agreement regarding how to proceed

    d. Additional strategies for using persuasion

        1) Educate the decision makers

        2) Discuss options

        3) Ask if a trial or partial policy, project, or program change is possible

        4) Suggest that a committee be formed to discuss and consider the proposed plan

        5) Creatively identify how target and action system members could spend more time together to develop communication channels and become familiar with the issues from both sides

        6) Appeal to the decision makers' sense of fairness, ethics, and right and wrong

        7) Develop a rational argument to support your proposed plan

        8) Specify to decision makers what the negative consequences of ignoring the identified problem might be

5.   Highlight 6.2: Being an Adversary and Pressuring

      a.   Strategies when pressuring for change

          1)   Circulate a petition to gain collective support and submit it to administration for consideration

          2)   Stage open confrontations regarding issues with decision makers during regular staff meetings

          3)   Inform sanctioning agencies from the external environment about the issue

          4)   Go to the newspapers, television, and radio with information that will bring agency problems to public attention

          5)   Encourage staff or clients to interfere deliberately with service provision

          6)   Initiate a strike

          7)   Organize concerned personnel and others, including clients, to picket the agency

          8)   Take the issue to the courts

          9)   Undertake formal bargaining

6.   Case Example—**Neutralize** opposition

H.   IMAGIN**E**: **Evaluate** progress

      1.   Evaluation serves two major purposes

          a.   Monitor the ongoing operation and activities involved in achieving a macro-level change

          b.   Target the end results of your macro intervention

      2.   Case Example—**Evaluate** Progress

IV.   **Application of IMAGINE to Macro Intervention**

A.   Changing Agency Policy

B.   Formal and informal agency policies

C.   Types of Changes in Agency Policy

1.   Highlight 6.3: Using PREPARE and IMAGINE to Establish a Culturally Competent, Empowering Organization

a.   Cultural competence in the organizational context—a set of congruent behaviors, attitudes, policies, and structures which come together in a system, an agency, or among professionals and enables that system, agency, or those professionals to work effectively in the context of cultural differences

b.   Cultural Incompetence: A Case Example

c.   Assessing cultural competence

1)   How responsible is the organization in responding effectively and efficiently to the needs of the culturally diverse people it serves?

2)   In what ways is the agency empowering its staff so that staff may, in turn, empower clients from diverse backgrounds?

3)   In what ways could services be administered differently in response to the needs of the agency's culturally diverse client population?

4)   What is the organizational vision with respect to the culturally diverse community?

5)   How might you determine that the goal of cultural competence has been achieved?

d.   Recommendations for attaining cultural competence

e.   Responding to the juvenile justice system critique

2.   Changing agency goals

3.   Changing policies on personnel practices

4.   Changing policies on practice procedures

5.   Using IMAGINE to change agency practice procedures

Exercise 6.1: Targeting Policies for Change

A.   Brief Description

Using a small group format, students apply the first four steps of IMAGINE model to a university, college, or department policy they feel merits change.

B.   Objectives

Students will:
1.   Review the IMAGINE process for pursuing policy change.
2.   Discuss how the first four steps of the process might be applied to pursue a policy change.

C.   Procedure
1.   Review the IMAGINE process and the material on changing agency policy.
2.   Ask students to identify a university, college, or department policy they would like to see changed. This might involve anything from parking fees to grading procedures to the department's course prerequisites.
3.   Divide the class into small groups of four to six.
4.   Ask the groups to follow the first four steps in the IMAGINE process for pursuing the designated policy change. The model is outlined below in a box under "Instructions for Students." Ask the groups to designate at least one spokesperson to take notes and subsequently share the group's plan with the entire class.
5.   After about 30 minutes, ask the small groups to terminate their discussions and participate in a full class discussion.
6.   Ask group representatives to share their summaries of the discussion. Encourage participation from all class members.

D.   Instructions for Students

An outline of the IMAGINE process for policy change is provided in the box below.

An Outline of the First Four Steps in the Imagine Process: Pursuing Policy Change

IMAGINE Step 1: Develop an Innovative **Idea.**
IMAGINE Step 2: **Muster** support and formulate an action system.
     Identify the macro client system.
     Identify the change agent system.
     Identify the target system.
     Identify the action system.
IMAGINE Step 3: Identify **assets.**
IMAGINE Step 4: Specify **goals** and action steps to attain them.

---

1.   Select a university, college, or department policy you feel is in need of change.

2.   Discuss how you might apply the first four steps of the imagine process (as summarized in the box above) to initiate change in this policy.

3.   Address the following questions:

        a.   What difficulties were you faced with in trying to follow the steps?
        b.   What additional information would be helpful?
        c.   What have you learned about changing policy from this experience?

E.   Commentary
This activity may also be conducted by holding a full class discussion without breaking students down into small groups

---

Exercise 6.2: Using Persuasion

A.   Brief Description
The class is broken down into pairs for the purpose of a role play. One member of the dyad plays a worker attempting to persuade the other member, playing an agency director, to pursue a policy change. Ensuing discussion focuses on the process, positive aspects, and difficulties of persuasion.

B.   Objectives
Students will:
1.   Dramatize a simulated macro situation involving persuasion.
2.   Appraise the persuasion process.

C.   Procedure
1.   Review the content in the text on neutralizing opposition, including that on communicating with decision-makers, logical administrative reactions, phases of resistance, and collaborative and adversarial strategies.
2.   Read the material included below under "Instructions for Students" including worker role, suggestions for persuasion, and agency director role.
3.   Divide the class up into pairs. Instruct one member of the dyad to play a worker and the other an agency director. Students can arbitrarily decide who plays whom. Read the role player descriptions cited below under "Instructions for Students." The worker in the role play should try to use the suggestions for persuasion presented in the text to persuade the agency director to the former's point of view. Inform students that the role play will take about ten minutes.
4.   After about ten minutes, arbitrarily halt the role play for a full class discussion. Address the questions identified in "Instructions for Students" below.

D.   Instructions for Students
Divide up into pairs where one will arbitrarily play the worker and the other the agency director described below.

> ***WORKER ROLE:*** You are a case manager at an agency that provides diagnosis, treatment, and residential care for clients who have cognitive disabilities. The agency's policy for interdisciplinary treatment staffings is to include the designated client's MSW social worker (who provides therapy), psychologist, psychiatrist, physician, and nursing staff. Interdisciplinary treatment staffings are meetings held biannually for each client where staff involved with the client report the client's progress, discuss new treatment plans as necessary, and make specific recommendations for service provision.
>
> The problem is that you, as the client's case manager, are not invited to the staffings. You feel this is ridiculous because you are the one who works directly with clients on a daily or weekly basis and are charged with overseeing all service provision. The rationale for your

exclusion is that you don't have a graduate degree. This makes no sense to you because nursing staff are included and they don't necessarily have graduate degrees either. You approach the agency director who is responsible for establishing much of agency policy and seeing that staff adhere to it.

You have made an appointment to meet with the agency director. Use the suggestions for persuasion proposed in the box below and any others you can think of to persuade the director to amend policy to include you and other case managers in multidisciplinary treatment staffings.

Suggestions For Persuasion

1. Establish something you have in common with the agency director.
   (Suggestion: Concern for the clients' wellbeing and best interests.)

2. Share honest feelings.
   (Suggestions: Share your sincere desire to improve service provision. Empathize with the agency director's position as agency policy is not all that easy to change.)

3. Educate the decision-makers.
   (Suggestions: Elaborate on your role as case manager—without being condescending. Inform the director of the extra time it takes for you and other staff to communicate about treatment plans because you can't attend treatment staffings.)

4. Discuss options.
   (Suggestion: Discuss the potential advantages and disadvantages of your proposed plan.)

5. As if a trial or partial policy change is possible.
   (Suggestion: Is it possible to include the case manager in staffings for a temporary period of time on a trial basis?)

6. Suggest that a committee be formed to discuss and consider the proposed plan.

7. Creatively identify how spending more time with other team members during staffings could develop communication channels and become familiar with the issues from both sides.

8. Appeal to the agency director's sense of fairness, ethics, and right and wrong.
   (Suggestion: What is the most ethical approach to service provision for clients?)

9. Develop a rational argument to support your proposed plan.

10. Specify to the agency director what the negative consequences of the identified problem might be.
    (Suggestion: How will ignoring the problem result in costs to the director, the client, and the agency.)

AGENCY DIRECTOR: You are very busy overseeing numerous aspects of agency functioning. You are plagued by budget cuts, pressure from regulatory agencies to comply with codes, and various staffing problems. (For example, a former employee is suing the agency for sexual harassment by a psychologist who supervised her.)

You are very busy and have little time to waste on complaints or whining. You have agreed to see the case manager because you feel it is your responsibility to be in touch with your

After the role play, address the following questions in a full class discussion.
- a. What happened during the role play?
- b. Which suggestions for persuasion worked and which didn't? Explain.
- c. What other suggestions do you have for successful persuasion?
- d. From this experience, what have you learned about the persuasion process?

E. Commentary

This exercise may also be performed by asking two volunteers to conduct the role play before the rest of the class with the other students observing.

Exercise 6.3: Identifying Macro Client, Action, and Target Systems

Read the following vignette and identify the systems involved.

You are a hospital social worker who works with patients in the geriatric unit. Their problems typically include broken bones, onset of diseases such as diabetes, increasing mental confusion, and many accompanying physical difficulties. Patients usually remain hospitalized two days to two weeks. Most patients come to the hospital from their homes, and your job often involves placing patients in more structured settings because injuries or diseases have restricted their ability to function independently. Many are placed in health care centers (nursing homes).

You have been assigned Olga, 82, who fell and broke her hip. She also has diabetes and is increasingly incontinent. Prior to her fall, she barely subsisted in a second story one-room apartment, dependent on her monthly Social Security check for survival, and she has consumed all of her meager savings. She is an extremely pleasant woman who continues to emphasize that she doesn't want to be a burden on anyone. All of her family are dead. You worry that placement in an inferior setting will be tortuous for her if she doesn't receive the relatively intensive care she needs.

You notice that nursing homes vary dramatically in their levels of care, their appearance, the attention they give to patients, their ratios of staff to patients, the activities they offer, and their overall cleanliness. Patients with private insurance can easily enter one of the better facilities, while impoverished patients on Medicaid must go to inferior settings. You consider this both unfair and unethical.

You see yourself as a possible change agent. At least three of your colleagues in the hospital's social work unit have similar concerns about their own clients and the hospital's elderly clients in general. Your immediate supervisor is not really an "eager beaver" when it comes to initiating change, but you think you might be able to solicit some support from her. You are not certain whether upper levels of hospital administration believe that nursing home conditions are any of their business. In your state all nursing homes must be licensed, but licensing regulations require the maintenance of only the most minimal standards.

a. Identify the macro client system in this case.

b. Who might make up the action system?

c. Who might be your target system?

Step 3: IMAGINE—Identify *Assets*

Whatever the type of macro level change, a change agent must determine what *assets* are available to implement the change. Assets are any resources and any advantages you have that will help in your proposed change process. Assets can include readily available funding, personnel who are able and willing to devote their time to implementing the change, and office space from which the change activities can be managed.

Exercise 6.4: Identifying Assets

Read the following case scenario and identify the assets it reveals.

Louise, a financial counselor at a private mental health agency, knows that the agency has access to special funding through personal donations made on behalf of persons "with special needs." She is not certain how the administration defines "special needs." But since the agency is privately owned, it is not subject to the same requirements and regulations that would limit a public agency. Louise learned about this special fund via the informal agency grapevine. It has never been publicly announced.

Louise is working with several families whom she feels are in exceptional need. Their problems—including unemployment, depression, mental illness, poverty, unwanted pregnancy, and truancy—make them truly multiproblem families. Neither her agency nor any local public agency has been able to provide adequate resources for these families. Louise has established clear documentation of their extreme circumstances.

Having worked at the agency for eight years, she feels she has gained substantial respect for her work and her ideas. She knows one member of the agency's board of directors fairly well, because she's worked with him on several projects in the past. (A board of directors is "a group of people empowered to establish an organization's objectives and policies and to oversee the activities of the personnel responsible for day-to-day implementation of those policies," and board members are often highly respected and influential volunteers from the community (Barker, 1995, p. 39). Louise might be able to contact this man to get information about the special-needs funding.

She is aware, however, that her agency administration discourages workers from seeking access to this "secret" fund. Amounts available are limited, so the administration must dispense these funds extremely cautiously. In any case, Louise decides to approach the agency's Executive Director and request funding for the families in need.

Identify the assets available to Louise.

Step 4: IMAGINE—Specify *Goals* and Objectives

After formulating an innovative idea, mustering support from others, and identifying assets, it is time to specify your goals and objectives in the macro change process. You have already identified your primary goals during your assessment of macro change potential in chapter 5. Goals give you direction, but primary goals are usually so broadly stated that it is virtually impossible to specify how they will be achieved. For example, you might want to improve conditions in the Family Planning Center where you work. In order to accomplish this, you must break down that primary goal into a series of objectives. An objective is "something toward which effort is directed, an aim . . . or end of action" (*Webster's Ninth New Collegiate Dictionary*, 1991, p. 815). Objectives or subgoals are smaller and more easily achieved. In a sense, these behaviorally specific subgoals are stepping stones on the way to the accomplishment of the primary goal.

What does "improving conditions in a unit at a residential treatment center" really mean? Objectives en route to this goal might include painting the walls, improving the disciplinary system, and/or developing recreational groups. Of course, these limited objectives also break down into smaller specific steps: Who will paint the walls? When will the job be done? Who will pay for the work?

Establishing objectives involves specifying "the steps that must be taken and the time needed to reach those objectives" (Barker, 1987, p. 64). Two necessary ingredients in objective-setting, then, include the *steps* involved in the intervention process and *time limitations* for each step. The basic formula for delegating responsibility is to specify *who* will do *what* by *when*. "Who" is the individual or group assigned to a task. "What" is the task itself. "By when" sets a time limit so that the task is not forever postponed. Sometimes one task depends upon another and they must be accomplished in sequence. For instance, before A can paint the office, B has to purchase the paint—which he can't do until C is empowered to spend the money.

The following are examples of objectives:

Harry Carey **(who)** will notify all unit colleagues about the upcoming in-service **(what)** by noon on March 15 **(when)**.

I **(who)** will write a five-page paper describing the new treatment approach **(what)** by 9:00 A.M. on Friday, October 13 **(when)**.

Ms. Fidgety **(who)** will contact the designated community leaders for information about housing needs **(what)** by next Tuesday **(when)**.

In addition to being specific, objectives should be measurable. That is, it is important to specify exactly when and how an objective will be met. For example, if your objective is to contact five designated community leaders, you have not met your objective until you have established contact with *all five*.

Exercise 6.5: Establishing Goals and Objectives

Read the following case scenarios, and identify the initial goals that would lead to the desired ends. Use the **who** will do **what** by **when** formula. Then list some objectives or subgoals that would help in achieving the larger goal. (Note that an arbitrary number of four goals and objectives are cited for each case vignette. You are free to establish more or fewer goals as you see fit.)

Vignette #1: Horace, a state parole agent, is a member of a Task Force to Curb Substance Abuse in his community.[1] He attends the first of a series of meetings aimed at facilitating a range of educational, prevention, and treatment programs to obliterate substance abuse among youth, especially delinquents. Other members include Bainbridge, a local judge; Uzzia, a lawyer working for the county to represent juveniles accused of felonies; and Wahkuna, a retired social worker who was an alcohol and other drug abuse counselor. They decide they need more information to determine the extent of the problem: How prevalent *is* drug abuse in this area? What prevention tactics are currently in use? What treatment facilities (type and quantity) are now in place? What diagnosis and assessment mechanisms would be appropriate? What treatment approaches are likely to be most effective?

Goal:

Objectives:

Goal:

Objectives:

---

[1] A task force is "a temporary group, usually within an organization, brought together to achieve some previously specified function or goal" (Barker, 1991, p. 235).

Goal:

 Objectives:

Goal:

 Objectives:

Vignette #2: Marelda is a social worker at a homeless shelter in a large northeastern city. Facilities are simply inadequate to provide the necessary resources—including food, clothing, and shelter—for hundreds of homeless families. Suddenly Marelda has a brilliant idea. Why not make arrangements with the dozens—perhaps hundreds—of fast-food restaurants in the area to collect their unused food and distribute it to people in need? At the end of a day, remaining food is simply thrown out and goes to waste. Marelda begins to consider what support from friends and colleagues she might elicit, and how she might go about contacting fast-food restaurants and persuading them to support her cause.

Goal:

 Objectives:

Goal:

 Objectives:

Goal:

 Objectives:

Goal:

 Objectives:

Vignette #3:[2] Brian is a hospice social worker. The hospice movement rests on a philosophy of caring and an array of programs, services, and settings for people with terminal illness. Hospice services are usually offered in nonhospital facilities with homelike atmospheres where families, friends, and the significant other can be with the dying person (Barker, 1995, p. 171).

 Brian sees increasing numbers of gay patients entering the facility. He is aware of the special "issues of stigma, homophobia, and the cumulative effects of stress" experienced by gay people along with the devastating effects of their terminal illness (Dworkin & Kaufer, 1995, p. 41). He considers two possibilities. First, can he initiate support groups for patients, their families, and their partners? Second, to what extent are other hospice staff aware of the special issues facing gay people? Could the agency initiate in-service training to address this potential need? Brian thinks the hospice director would probably be very supportive of these his ideas—*if* Brian can figure out just how to implement them.

Goal:

 Objectives:

---

[2] This vignette is based on an account in J. Dworkin & D. Kaufer, "Social Services and Bereavement in the Lesbian and Gay Community," Vol. 2, No. 3/4, 1995, pp. 41-60.

Goal:

Objectives:

Goal:

Objectives:

Goal:

Objectives:

Step 5: IMAG<u>I</u>NE—*Implement* the Plan

In IMAGINE's fifth step, you actually *implement* or undertake the established plan. The plan's goal or desired result is to establish the macro change.

Step 6: IMAG<u>I</u>NE—*Neutralize* Opposition

Neutralizing opposition means overcoming or circumventing people and groups that might oppose or block macro change. The macro change process does not usually involve a direct linear thrust whereby all objectives proceed perfectly as planned. People change their minds. New elements such as funding cuts appear on the scene—seemingly out of nowhere.

Presenting your plan to your target system is a critical point in the macro change process. Before you do this, determine who—in your ideal version of events—will assume what roles. *Role determination* means deciding in advance who will attend the meeting and who will contribute what. It is wise to choose action system members who you think will have the strongest positive impact on the target system (for example, decision-making administrators). You want to maximize your potential to influence decision-makers on your behalf. Next, you should determine who will introduce the idea, who should present the rationale, who should respond to what types of questions, and so on.

Second, before a formal meeting, you must decide how *you will describe and portray the issue, your concern, and your recommendations for change.* This should be crystal clear in your mind. Try to anticipate any arguments against the proposal, and formulate responses to those arguments. For example, suppose administrators say that the proposal will cost too much or that existing staff would not be able to complete the necessary tasks. How will you answer them? It is extremely important that you examine and understand the change from an administrative point of view, and that you be able to respond to administrative objections. After all, administrators may have constraints such as licensing regulations or funding requirements of which you are unaware.

In neutralizing opposition, you may pursue a range of strategies from "persuading" to "pressuring" (Austin, Kopp, & Smith, 1986, pp. 123-28). Persuading means using logical and convincing arguments to bring decision-makers around to your point of view. It works best when decision-makers are not dead set against your proposal and are open to rational arguments and innovative ideas.

There are three basic ways to initiate persuasion.

- First, *establishing something in common*—that is, presenting some aspect of the problem or proposed solution with which you know both action and target systems will agree. For example, you might say, "I know that we all are seeking effective service delivery for our clients."

- Second, *sharing honest feelings*—which may entail getting right to the point, even if the target system receives the point negatively. For instance, you might say, "I understand that you are opposed to a major change. However, I feel it is necessary to share my serious concerns with you."

- Third, the *blunt assault*—a step beyond just sharing your feelings. (This approach should be used rarely, because it comes close to pressuring.) For example, you might say, "I have to be honest. I totally disagree with your position, and I will be forced to fight you on this one. Let me explain to you why I feel so strongly. . . ."

Austin et al. (1986) cite additional persuasive strategies.

- Educate the decision-makers by providing detailed, specific information.
- Help decision-makers understand the problem and see it more clearly from your point of view.
- Discuss options and potential solutions to your described problem. Review the advantages and disadvantages of each.
- Appeal to the decision-makers' sense of fairness, ethics, and right and wrong. What is the most ethical approach to service provision for clients? What goals are most important for the agency to pursue?
- Develop a rational argument to support your proposed plan. Choose information that strongly supports your macro proposal.
- Finally, specify to decision-makers what the negative consequences of the identified problem might be. What will ignoring the problem or maintaining the status quo cost them in money, morale, public opinion, etc.?

Pressuring is a much "pushier" approach than persuading because it means using force and even coercion to achieve your goals. As a result, it involves much higher potential risks than persuading. Decision-makers are far more likely to react with hostility and dogged resistance. Use pressuring only when three conditions are present (Austin et al., 1986).

- First, you have tried everything else, including persuasion, and nothing has worked.
- Second, you are determined to pursue this macro change for the sake of your clients.
- Third, you believe you have a reasonable chance of attaining your goals. Otherwise, why waste your energy and expose yourself to risk?

Pressuring strategies include circulating a petition to gain collective support, calling on sanctioning agencies in the external environment (such as regulatory agencies, referral agencies, or powerful political entities), going to the media, or initiating a strike or lawsuit. Please note, however, that an administration may feel betrayed by Benedict Arnolds who air the agency's dirty laundry for all the world to see.

Step 7: IMAGINE—*Evaluate* Progress

In the final step in the IMAGINE macro change process, you *evaluate* the intervention's progress and effectiveness. Evaluation can focus on either the *ongoing operation* and activities involved in achieving a macro level change, or on the *results* of the effort. How effective is or was the change effort?

Changing Agency Policy

IMAGINE can also be applied to changing an agency policy. Policy is "the explicit or implicit standing plan that an organization or government uses as a guide for action" (Barker, 1991, p. 175). Policies thus provide rules or directions for the functions and activities of a macro system. Policy's purpose is to provide rational, predictable guidelines for a system's operation, especially with respect to how resources are distributed (Kettner et al., 1985). Thus, policy dictates what should and should not be done in the agency setting, especially with respect to how resources are distributed (Kettner et al., 1985).

Policy changes may be aimed at agency goals (for instance, what clientele the agency intends to serve), practice procedures (such as using crisis intervention rather than behavioral methodology, or vice versa), and personnel practices (such as workers' hours) Any time a worker decides to pursue an agency policy change, she should first answer two questions (Netting et al., 1993).

- Will the change result in improved service delivery and resources allocation for clients?
- Will the change result in improved working conditions for staff, enabling them to better serve their clients?

The bottom line is that, whatever the type of policy change, the ultimate beneficiaries of that change should be your clients.

Apply IMAGINE to the following case example by responding to the subsequent questions.[3]

Hsi-ping is a worker for the Comeasyouare County Department of Human Services. She and most other staff disagree with many policies initiated by Marcus, the agency director. Workers commonly refer to Marcus as Mr. Scrooge. They frequently question his decisions, which they believe are based on financial variables rather than clients' welfare.

The latest problem is Marcus's decision to stop sending letters to clients without telephones. These letters announce that a particular worker will visit a client's home at a designated time. If that time is inconvenient, the client is asked to contact the worker to reschedule the visit. The letter then adds that the worker is looking forward to talking with the client. These letters have traditionally been sent out far enough in advance to allow clients to accommodate their own schedules or let the worker know beforehand that the time is inconvenient. Apparently, Marcus and his Chief Financial Manager, Millicent (often referred to as Ms. Scrooge), have figured out these letters cost the agency about five dollars apiece to send—including worker time, secretarial time, paper, postage, and any other agency efforts expended. Hsi-ping thinks Millicent read the five-dollar figure somewhere in a financial magazine and magically transformed it into a fact. She has a number of problems with the policy even if the figure is accurate.

- First, it ignores clients' right to privacy, respect, and dignity. Dropping in on people unannounced is inconsiderate and simply rude.
- Second, it violates clients' right to self-determination because it does not allow them any input in setting meeting times.
- Third, it complicates both workers' and clients' lives. There is no guarantee that workers will arrive at convenient times for clients or that clients will even be at home.

Hsi-Ping thinks about who might agree with her that this policy is unacceptable. She knows other staff in her own unit agree with her, but many of them are fairly new and would probably be hesitant to speak up. Hsi-Ping's supervisor Sphinctera follows regulations to the letter—even to the comma—without question. Nevertheless, Hsi-Ping likes Sphinctera, so she decides to share her feelings about the problem and see what reaction she gets.

Much to Hsi-Ping's amazement, Sphinctera is very supportive of Hsi-Ping's position. Apparently, Sphinctera is tired of the agency's many policy changes and has difficulty keeping up with them. This no-letter policy is just too much. Sphinctera even comes up with an idea. Why not send out postcards announcing home visits? The cards could be preprinted for a nominal cost, workers could then address them, fill in the proposed visiting time, sign them, and send them out themselves.

It's a fine compromise—but Sphinctera hesitates to make waves and wants more information and more support before she will propose her idea to Marcus. Hsi-Ping volunteers to talk to her other colleagues in the unit, and verifies that they generally agree with her. One worker, Ruana, emphasizes her relief that someone else is addressing the problem. She tells Hsi-Ping about a home visit she made the day before, an unannounced visit because of the no-letter policy. It took her about an hour to get to the client's home and back. Since the client wasn't there, Ruana's time was wasted—at a cost to the agency of about $11 in salary for Ruana's wasted time and about $12 in mileage reimbursement. Even if Millicent and Marcus are correct that letters cost the agency $5, Ruana's useless trip cost $23, so the agency lost $18 under the new procedure. Imagine multiplying this by the hundreds of home visits workers regularly make.

Hsi-Ping reports her findings to Sphinctera. Together they decide to address the issue with Marcus. Sphinctera suggests doing so at one of the agency's regular staff meetings when staff are encouraged to voice their ideas and concerns (whether or not administrators are paying attention). She

---

[3] The idea and some details presented in this case example are taken from "The Appointment Letters," by G. H. Hull, Jr. In R. F. Rivas & G. H. Hull, Jr., *Case Studies in Generalist Practice* (Pacific Grove, CA: Brooks/Cole, 1996, pp. 150-53.)

encourages Hsi-Ping to raise the issue because it was originally Hsi-Ping's idea. Hsi-Ping thinks Sphinctera is really afraid to initiate it herself, but she agrees to do the talking and thanks Sphinctera for her support.

At the next staff meeting, Hsi-Ping expresses her concern about the no-letter policy. She takes a deep breath and is careful to speak with little emotion and no hostility. She presents the financial facts that support her proposal and emphasizes that she shares Marcus's concerns about the agency's finances. She then offers her suggestion and its rationale, adding that sending postcards was really Sphinctera's idea. Hsi-Ping adds that the postcards would not violate clients' confidentiality or privacy rights because they would carry no identifying information.

When she finishes, the eighty staff members in the room are dead silent for a few painful moments that seem like an eternity. Finally, six hands shoot up at once. One after another, staff support the idea. Hsi-Ping watches Marcus for some reaction. He looks straight ahead, says nothing, and pulls at his chin in his usual thoughtful gesture. Finally, he says, "You know, I think you just might have something here. Let's give it a try."

Hsi-Ping is overjoyed. She did it! She actually did it. She effected a substantive change in agency policy. Two days later Marcus sends a memo around the agency informing workers of the new change. Workers are generally pleased (although some old-timers still grumble that the letters were better). Marcus continues to seek new ways to cut costs—and, Hsi-Ping sometimes thinks, to make workers' lives miserable. However, the no-letter battle has been won and Hsi-Ping certainly is proud of that accomplishment.

Follow the seven steps in IMAGINE and respond to the questions below:

Step 1: IMAGINE—Start with an Innovative *Idea.*

A.   Summarize the problem presented above and describe the innovative idea for a solution. Explain the pros and cons of this idea.

B.   Describe the innovative idea for a solution.

C.   Explain the pros and cons of this idea.

Step 2: IMAGINE—*Muster* Support and Formulate an Action System. Identify the following systems portrayed in the case scenario above.

Macro client system:

Change agent:

Target system:

Action system:

Step 3: IMAGINE—Identify *Assets.* Identify the assets in Hsi-Ping's favor and explain why each is important.

Step 4: IMAGINE—Specify *Goals* and Objectives. Identify the major goal Hsi-Ping wished to accomplish.

4a.   Identify specific objectives necessary for leading up to this goal. Use the *who* did *what* by *when* format.

Step 5: IMAGINE—*Implement* the Plan. Evaluate and discuss the effectiveness of Hsi-Ping's implementation of her plan.

Step 6: IMAGINE—*Neutralize* Opposition. Explain how Hsi-Ping determined who would assume which roles in the change effort.

6a. Discuss the interpersonal dynamics determining who actually presented the issue and proposed recommendations.

6b. Explain how Hsi-Ping used persuasion to pursue her goal. What specific techniques did she use?

6c. How might Hsi-Ping have used pressuring to attain her goal? What effects might pressuring have had?

Establishing a Culturally Competent Organization

There is one particular dimension of agency policy that may merit your attention when you are considering a possible macro change—cultural competency. *Cultural competence,* in an organizational context, is "a set of congruent behaviors, attitudes, policies, and structures which come together in a system, agency or among professionals and enables that system, agency or those professionals to work effectively in the context of cultural differences" (Benjamin, 1994, p. 17; Cross, Bazron, Dennis, & Isaacs, 1989, p. 13).

Cultural competence, then, is a multi-focused, unifying thread involving staff behaviors and attitudes in addition to agency policies and formal structure. Every aspect of an agency's performance should be sensitive and responsive to the cultural diversity of its clientele. How can the agency make clients from diverse cultural backgrounds feel as comfortable as possible in accessing agency services? How can practitioners best communicate with clients from diverse cultures? How can staff be taught to maximize their own cultural competence? What agency policies, practices, and goals work for or against cultural competence?

You will probably be employed by some social services agency. Will that agency be culturally competent? You might assume, "Well, of course. It's the only ethical way to be," or *"All* social workers are trained to be sensitive to cultural diversity." In fact, agencies may not be culturally competent or even sensitive. Almost all agencies can improve upon or expand their cultural competence. They can provide continuing education for employees or expand the range of their competence concerning specific cultural groups. They can take a long, hard look at the entire concept of cultural competence and make major revisions in their agency mission statements and overall goals.

After undertaking the PREPARE process, you might decide to pursue a macro level change to raise the level of cultural competence in your organization.

Exercise 6.7: Assessing an Organization's Cultural Competence

---

Make an appointment with a worker or administrator at a social services agency in your area. (If necessary, you can conduct this interview by phone.) Solicit answers to the following five questions aimed at assessing an organization's cultural competence (Mason, 1994). Examples of questions you might use for further clarification are presented in parenthesis following each question.

1. *How responsible is the organization in responding effectively and efficiently to the needs of the culturally diverse people it serves?* (Does the agency have a good understanding of its clientele's cultural diversity? Must further research be performed to identify target client groups? To what extent are staff culturally competent in their individual interactions with clientele? What types of training and education could improve employees' cultural competence?)

2. *In what ways can a culturally competent staff—regardless of individual workers' cultural backgrounds—assist the agency in actualizing its mission of cultural competence?* (How can staff work together to best serve clientele from culturally diverse backgrounds? How can staff help each other obtain relevant knowledge and skills?)

3. *In what ways could administration of services be changed to bring about a more effective response to the needs of the agency's culturally diverse client population?* (Are services readily accessible to culturally diverse client groups? If not, how might the agency make such services more accessible? Is the communication between staff and clients as effective as it could be? Should workers be fluent in languages that will allow them to deal more effectively with clients from diverse cultural groups? Can agency personnel solicit information from community leaders or from clients to help them identify and pursue more culturally competent provision of services?)

4. *What is "the vision of services" to the culturally diverse community (Mason, 1994, p. 5)?* (How might you best "envision the system as it should be and . . . identify ways of funding such a system" [Mason, 1994, p. 5]? How can you maximize the involvement of people who represent the diverse cultures your agency serves? How might you empower community residents? Can you and others helping you identify new potential resources for the community and the agency? Such resources might include "assisting with staff and board recruitment, encouraging . . . donations, identifying advocacy resources, and promoting parent or community education and support groups" [Mason, 1994, p. 5].)

5. *How can you determine that the goal of cultural competence has been achieved?* (What specific goals and objectives can you identify that would clearly make your agency more culturally competent? What task groups might you and the agency establish to review progress, refine recommendations, and keep efforts on task?)

Chapter 7
IMAGINE Project Implementation and Program Development

I.   **Introduction**

II.   **Initiating and Implementing a Project**

    A.   **I**MAGINE: Develop an innovative **Idea**

        1.   Highlight 7.1: Examples of Projects in Macro Practice

            a.   Meeting clients' special needs

            b.   Fundraising projects

            c.   Evaluating effects of agency or community changes

            d.   Evaluating new intervention approaches

            e.   Implementing internal agency changes

            f.   Providing internal services to your agency staff

    B.   I**MA**GINE: **Muster** support

    C.   IM**A**GINE: Identify **Assets**

    D.   IMA**G**INE: Specify **Goals**, objectives, and action steps to attain them

    E.   IMAG**I**NE: **Implement** the plan

        1.   Figure 7.1: Examples of Amended PERT Chart Formats

        2.   PERT charts illustrate objectives, and action steps

        3.   PERT charts portray specific tasks

        4.   PERT charts depict task sequence

        5.   PERT charts and necessary resources

        6.   PERT charts establish a time frame

        7.   Advantage of PERT charts

        8.   Case Example: A PERT chart for developing an inservice training project

        9.   Figure 7.2: An Example of a PERT Chart for Developing an In-service Training Program

    F.   IMAG**I**NE: **Neutralize** opposition

G.   IMAGINE: **Evaluate** progress

    1.   Projects and diversity

    2.   Highlight 7.2: A Project Example: Substance Abuse Prevention for Puerto Rican Adolescents

        a.   Nuevo Puente (New Bridges)

        b.   Resilience—the strength and ability to resist risk-taking behavior

        c.   Self-esteem—one's inner sense of one's own value

        d.   Coping strategies—behaviors and choices used to contend with and survive stress

        e.   Three Kings' Day—Puerto Rican holiday

        f.   Community assets assessment—a systematic appraisal of the community's strengths

III.   Developing a Program

A.   Highlight 7.3: Why Program Development Is Relevant to You

B.   **I**MAGINE: Develop an Innovative **Idea**

    1.   Work with your client system

    2.   Articulate the proposed program's purpose

        a.   Clearly define and document the unmet client needs

        b.   Identify the clientele who will receive services

        c.   State the services the program would provide

    3.   Highlight 7.4: Ethical Questions and Critical Thinking about Public Assistance: Empowerment or Oppression for Women?

        a.   Personal Responsibility and Work Opportunity Reconciliation Act (1996)

        b.   Temporary Assistance for Needy Families (TANF)—replaced Aid to Families with Dependent Children (AFDC)

  c. TANF and Work

    1) Caroline Center—a career and learning resource center for women founded by the School Sisters of Notre Dame

    2) Enabling women to leave welfare and become self-sufficient

  d. TANF and Health

  e. TANF and Family Structure

    1) Family structure—the nuclear family as well as alternatives to nuclear family which are adopted by persons in committed relationships and the people they consider to be family

    2) How ethical is it for government to regulate the childbearing behavior of poor women?

  f. TANF and Day Care

  g. Child Care in Denmark Versus Wisconsin: An International Perspective

C. IMAGINE: **Muster** support

 1. Allocate responsibilities to a designated task group or advisory council

 2. Advisory councils/boards—committees created outside of the organization's formal power structure that meet to provide information and feedback

D. IMAGINE: Identify **Assets**

 1. Prepare the agency for change

 2. Consider implementing a feasibility study—a systematic evaluation of the resources necessary to achieve your program development goals

 3. Solicit the financial resources you need to initiate the program

E. IMAGINE: Specify **Goals**, objectives, and action steps to attain them

 1. Consider developing a PERT chart—a tool for plotting your intervention plan in a linear manner

 2. Describe how the program will provide services

F. IMAGINE: **Implement** the plan

 1. Get the program going

 2. Nurture participating staff's support

 3. How about a trial run?

4.   Consider starting out small

5.   Formalize any contracts that might be needed (purchase-of-service contracts—formal agreements between one or more organizations where one organization purchases some specified service within a designated time period from one or more other agencies)

G.   IMAGINE: **Neutralize** opposition

1.   Anticipate a "honeymoon period"

2.   Maintain administrative support

H.   IMAGINE: **Evaluate** progress and effectiveness

1.   Monitor daily activities and evaluate program impact

2.   Monitor your program

3.   Perform an impact analysis

4.   Establish how services will be provided on an ongoing basis

a.   Standardized procedures for continued implementation of the program should be clearly defined

b.   The new program should be linked as much as possible with other units and aspects of the organization

c.   The program's importance should be established within the context of other programs and services in the community

d.   Develop an intelligence and feedback system

IV.   **Program Development: A Case Example**

A.   Highlight 7.5: Program Development Ideas are Endless

1.   Sanctuary for young homeless new mothers

2.   Housing development for non-heterosexual seniors

B.   IMAGINE: Develop an innovative **Idea**

    1.   Highlight 7.6 What is Sexual Harassment?

        a.   Title VII of the Civil Rights Act of 1964 covers discrimination on the basis of sex, along with discrimination on the basis of race

        b.   Two major dimensions to the definition

            1)   The concept of *quid pro quo* (I'll scratch your back if you scratch mine)

            2)   Creation of a hostile environment

        c.   Equal Employment Opportunity Commission expanded the definition of sexual harassment to include gender harassment (1993)

C.   IMAGINE: **Muster** support

D.   IMAGINE: Identify **Assets**

E.   IMAGINE: Specify **Goals**, objectives, and action steps to attain them

    1.   Establishing a Sexual Harassment Awareness Program for Employees (SHAPE)

    2.   Figure 7.3: A PERT Chart for the Sexual Harassment Awareness Program for Employees (SHAPE)

    3.   Description of SHAPE

    4.   The SHAPE coordinator's role

        a.   Educational programming

        b.   Providing support for victims

        c.   Counseling

        d.   Formal grievance procedure

        e.   Informal indirect action

        f.   No action

    5.   Planning the program: Development of a PERT chart

        a.   Figure 7.4: A Budget Summary for SHAPE

        b.   Initial planning

        c.   Education

              d.   Public relations

              e.   Counseling

              f.   Evaluation of SHAPE functioning

     F.   IMAGINE: **Implement** the plan

     G.   IMAGINE: **Neutralize** opposition

     H.   IMAGINE: **Evaluate** progress and effectiveness

Experiential Exercises and Classroom Simulations

Exercise 7.1: Imagine A Program

A.   Brief Description
        Using a small group format, students discuss how the first three steps of the IMAGINE process
        might be applied in an agency requiring program development.

B.   Objectives
        Students will:
        1.   Review the IMAGINE process for pursuing program development.
        2.   Discuss how the first three steps of the process might be applied to program development
                in response to a vignette describing a macro scenario.

C.   Procedure
        1.   Review the material in the text on using the IMAGINE process to develop a program.
        2.   Read the vignette below which describes a programmatic need in the macro context of a
                Veterans' Administration Hospital.
        3.   Divide the class into small groups of four to six.
        4.   Ask the groups to discuss the first three steps of the IMAGINE process to begin program
                development in the vignette described below under "Instructions for Students." Instruct
                them to follow the instructions and address the questions provided after the vignette.
                Indicate that they should select a group representative who should be prepared to report
                to the entire class the small group's findings.
        5.   After about 20 minutes, ask the small groups to terminate their discussions and
                participate in a full class discussion regarding their findings.
        6.   Ask the representative from each group to share her or his summary of the discussion.
                Encourage participation from all class members.

D.   Instructions for Students
        Read the vignette below. Respond to the subsequent instructions and questions concerning the
        application of the first three steps of the IMAGINE process to program development as it might
        apply to the vignette.

VIGNETTE: You are a social worker in a Veteran's Administration (VA) Hospital in East LA. The VA, a federal organization initially established in 1920, provides a wide range of services to people who have served in the military in order to enhance their overall health and welfare; services include those directed at physical and mental illness, vocational training, financial assistance, and a host of others (Barker, 1999). Specifically, you work in a unit that provides short-term housing and alcohol and other drug (AODA) treatment for homeless veterans. The problem is that you're finding that more and more of your clients come to you and tell you they simply can't find any full-time jobs, even for minimum wage. You find yourself thinking more and more frequently to yourself, "Even a full-time minimum wage job is pretty much a bummer in terms of taking care of yourself."

     The issue you really feel boils down to adequate job training. Why can't the VA provide educational and vocational training, or else finance its purchase through some other agency? You have looked and looked for resources for your clients. They need to get back on their feet again. They need work that is relatively permanent, provides an adequate standard of living, and enhances their self esteem. What you and your clients really need is a job-training program with a strong educational component. But there isn't one. Now what?

1.   IMAGINE Step 1: Develop an innovative **idea.**
     Propose and describe a program that you feel would meet clients' identified needs.

2.   IMAGINE Step 2: **Muster** support.
     Who might be appropriate action system members from the agency and community in this situation? Explain why.

3.   IMAGINE Step 3: Identify **assets.**
     What variables might exist that could support your change efforts?

     a.   Who else in the agency might be called upon for support (other than action system members)?
     b.   How might you work to enhance your own power?
     c.   What potential funding sources might you pursue?

E.   Commentary
This activity may also be conducted by holding a full class discussion without breaking students down into small groups

---

Exercise 7.2: Identify an Innovative Program

A.   Brief Description

B.   Objectives
Students will:
1.   Identify an innovative program operating in their macro environment.
2.   Assess various aspects of its functioning and usefulness.

C.   Procedure
1.   Give students the assignment of identifying a local, state, or national innovative social services program.
2.   Read the assignment as it is discussed below under "Instructions for Students."

3. The assignment may be used in any of five ways:
   a. Have students bring their findings to class to participate in a full class discussion.
   b. Have students bring their findings to class for participation in small group discussions.
   c. Have students turn in a written assignment for a grade.
   d. Have students present brief oral reports to the class regarding their findings.
   e. Assign students to small groups who complete the assignment together.

D. Instructions for Students

Identify a program providing some kind of social services which you feel is innovative and especially useful. You may select a local, state, or national program. You may find your information in newspapers or news magazines, from public documents, on the Internet, or directly from agencies.

Answer the following questions and be prepared to share your findings with the rest of the class.

1. What is the program's name?

2. What is the program's purpose?

3. Whom does the program serve?

4. What client needs does it meet or problems does it address?

5. How large is the program?

6. How is the program structured regarding staffing, internal organization, and power structure?

7. Who provides funding for the program?

8. What are your reasons for identifying it as an innovative program?

9. How useful is the program?

10. How is the program's effectiveness evaluated?

Exercise 7.3: Creative Projects

Read the following case vignettes and respond to the questions about potential project implementation.

Vignette #1: Manuela is a Protective Services Worker who helps "legal authorities with investigations to determine if children are in need of such services, help[s] children get services when needed," and provides family counseling (Barker, 1995, p. 56). Most of her clients are very poor, and since Thanksgiving is approaching, Manuela worries that many of them will be unable to have much food at all, let alone a grand turkey celebration.

What types of projects could Manuela initiate? Specifically, how might she go about doing so?

Vignette #2: Dougal is a counselor at a large urban YMCA. He organizes and runs recreational and educational programs for youth, functions as a positive role model, and provides informal counseling. Recently, he learned that the county social services agency had contracted with an expert on gang intervention to run a four-day in-service program for its staff. Dougal thinks it would be extremely helpful to the staff at the "Y" if they could somehow participate in such a program.

What sort of project might Dougal initiate to get in-service training for the "Y" staff? Specifically, how might he go about doing so?

Vignette #3: Jarita works at a Planned Parenthood organization where she does contraception and pregnancy counseling. She is also invited to give educational presentations to large groups of people. She finds that over the years her job has significantly changed: Whereas she once dealt primarily with contraception counseling, she now spends more time providing sex education, especially with respect to AIDS. Along with the changes in her job, many other changes have occurred in the agency over the past ten years. For one thing, it is much larger than it was when Jarita began working there. More restrictive state legislation has affected the referral process for abortions. Much more emphasis is now placed on sex education. Jarita observes that the agency policy manual has simply not kept up with the agency's progress and development. Even some personnel policies such as insurance coverage have changed significantly over time. Simply put, the policy manual is colossally out of date.

What sort of project might Jarita pursue in dealing with this concern? Specifically, how might she go about doing so?

Program Evaluation and Review Technique (PERT)

To initiate a project and follow the IMAGINE process described in chapter 6, you need a specific plan. A project design or plan is like a map of the entire project from beginning to end. One useful way of formulating and illustrating a plan is through the use of a PERT (Program Evaluation and Review Technique) chart (Federal Electric Corporation, 1963). PERT charts are flow charts or time charts "that show what steps need to be taken in what order"; "such charts can help [action] group members anticipate and reduce problems while providing a sense of direction for projects" (Rubin & Rubin, 1992, p. 402).

PERT charts illustrate a sequence of tasks or activities in the order in which such tasks should be done to achieve a designated goal. When you create a PERT chart, you must first define your goal and then break it down into a series of steps. Figure 7.1 illustrates a variety of PERT formats. Each has the same goal—being prepared to present informational findings at an agency meeting. Specific tasks are depicted in the order they must be accomplished. For example, you need to gather information before you can complete a report on that information.

You can depict PERT chart tasks either horizontally or vertically by picturing necessary activities in boxes connected by horizontal or vertical lines. Each horizontal or vertical sequence of activity boxes connected by lines reflects a plan for achieving that particular goal.

PERT charts also establish a time frame, an estimate of how long it should take to complete each task and reach the primary goal. In figure 7.1 the horizontal formats have time lines on the bottom and top of the charts, respectively. The vertical chart has the time line located on its left-hand side. The time lines in these charts illustrate weekly deadlines for achieving each of the four objectives necessary to attain the goal. The idea is to complete each objective and arrive at the goal by the indicated target completion date. When developing a PERT chart, be realistic about how much time it will take to complete each task. Each PERT format in figure 7.1 depicts completion of the following tasks in the following order: (1) gathering information by February 7; (2) completing the report by February 14; (3) reviewing the report with your supervisor by February 21; and (4) presenting the report findings at a designated meeting by February 28. The timelines can employ virtually any unit of time—hours, days, weeks, months. Figure 7.1 uses weekly units.

PERT charts may take a number of forms, and individual tasks can be illustrated in various ways. For example, you can use sequentially connected circles or simple statements instead of boxes. A very complicated chart could use a series of letter or number codes to indicate tasks or time frames instead of writing them all out. In such cases, whoever creates the chart adds a key to the code.

For purposes of simplicity and clarity, the PERT chart in figure 7.1 shows how *one* task is accomplished by *one* person. In reality, however, multiple tasks must often be accomplished simultaneously by different members of the action system, and some tasks may depend on the completion of others. For example, another member of your action system is developing a list of resource people for the in-service program, and you need that data to complete your report. PERT charts become more complex as tasks and participants increase in number.

Figure 7.2 is a PERT chart for initiating an agency in-service training program. Provision of in-service training is the goal. That goal is broken down into a sequence of steps, and a time frame is established for achieving each step. When you decide what steps to take, you must consider a number of consecutive variables.

- First, a staff interest survey will help you establish what direction the in-service will take.
- Next, administrative approval is required for survey administration. Time must be allowed for distributing the questionnaire and for staff to complete it.
- Questionnaire results should then be communicated to administration.
- Arrangements for in-service speakers must be made.
- Finally, publicity and announcements should be used to notify potential participants of the in-service's time and location.

Figure 7.1: Examples of Amended PERT Chart Formats

Horizontal Format with Time Line at Bottom:

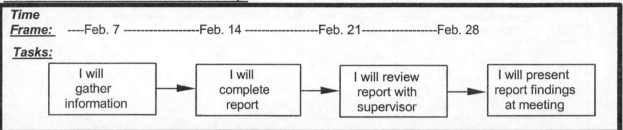

Horizontal Format with Time Line at Top:

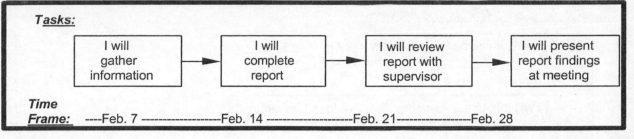

Vertical Format with Time Line at Left-Hand Side

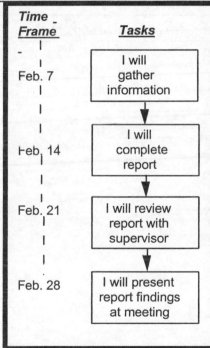

As illustrated here, PERT charts can assume either a horizontal or vertical format. Horizontal formats can depict a time line either at the bottom or top of the page. Vertical formats usually depict time lines on the left-hand side of the page. The important thing is that the time frame for the completion of each task is very clear. The other critical thing is that tasks be illustrated in their correct sequence. Generally speaking, the completion of one task depends upon the prior completion of the task listed sequentially before it. Hence, you can clearly illustrate your plan for completion of some designated goal in a step-by-step sequence.

161

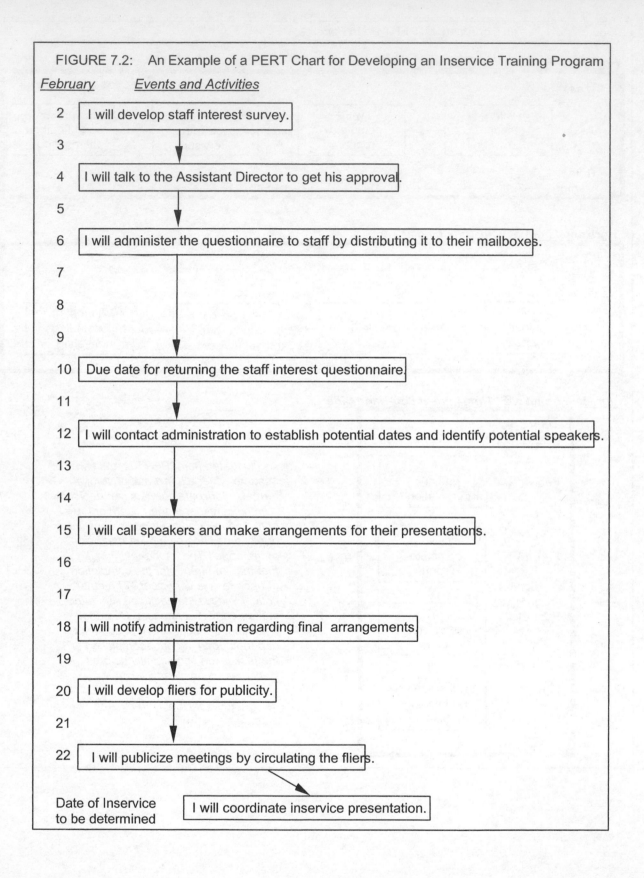

FIGURE 7.2: An Example of a PERT Chart for Developing an Inservice Training Program

February   *Events and Activities*

2   I will develop staff interest survey.

3

4   I will talk to the Assistant Director to get his approval.

5

6   I will administer the questionnaire to staff by distributing it to their mailboxes.

7

8

9

10   Due date for returning the staff interest questionnaire.

11

12   I will contact administration to establish potential dates and identify potential speakers.

13

14

15   I will call speakers and make arrangements for their presentations.

16

17

18   I will notify administration regarding final arrangements.

19

20   I will develop fliers for publicity.

21

22   I will publicize meetings by circulating the fliers.

Date of Inservice   I will coordinate inservice presentation.
to be determined

Exercise 7.4: Developing a PERT Chart

Select a campus issue (for example, lack of adequate, inexpensive campus parking; difficulties getting into required course sections; or problems in the field placement assignment process) that you feel is significant. Think carefully about how you might implement a macro level change if you had the time and energy. Would you develop and conduct a survey to establish the significance of the issue and gain support? Which administrators would you approach about the issue? How would you present your position and your plan? Would fundraising or grant writing be necessary to achieve your goal?

Develop a PERT chart below. Be sure to identify the primary goal, establish a sequence of tasks, and propose a time frame for task completion. You may choose to develop a PERT chart with other students. Brainstorming can be helpful. In that case you may establish a PERT chart with concurrent task sequences for each individual involved.

Exercise 7.5: PERT Role Play

The role play below requires five characters: two unit counselors (change agents); the school's principal; a social work therapist; and the unit counselors' supervisor. In order to reflect real professional life, each character has a professional and individual personality, and a personal agenda. The practice setting is Getalife, a residential treatment center for male adolescents with severe behavioral and emotional problems. To conduct the role play, follow the directions below:

1. Five students should volunteer for or be assigned the roles explained below. Remaining students should observe the role play and record their impressions on the Feedback Form included here. Role players should *not* record observations on Feedback Forms because that distracts from their role enactment.
2. Each role player should then read out loud his or her respective lines.
3. Review the organizational chart included below to understand the agency's chain of command.
4. Begin the role play and allow it to continue for approximately 20 minutes. The instructor should be responsible for halting the role play after the time has elapsed.
5. After the role play is halted, the entire class should discuss critical points, constructive techniques, and suggestions for improvement concerning what occurred. Use the feedback forms to aid in discussion. Role players may share their perceptions concerning their roles and what transpired.

__Unit Counselor #1__: Your job is to supervise daily living and recreational activities for Getalife's residents, to implement individual residents' behavioral programming, to keep records, and to participate in the residents' group counseling sessions. You also periodically attend staffings where individual case plans are established, implemented, and updated. You work in the Box Elder Unit which includes fourteen boys ages 13 to 15. You have worked for the agency for two years, like your job, and feel you can make valuable contributions to residents' well-being. You are especially concerned about residents' need for sex education. Many—perhaps most—of the center's residents have been sexually active. You know this from talking with residents, reading records, and attending staffings where such information is shared and addressed.

You can't think of anyone in the residential center—including child-care workers, teachers, social workers, or administrators—who has an expertise in this area. You set up a meeting with the head child-care worker (your direct supervisor), the residential unit's social work therapist, and the school's principal to establish a plan. You have already explained to them your general idea so that they will have time to think about the issues prior to the meeting. You have discussed your ideas in greater depth with Unit Counselor #2 who seems to agree strongly with you and is willing to help you conduct the meeting. Together you hope to convince this group of the usefulness of your plan. You intend to establish a PERT chart for how to go about setting up a series of sex education sessions for your unit's residents.

You feel that sex education is tremendously important. You have a 14-year-old sister who is pregnant, and that adds to the significance of this issue for you. You are happy that Worker #2 agrees with you and is willing to help you pursue a sex education program for the Box Elder Unit. However, you believe that you are more committed to the issue than Worker #2, and you would like to apply some pressure on Worker #2 to take on more responsibility for planning and implementing the program.

Unit Counselor #2: You work in the Box Elder Unit with Worker #1 who has talked to you about the sex education proposal. You think that sex education is a very important need for the boys in the Box Elder Unit, but you are pretty busy with your job and you are going to school part-time. You'd like to get the sex education program going, but you don't have much extra time for planning or implementation. You like and respect Worker #1, and you realize that Worker #1 is extremely committed to the issue. It seems logical to you that Worker #1 should take on the most responsibility for planning and implementation. You are willing to expend substantial energy to get a PERT plan in place, but you would then like to minimize your involvement in the plan's implementation.

The Center's School Principal: You supervise six special education teachers and their six respective assistants in Getalife's on-grounds school. You have been with the center for three years, and you believe that anything related to education comes under the school's responsibility. Right now, the school is pressed for resources, and you consider sex education a frill that the school can't afford to address. What's more, in your opinion none of the current educational staff has any expertise in this area, and you wonder whether they would feel comfortable teaching about sexuality. All in all, you resent having to attend this meeting. You wish that the two workers would just drop the subject and mind their own business. You also don't much like the Box Elder Unit's social work therapist. You see the therapist as an ineffective employee in a cushy job. You believe that a good education will offer the adolescent residents more hope for their futures than is likely to come from talking about their feelings with some social worker in hocus-pocus, psychobabble therapy. In short, you have very little confidence that the social workers can accomplish much.

You don't plan to support this "sex plan," and you're coming up with a list of reasons that it's a dumb idea. If in the end the group decides to implement it anyway, you definitely want the programming to be provided by an expert from outside the agency. On this point you do not intend to budge.

The Box Elder Unit's Social Work Therapist: You are an MSW charged with providing the adolescents in your unit with one hour of individual therapy and two hours of group therapy each week, in addition to any family counseling that is deemed necessary. You also assist staff in developing behavioral programming, coordinate residents' individual plans through periodic staffings, write staffing summary reports, coordinate staff activity in implementing treatment recommendations, and monitor residents' progress. You have been with the agency for almost six months.

You are a relatively new "gung-ho" social worker, anxious to do your job and do it well. You have finally been able to get your bearings after six months of struggling to figure out how the agency operates and what you're doing with your clients. You have had some difficulty working with both the school principal and the head child-care supervisor. Both seem to resent any suggestions you make for treatment and your efforts to implement treatment plans in the unit and in the school. Without consistency and follow-through, it's hard to get your clients' behavioral programming to work. The principal is especially difficult to work with and very protective of school turf. The head child-care supervisor is more easy-going but appears to "know everything." You feel the supervisor treats you rather condescendingly and doesn't always come through after promising that something will get done. You think the supervisor is pretty passive-aggressive.

You really like the idea of implementing the sexuality programming. You took a sexuality course in college and have had some subsequent training, so with some brushing up on the content you think you could present a really good program. You also feel it would enhance your relationship with your clients.

The Unit Counselors' Supervisor: You supervise all the counselors (child-care) for the residential center's six units—a total of 58 full-time and part-time staff. You are responsible for scheduling their shifts, supervising their work, and arranging for training to meet ongoing treatment needs. You have an associate's degree from a local community college and have been in your current position for the past 17 years.

Since you have been at the agency an awfully long time, you believe that you really know what's going on. These young whippersnappers on the staff come and go, but you maintain continuity for ongoing treatment and care. You also feel that you're pretty much "a natural" with the kids. You don't need a lot of fancy degrees to work effectively with the residents and develop caring and consistent programs for them. You feel you've helped many, many young people get their acts together. You haven't as yet developed confidence in the social work therapist's ability to work effectively with the residents. The social worker seems to you to have promise, but still needs more experience. You think the school principal is rather cocky, but then you've seen half a dozen principals come and go. You're pretty easy-going and are willing to work with the principal's "eccentric" behaviors and needs.

You attend this meeting out of respect for your two Potawatomi Unit Counselors. You like to encourage your staff to develop new ideas. You also like to present opportunities for them to do so. You feel that it would be best for the agency if some in-house staff did the programming. After all, this idea is basically a fad or frill. Why should the agency expend its scarce resources to pay some expert to come in? Why not have some volunteer staff do the sex ed programming and, essentially, get it over with?

PERT Role Play Organizational Chart

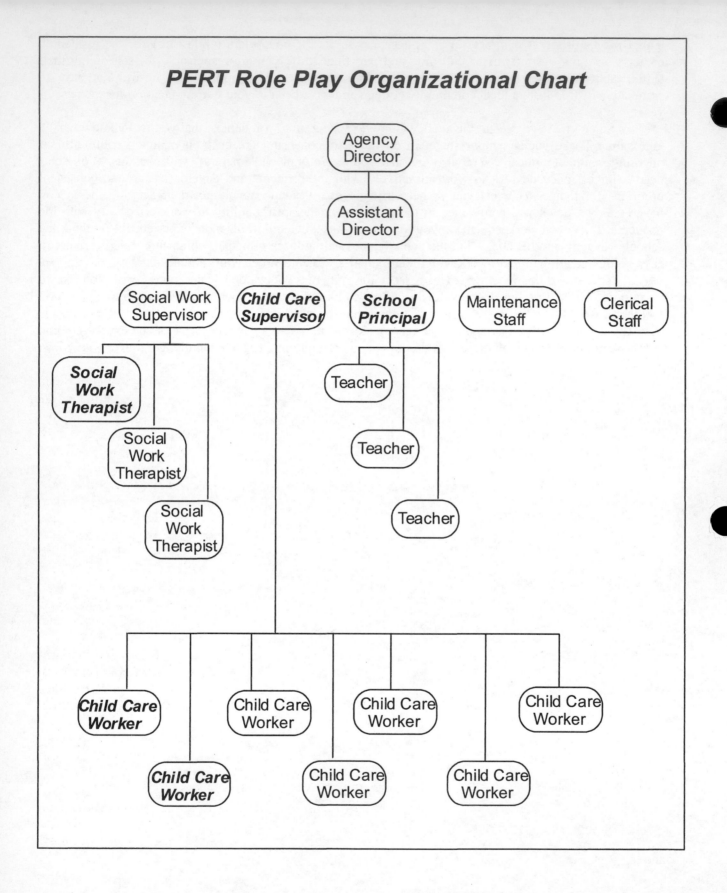

Role Play Feedback Form

1.   What were the critical points or major issues addressed in the role play?

2.   What especially helpful techniques and approaches were used? Please be specific.

3.   What specific suggestions for improvement can you make? For example, how could issues have been addressed more effectively?   What alternative responses might have solicited more information or cooperation? Please be specific.

Program Development

In addition to initiating agency policy changes and implementing projects, you may have the opportunity within your agency to set a whole new program in motion. A program is "an aggregate of actions directed toward accomplishing a single goal" (Rapp & Poertner, 1992). Program development can range from expanding services in an existing agency unit to developing a whole new organizational unit or even an organization itself. There are times in a worker's career when resources and services desperately needed by clients do not exist. At these times, workers must determine whether it is possible, practical, and worth their effort to pursue the development of some new program. Often workers are not alone in their concerns. There may be others—including clients, administrators, colleagues, and persons in the community and other agencies—who also support the establishment of badly needed services.

In most cases workers' job descriptions—established by others working for "The System"—will not include the pursuit of macro changes such as program development.[1] Nevertheless, it is part of professional responsibility to pursue macro change when necessary. You can't assume that the administration will always respond to a given need. It may be up to you to become the change agent.

As with policy change and project implementation, both the PREPARE assessment and the IMAGINE implementation processes can be applied to program development. In this case we will use IMAGINE. Step 1 is coming up with an innovative *idea* to address some programmatic need. During this phase, it is important to work with the client system. For example, if you want to start a homeless shelter program, input from the homeless people who will be involved is absolutely necessary, and so is a clear articulation of the program's purpose. For instance, you might want to renovate an unused building in a designated area of town to provide specified services to a certain number of homeless people who fulfill stated eligibility requirements.

Step 2 in **IMAGINE** involves *mustering* support for your efforts. Carefully choose action system members with the necessary motivation and expertise, and with the ability to work together toward your identified goal. An action system can solicit information and resources, clarify goals and objectives, and fight for community support for the proposed program (Hasenfeld, 1987).

IMAGINE's Step 3 is identifying *assets*. What variables will aid you in the program development process? Who else in your agency will assist and support you? Are there ways to enhance your own power and influence within the agency and community (e.g., by increasing your expertise in the area you've targeted or by ferreting out facts to support your proposal)? What potential and actual funding sources are available to you (Hasenfeld, 1987)?

Step 4 in IMAGINE is specifying *goals* and objectives. Using the *who* will do *what* by *when* format and formulating your plan according to a PERT chart can be helpful. Who will be served by your proposal? What services will be provided? What steps must be taken to accomplish effective service provision?

Actual program *implementation* is Step 5 in IMAGINE. During this phase it is important to monitor participating staff and solicit their support. Other suggestions for implementation include making a trial run before fully implementing your plan. This allows you to iron out any potential "bugs" and to start out small.

---

[1] A job description identifies the specific tasks and responsibilities that make up your job.

IMAGINE's Step 6 is the *neutralizing* of opposition. Carefully observe participating staff's reactions to the program as it develops and seek administration support for your plans.

Finally, Step 7 in IMAGINE is evaluating your progress and effectiveness. You accomplish this through day-by-day monitoring of the agency's performance to determine how efficiently and effectively services are actually being provided (Rubin & Rubin, 1992). This evaluation also requires you to discern who is really being served and how much progress has been made in helping these clients (Rubin & Rubin, 1992). An effective evaluation can lead to the establishment of new programs to provide services on an ongoing basis (Brager & Holloway, 1983; Hasenfeld, 1987). How will the new program fit in with and be linked to other agency units and staff? How will permanent funding be established and maintained?

Exercise 7.6: Creative Program Development

The three vignettes below illustrate dilemmas that prevent direct service workers from providing needed services. Each sets the stage for program development from a generalist practitioner's perspective. Consider each situation, then answer the subsequent questions about program development based on the first three steps in the IMAGINE process.

Vignette A: You are a social worker in a Veteran's Administration (VA) Hospital in East L. A. The VA, a federal organization initially established in 1920, provides a wide range of health and welfare services to people who have served in the military. Services may be directed at physical and mental illness, vocational training, financial assistance, and a host of other needs (Barker, 1991, p. 247). You work in a unit that provides short-term housing and alcohol and other drug (AODA) treatment for homeless veterans. You're finding that more and more of your clients tell you they simply can't find any full-time jobs, even for minimum wage. You can't help thinking, "Even a full-time minimum wage job is pretty much a bummer in terms of taking care of yourself."

The problem, in your opinion, is a lack of adequate job training. Why can't the VA provide educational and vocational training, or purchase such services through some other agency? You have looked and looked for resources for your clients. They need to get back on their feet again, which means finding relatively permanent work that provides an adequate standard of living and enhances their self-esteem. What you and your clients really need is a job-training program with a strong educational component. But no such program is available. Now what?

IMAGINE Step 1: Develop an innovative *idea*.

Propose and describe a program to meet these clients' identified needs.

IMAGINE Step 2: *Muster* support.

Who in your agency and/or community might be appropriate action system members for this macro change? Explain why.

IMAGINE Step 3: Identify *assets*.

What variables can you suggest that would support your change efforts?

In addition to the action system members you listed above, who in the agency might you call upon for support?

How can you enhance your own power?

What potential funding sources might you pursue?

168

Vignette B: You are an intake worker for the Sheboygan County Department of Social Services. The county is primarily rural with a smattering of small towns. Your primary job is to take calls from people requesting services, gather initial information about them and their problems, provide them with some information about county services, and make appropriate referrals to the agencies whose services they need.

You are alarmed at the growing number of calls concerning elderly people having difficulty maintaining themselves in their own homes. Most are calls from neighbors, relatives, or the elderly people themselves. Examples of concerns include: worries about falling and remaining stranded for days; forgetfulness (such as leaving the stove's gas burner on); lack of transportation to get to a critical doctor's appointment; difficulties in understanding complicated health insurance and Medicare reimbursements; and depression due to loneliness and isolation.

After you receive such calls, you typically refer the callers to the Department's Protective Services for the Elderly unit. However, you know all the unit can usually do is make an assessment home visit and either refer the client to a local nursing home or terminate the case. That's depressing. Many of these people just need company and supportive help to maintain their independent living conditions. You have heard of such programs in other parts of the state. It would be great to have a program through which staff could visit similar clients, help them with daily tasks, transport them to recreational activities, and generally provide friendly support. Such a program would help these elderly people remain in their own homes. Can you initiate such a program?

IMAGINE Step 1: Develop an innovative *idea*.

Propose and describe a program that you feel would meet clients' identified needs.

IMAGINE Step 2: *Muster* support.

Who in your agency and/or community might be appropriate action system members for this macro change? Explain why.

IMAGINE Step 3: Identify *assets*.

What variables can you suggest that would support your change efforts?

In addition to the action system members you listed above, who in the agency might you call upon for support?

How can you enhance your own power?

What potential funding sources might you pursue?

Vignette C: You are a state probation officer. You notice a significant increase in your caseload (that is, the clients assigned to you) of men repeatedly committing acts that in your state are considered misdemeanors. A misdemeanor is a minor crime—less serious than a felony—that generally results in incarceration of less than six months (Barker, 1991, p. 146). These men, for example, are speeding while driving under the influence, shoplifting items such as CDs, and even urinating when driving a car. (This last incident actually happened, although it's hard to picture.) As their probation officer, you see these "dumb" things getting them several-hundred-dollar fines and several-month jail sentences. You think this is senseless. There must be a better way to deal with this problem and to make these men more responsible for their behavior.

At a conference you hear about a "deferred prosecution" approach in an adjoining state. This program provides men arrested for such misdemeanors with alternatives to fines and jail terms. They can opt to participate in a 12-week group run by two social workers. Group sessions focus on enhancing self-esteem, raising self-awareness, improving decision-making skills, developing better communication skills, and encouraging the analysis of responsible versus irresponsible behavior. The program was initially funded by a grant (often referred to as "soft money," meaning temporary and limited funding), but it was so successful that the state now implements and pays for it in several designated counties with "hard money." ("Hard money" means relatively permanent funding that becomes part of an organization's regular annual budget.) Men who participated in the program had a significantly reduced recidivism rate. *Recidivism rates* in this context refer to the proportion of offenders who continue to commit misdemeanors. A recidivism rate of 25 percent, then, would mean that of 100 men, 25 committed additional misdemeanors and 75 did not.

You think, "What a wonderful idea!" You begin to investigate how you can initiate such a program in your agency.

IMAGINE Step 1: Develop an innovative *idea*.

Propose and describe a program that you feel would meet clients' identified needs.

IMAGINE Step 2: *Muster* support.

Who in your agency and/or community might be appropriate action system members for this macro change? Explain why.

IMAGINE Step 3: Identify *assets*.

What variables can you suggest that would support your change efforts?

In addition to the action system members you listed above, who in the agency might you call upon for support?

How can you enhance your own power?

What potential funding sources might you pursue?

Chapter 8
Understanding Neighborhoods and Communities

I. **Introduction**

II. **The Role of Social Workers in Neighborhoods and Communities**

    A.   National Association of Social Workers Code of Ethics

    B.   Council on Social Work Education

    C.   Generalist practitioners' typical activities

        1.   Assessing needs through use of interagency committees

        2.   Identifying service gaps, and recommending new programs

        3.   Advocating for policy changes in response to needs identified by grassroots community organizations

        4.   Participating in professional association action groups

III. **Defining Community and Neighborhood**

    A.   Traditional communities—encompass places like cities, towns, and villages, identifiable geographical entities

    B.   Nontraditional communities—nonplace or nongeographic communities (i.e. legal community), also known as identificational communities

    C.   Common components of traditional definitions of communities

        1.   Community occupies a shared physical space

        2.   Community members interact with each other differently than they interact with people outside the community

        3.   Community members often form a strong affiliation and identity with their community

    D.   Neighborhood—a region or locality whose inhabitants share certain characteristics, values, mutual interests, or styles of living

        1.   A community is composed of many neighborhoods

        2.   The degree of neighborhood identity is often even greater than the sense of identity found in the larger community

E.   Functions of communities

1.   Socialization—transmission of values, culture, beliefs, and norms to new community members

   a.   Values—those principles a group considers important

   b.   Culture—includes customs and ways of doing things

   c.   Beliefs—ideas that members assume are true, but may not be verifiable

   d.   Norms—a community's expectations for how its members should act

2.   Production, distribution, and consumption of goods and services

3.   Social control, which involves setting limits on behavior by creating and enforcing laws via police and other official bodies

4.   Mutual support, meaning that community members take care of one another

5.   Providing for the participation of its residents

6.   Highlight 8.1: Examples of Two Communities

F.   Types of communities

1.   Most common classification system is size

   a.   Metropolitan communities—vary in size from about 50 thousand to several million residents, they are large cities that serve as the surrounding area's business and economic center

   b.   Nonmetropolitan communities differ from metropolitan communities mainly in terms of size

      1)   Small cities (15,000-50,000)

      2)   Small towns (8,000-20,000)

      3)   Rural (under 10,000)

      4)   Reservation—located on Native American reservations recognized by the federal government

      5)   Bedroom—predominantly residential in nature

      6)   Institutional—one major employer that may overshadow the whole surrounding area

2.   Classified by ethnic composition or degree of homogeneity/heterogeneity

3.   Boundaries of cities are easily identified; community boundaries may be more diffuse

IV.   Using the Systems Perspective

A.   Figure 8.1: A Social Systems Model

B.   Change agent system—refers to worker or agency to whom a "problem" is reported

C.   Target system—includes those individuals, organizations, or community elements that need changing

D.   Client system—consists of those who will benefit directly or indirectly from the change

E.   Action system—those individuals, groups, or other entities that will carry out the effort to cause change

V.   The Community as an Ecological and Social System

A.   Ecosystems or ecological theory emphasizes the importance of the transactions between systems within an environment

B.   Every community can be viewed as a social system with all the associated characteristics

1.   Boundaries—borders or dividing lines

2.   Homeostasis or equilibrium—attempt to maintain the status quo when threatened by outside stressors

3.   Task and maintenance functions—communities seek to maintain a range of services, attend to the needs of multiple audiences, and respond to special-interest groups

4.   Primary groups and service clubs

C.   Social structural theory—focuses on understanding how various subsystems affect the individual and group

D.   Human behavior theories—the roles of adaptation and stress are useful in understanding how and why individuals behave in a certain manner when dealing with larger systems such as communities

E.   Rational theories—actions and feelings arise from our thinking process

VI. Additional Perspectives on the Community

A. Highlight 8.2: Key Concepts for Understanding Communities

   1. Competition—the struggle within a community by various groups, all seeking to have their interests and needs considered more important than others' needs

   2. Centralization—the practice of clustering business services and institutions in one area of a city

   3. Concentration—the tendency of certain groups (particularly ethnic groups) to cluster in a particular section of neighborhood of a community

   4. Gentrification—a pattern whereby upper-middle-class families move back into downtown and near-downtown residential areas, turning second floors of businesses into lofts and rehabilitating large older homes

   5. Invasion—a tendency of each new group of in-migrants to force out or replace existing groups previously living in a neighborhood

   6. Succession—the replacement of the original occupants or residents of a community or neighborhood by new groups

B. Competition

   1. Communities are often battlegrounds for groups and organizations competing for resources

   2. Competition is essentially a political activity in which many valid needs vie with other equally valid needs

C. Centralization

   1. Communities, through zoning and other land-use restrictions, frequently attempt to centralize certain businesses in specific areas

   2. Zoning laws are why subdivisions of expensive homes are approved and rules established excluding less-expensive homes

D. Concentration

   1. Housing in an area may cost less

   2. Oppression and discrimination often results in housing segregation

E. Invasion—primary affects housing

F. Gentrification—those forced out are often lower- or fixed-income elderly

G. Succession—can continue indefinitely in some areas of a community

H. Concepts characterize real life

174

VII. Community Resource Systems

    A.   Informal—include family members, coworkers, friends, neighbors, and others who provide emotional, social, or more tangible types of support

    B.   Formal—membership organizations including social or fraternal organizations

    C.   Societal—institutionalized organizations or services, such as private and public social service agencies

    D.   Figure 8.2: Community Resource Systems

        1.   Government units

        2.   Spiritual/religious groups

        3.   Professional groups

        4.   Social service agencies

        5.   Business/trade groups

        6.   Civic groups

        7.   Consumer groups

        8.   Educational organizations

VIII. Demographic Development of Communities

    A.   Urbanization and Suburbanization

        1.   Urbanization—the trend in which multitudes of people move to large metropolitan areas and away from rural, outlying areas

        2.   Suburbanization—residents deserted large cities and moved to smaller communities nearby

        3.   White flight—the most upwardly mobile members of our society, composed disproportionately of white, middle-class Americans moving out of the central city

        4.   Blockbusting—a form of social and economic injustice in which realtors tamper with the natural buying and selling trends in a community or neighborhood

B.   Gentrification

    1.   Rehabilitation of rundown buildings improves the quality of life in a community and prevents further deterioration

    2.   The process eventually hurts low-income families and individuals who may have few other housing choices

C.   Rural communities

    1.   Rural communities often have many of the same problems that urban areas have, but fewer of the services needed to cope

    2.   Strong value systems in rural areas and the pressure to conform to longstanding traditions may make it more difficult for newcomers to fit in

    3.   Rural residents are often more willing to help each other in times of need

    4.   A community belief in self-reliance may result in opposition to development of new societal resources

    5.   Highlight 8.3: Social Work in Rural Areas

        a.   Rural areas frequently suffer from a variety of problems including few resources, no public transportation systems, isolation of resource providers, and a loss of anonymity usually available in more urban areas

        b.   Rural residents tend to rely on themselves for problem solving, value high levels of autonomy, and prefer informal to formal resource systems when help is needed

        c.   In times of crisis, rural dwellers are more likely to consult their spiritual advisor than a mental health professional

        d.   About one-third of social workers in rural areas tend to be engaged in advocacy, program development, management, education, and training

        e.   Generalist practice, with its broad range of skills, is especially appropriate and practical for rural environments

D.   Where is the best place to live?

IX.   **Social Stratification**

A.   Social stratification—the division of a society into categories (e.g., income or social class)

    1.   Used for needs assessments and to better understand our society and the vast disparities within it

2. Can be used to discriminate against groups who differ by gender, race, sexual orientation, or other characteristics

3. Underclass—a term that refers to the poorest of the poor

X. Community Economic Systems

A. Economics systems—whether at the national, state, or local level, are concerned with the production, distribution, and consumption of goods and services

1. Underground economic system—consists of off-the-books businesses (such as some child- and lawn-care enterprises), bartering, and even gambling

2. Underclass—refers to members of a community who feel alienated from the community and hopeless about the future

3. The enormous emphasis communities place on recruiting new businesses is testimony to the importance of the economic system on the local level

4. There is often tension and competition in the community between the goals of a healthy economy and concerns about the environmental impact of new industries

5. An environmental justice issue is the tendency for urban growth to occur through development of farmland, green areas, and previously undeveloped rural areas while ignoring deteriorating inner cities or neighborhoods where new jobs and housing rehabilitation are badly needed

6. You cannot overestimate the importance of the economic system

XI. Community Political Systems

A. Formal organizations and informal political processes

1. Federal government—funds many social programs, maintains the U.S. monetary system, oversees interstate commerce, provides for the national defense, and protects the civil rights of U.S. citizens

2. State governments—fund a significant portion of the health and mental health services provided by social workers and others, and play a role in education, providing financial support for local school districts and enforcing rules regarding how this financial support is spent

3. Local governments (county or city)—often provide health and social services, fire and police services

B. Formal structure of the community political system

   1. Official governance structure, consisting of elected officials, the city bureaucracy, the staff who carry out the city functions, and appointed committees

      a. Highlight 8.4: Governmental Activities in the Community

         1) Designing community programs

         2) Allocating funds

         3) Providing services for citizens

         4) Building projects

         5) Awarding and supervising contracts

         6) Determining and enforcing laws

         7) Making and enforcing regulations

         8) Negotiating agreements

         9) Mediating disputes

         10) Planning for the community

   2. Citizen participation

      a. Formal citizen involvement through organizations such as the Chamber of Commerce

      b. Informal involvement through the personal power and influence of individual community members and through the power structure

XII. Power in the Community

A. Defining power

   1. Power—the capacity to move people in a desired direction to accomplish some end; also the ability to prevent someone from doing something they want to do

   2. Highlight 8.5: Power at Work

B. Types of power

   1. Potential power—power that has not yet been exercised, it exists when we can influence others but have not done so

   2. Actual power—the *use* of power to influence others

C.	Sources of power

    1.	Financial asset

    2.	Business ownership

    3.	Community status

    4.	Possession of information

    5.	Links to other individuals, groups, or organizations with power

    6.	Methods of detecting power

        a.	Reputational approach—involves simply asking others about who has power

        b.	Issues approach—assumes that there are always important community issues under consideration and that those who are influential in addressing these issues are powerful people

        c.	Positional approach—assumes that those who hold various important positions in a community also have power

D.	Power and conflict

    1.	Power becomes more visible in times of community conflict

    2.	During conflicts you are most likely to observe those with power influencing the outcome

## XIII.	Neighborhoods

A.	Functions of neighborhoods

    1.	Social functions—include providing friendships, status, socialization, mutual assistance, and informal helping networks

    2.	Institutional functions—include providing employment, connecting new residents to older residents, providing access to specific services, and otherwise helping neighborhood members integrate

    3.	Political function—allowing members to become involved in the political process to influence elected and appointed decision makers

    4.	Economic functions—include provision of housing and places to shop. These are the functions most threatened by technology, changing demographics, and changes in the nature of businesses

    5.	Highlight 8.6: Goodbye to Geneva

B. Types of neighborhoods

    1. Composed of highly mobile residents who will be there for only a short time

    2. Consisting of residents who have lived there all or most of their lives

    3. Characterized by the lack of integrating mechanisms, they are almost disorganized in a social sense

    4. Transient neighborhoods with little cohesion are less likely to function as informal resource systems

    5. Ghetto—used to describe a section in which a specific ethnic group or people of color must live

    6. Slums—indicates they are run-down, deteriorating, or otherwise blighted

    7. Ethnic neighborhoods—where ethnic similarity among the residents is great. The degree of residential segregation that occurs in these neighborhoods challenges the image of the melting pot

C. Neighborhoods as helping networks

D. Neighborhood organizations

    1. It is estimated that there are over 100,000 neighborhood organizations in this country

    2. Highlight 8.7: Two Effective Neighborhood Associations

    3. Highlight 8.8: Neighborhood Organizations

    4. Highlight 8.9: Neighborhood Resources

E. Community and neighborhood resources

XIV. **Putting It All Together: Assessing Communities and Neighborhoods**

A. Useful sources of information for community assessment

    1. Census records, planning agency documents, and business development plans

    2. Newspapers, libraries, books about the community's history, and information from the Internet

    3. United Way and other existing data sources

    4. Database of important officials and individuals (key informants—knowledgeable persons in the community with special expertise in your area of interest)

B.   Highlight 8.10: A Model for Community Assessment

C.   Highlight 8.11: KidsPlace

Experiential Exercises and Classroom Simulations

Exercise 8.1: Nontraditional Communities

A.   Brief Description
Students differentiate between traditional and nontraditional communities.

B.   Objectives
Students will:
1.   Identify traditional and nontraditional communities of which they are a part.

C.   Procedure
1.   Ask students to list any communities of which they are a part.
2.   Ask them to indicate which of the communities are traditional and which are nontraditional.
3.   Lead a discussion about the differences and similarities of traditional and nontraditional communities in terms of their functions for members.
4.   Allow about 10 minutes for the first two steps and another 10 minutes for the discussion.

D.   Instructions for Students
List all communities of which you are a member. Make a note next to each community as to whether it is a traditional community or a nontraditional community.

E.   Commentary
Students can also complete this assignment in small groups

Exercise 8.2: Assessing Community Effectiveness

A.   Brief Description
Students discuss the effectiveness of their own community with respect to traditional community functions.

B.   Objectives
Students will:
1.   Apply community concepts to their own community
2.   Assess the extent to which their community performs specific functions

C.   Procedure
    1.   Discuss in class the traditional functions of communities.
    2.   Divide class into groups of four to six.
    3.   Ask each group member to look at his/her hometown and to assess how well that community performed the functions expected of a community. Share this information within the group.
    4.   Ask each group to record the functions which members believed were well performed and those which were less well performed. Ask them to suggest ways in which a less well-performed function could be enhanced.

Exercise 8.3: Context vs. Target

A.   Your first job out of school is in the foster care unit of a county social service agency. You work with adolescents placed in various community group homes. Lately several group home residents have commented on the rude treatment they receive from certain neighborhood residents. In the section below, give an example in which the community is the context for your practice and another in which the community is the target of change.

    1.   Community as Context:

    2.   Community as Target:

B.   Now you are the Director of Social Services for a nursing home. You recruit, orient, and serve clients for your facility (a for-profit organization). You are new to this position and wish you had someone to talk to about your work. A former professor suggests that you join the nursing home social workers association. You inquire about this group and learn that the nursing home social worker organization used to hold monthly meetings but has not met for a couple of years. Now what? Considering this situation, give an example in which the community is both the context for your practice and the target of change.

    1.   Community as Context:

    2.   Community as Target:

Definitions of Community and Neighborhoods
    Communities are typically defined in terms of certain characteristics. For instance, a community occupies a shared physical space where residents engage in social interaction and share a sense of identity as members. The physical space (like any social system) has boundaries—often, but not always, physical boundaries. The social interaction may occur in the context of work, play, religious celebration, or other activities.
    The sense of identify may be strong or weak. In fact, it may be stronger at some times than at others, and stronger for some residents than for others. Those who are new to the community or have a low level of social interaction may not feel this sense of identity as much as other residents.

The following are characteristics of the community of East Troy. Explain how each provides a context for social interaction and shared identity in the community.

General Motors Plant

Hochander Ice Rink

Bethel Synagogue

Southlake Mall

East High School

Eken Park

Community Functions

Communities serve a number of functions for residents, including socialization; production, distribution, and consumption of goods and services; social control; mutual support; and an opportunity for residents to participate with others (Warren, 1978). Table 8.1 highlights some of these functions.

Every community is composed of multiple neighborhoods. Neighborhoods are usually defined as geographical areas whose residents have similar lifestyles, values, and expectations (Barker, 1991). One's sense of identity with one's neighborhood may be strong or weak. Sometimes it exceeds one's sense of connection to the community.

Table 8.1: Community Functions

Function	Example
Socialization	Transmission of values, culture, beliefs, and norms to community residents
Production, distribution, and consumption of goods and services	Provision of food, clothing, housing, and other services
Social control	Enforcement of community norms through laws, police, ordinances, etc.
Mutual support	Informal social supports and formal services such as social work and other human services
Participation of residents	Recreational opportunities, religious celebrations, and socializing

Neighborhoods provide some, but not all, of the functions of a community. Because of their smaller scale, they cannot provide everything a resident will need. For example, some neighborhoods lack food stores, adequate housing, and social control. Mutual support may be weak or nonexistent. However, others offer multiple opportunities for mutual support, participation, and socialization. The extent to which a neighborhood mimics the functions of a community may affect its attractiveness to potential and current residents.

Using your hometown, describe the mechanisms of socialization used to help you learn the values, culture, beliefs, and norms of your community.

Exercise 8.6: Social Control

Again, using your own experience, identify one example of how the social control function of your community directly affected you.

Community Types

There are multiple ways to classify communities. One of the most obvious is according to size. We set relatively arbitrary definitions of communities. For instance, we say that the largest are *metropolitan,* but we apply this term to cities with several hundred thousand residents as well as to those with a million or more. The smallest communities are designated *nonmetropolitan,* and this category includes small cities, small towns, rural communities, American Indian reservation communities, bedroom communities, and institutional communities. What's more, these subdivisions are not necessarily mutually exclusive. For example, a small town or city may also be a bedroom community for a large city, and thus part of a metropolitan area. Many Native American reservations are also rural communities. The "company town"—as some institutional communities are called—is probably also a small town.

All this means that, while size is an important means of categorizing communities, it does not always tell us much about an area. A more useful category than size is based on the degree to which a community provides the full range of functions referred to above, and on the degree to which everyone in the community benefits from these provided functions.

We also characterize communities on the basis of their heterogeneity or homogeneity. A community may be heterogeneous in the sense that many races, ethnicities, or classes are represented within its boundaries. It may be homogeneous to the extent that such diversity is absent. These factors can have important implications for a community's sense of identity and for its ability to serve the needs of its residents.

Likewise a community may be characterized by its wealth or resources. An economically disadvantaged community may lack sufficient resources to resolve significant social problems, while a wealthy city may provide a high quality of educational opportunity for its children. These ways of characterizing communities are a shorthand means of understanding the potential of a community to perform its functions and serve residents' needs.

There is one more use of the term community that we need to consider. We often refer to groups sharing particular characteristics as communities—the social work community or the medical community—because they share a sense of identity. This type of community does not function in the way that the geographical communities we have described do. Thus, we often call them "non-place communities."

Exercise 8.7: Typing Your Hometown and Your Communities

A.   Identify your hometown by type on the basis of its size and degree of heterogeneity.

B.   Identify any non-place communities of which you are a part.

Communities from a System Perspective

Chapter 1 discussed the importance of the system framework for understanding the macro environment. We may view a community as a system composed of a number of subsystems (for example, neighborhoods). Or we can look at a community as a subsystem of the state in which it is located. Human beings are systems in their own right, but are also subsystems of their neighborhoods and communities. A neighborhood or community can further the growth and development of an individual or family, or it can limit or even destroy that subsystem's progress. As social workers we continually shift back and forth between attention to individuals, subsystems, and to the larger systems of which they are a part. This ability to look at both levels sequentially and/or simultaneously is a hallmark of social work practice.

Chapter 1 also introduced other systems terminology—client, change agent, target, and action systems—to designate the various roles involved in a change effort. For example, we usually refer to the social worker as the change agent, the person who undertakes to change the situation. The change agent may also be the person who identifies a problem or seeks a change opportunity—although this is not always the case. A client system (such as an individual, family, group, organization, or community) may bring the situation to the attention of the change agent. As the name implies, the target system is the one we seek to change, the target of our intervention. The action system includes all those who assist in bringing about change. If we are seeking the formation of a community task force to consider how best to deal with a recent drug problem, the task force is our action system and the drug problem our target.

As you can see, social workers are involved with a number of systems, and each system may be composed of a single individual or of many people, of a group or of multiple groups. Thus, a community (a large system) struggling with gang violence may be the client system. The gangs—which may individually or collectively be large in number—are the target. The action systems might include police, social agencies, and any other groups which take specific steps to remedy the situation. In our role as the change agent in a change-agent system (typically, an agency), we may also be part of an action system. Clearly, these roles are not mutually exclusive, so anyone can play multiple roles.

Exercise 8.8: Identifying Systems

In the following situation, identify the client, change agent, target, and action systems.

Livermore is a small East Coast city with a big problem. Situated along a major interstate highway, it has become a haven for street gangs and drug dealers because it has only a small police force and is less able than the nearby large city of St. Trump to arrest and prosecute these criminals. Mary Mercado moved to Livermore to escape the violence and crime in St. Trump. As a hospital social worker, she knew first-hand the effects of violence. Worried that her new city is going to end up like her old one, Mary talks with a few of her friends who suggest that she bring her concerns to the attention of her city council representative. Mary meets with Paul Hernandez and together they ask the city council to fund a small task force.

The task force (composed of Mary, Paul, another city council member, the city attorney, a probation and parole officer—a social worker—and the police chief) prepares a report recommending that the city take seven steps to reduce or eliminate the drug and gang problem in Livermore.

Identify the following systems:

client system

action system

change agent system

target system

185

The Community from Ecological and Social Systems Perspectives

Like our understanding of individuals, our understanding of communities is enhanced when we look at them from different theoretical perspectives. Here we will emphasize ecological, social systems, social structural, organization, and human behavior theories.

Ecological theory suggests that we can understand systems best by focusing on the transactions that occur between different systems. To understand what is transpiring in a neighborhood or community, then, we view that entity within its larger environment. For example, a prolonged downturn in auto sales in the United States may bring major problems to American automakers. As production is cut back, auto workers lose their jobs temporarily (through layoffs) or permanently (through downsizing). Companies that supply the auto companies with everything from food for the cafeteria to computer chips for the engines are also hurt. They reduce their work forces; employees have less money to spend on food, housing, clothes, and entertainment; and the communities and neighborhoods in which they live and work suffer.

Social systems theory directs our attention to such things as a community's boundaries and stressors, its relative emphasis on homeostasis versus change, and the various functions it performs for its residents. Suppose that county commissioners decide to move the lights from an abandoned baseball field located in a largely African-American community to another ball diamond in an adjacent predominantly white community. The uproar over such a decision will be tremendous. The county commissioners have the authority to move the lights, but they did not anticipate how violating the boundaries of a community (by taking the lights) would upset its residents. This stressor was a decision that affected two communities. Other stressors might include job losses, rapid growth, natural disasters, and any other major event (positive or negative) that upsets the homeostasis (or equilibrium) of the community.

Every community must perform a variety of tasks to ensure that the needs of residents and of the community as a whole are addressed. Some are task functions—garbage collection, police services, creation and upkeep of public parks—which ensure that the business of the community continues with relative efficiency. At the same time, the community must perform certain maintenance functions—such as celebrations of the founding of the community, recreational programs, and other activities and services that help people feel good about belonging to their community. Social systems theory recognizes that survival of any system requires fulfillment of its functions and successful interactions with other systems.

Social structural theory concerns the way the subsystems of a community work together to achieve the desired ends. For example, if the economic, political, health, and education subsystems are working in concert to make a community a better place to live, people are likely to feel positive about their community. If the economic sector is malfunctioning or otherwise not healthy, the other subsystems are likely to be effected. Each of these subsystems has an impact on the community and its residents. A school system that seeks the input of community residents will be viewed more positively than one that ignores or rejects such input.

Organizational theory emphasizes the importance of communication and authority to a community. The most effective communities are those in which communication lines are open, reciprocal, and valued. If residents do not perceive themselves as able to convey information to other systems, problems arise. Neighborhood residents affected by gang violence may stop calling the police if they perceive that no significant help is ever provided. This failure to communicate hurts the entire community. Similarly, if lines of authority are poorly delineated, people become discouraged because they really don't know where to go for help. If you are concerned about a deteriorating house in your neighborhood which is being used by street gangs, you naturally assume the city can do something about it. If you call the police and they refer you to the building inspector who refers you to the public health officer who says this should be handled by the police, you will not be anxious to seek such help again.

Various *human behavior theories* also provide perspectives useful for understanding communities. For example, cognitive theory explains why residents who have been rebuffed in their requests for police assistance in fighting neighborhood drug pushers will not expect help from the authorities and may simply stop trying to change things. Behavioral theories also suggest that if you are shot at while sitting in a lighted living room, you will change your behavior—that is, you will turn off the lights and stay away from your windows.

Each of these perspectives can help you understand what occurs in neighborhoods and communities.

Exercise 8.9: Which Theory Is Most Helpful?

Which theory is most useful in understanding each of these community situations?

A.   The largest employer in a community goes out of business, throwing hundreds of people out of work.

B.   A large community attempts to annex (take over) an adjacent smaller community.

C.   The business sector in a community is deteriorating. Business owners are resisting community attempts to revitalize the downtown area and are failing to improve their own businesses.

D.   The city council has passed a resolution calling for the city building inspector and the police department to work together to target deteriorated buildings and fine landlords who fail to keep up their properties. This is the first attempt to get these two bodies working together.

E.   Maria Hatcher no longer calls the police when shots ring out in her neighborhood. After all, the police have been unable to stop the violence since it began three years ago.

Other factors also contribute to an understanding of communities and neighborhoods.

- Centralization: Certain businesses or industries are clustered together in a specific section of the community. Central business districts and industrial or business parks are two good examples of this phenomenon.
- Concentration: Groups tend to locate in the same parts of a community for reasons that include the cost of housing, ethnic or racial discrimination in other parts of the community, or a desire to live near people with similar backgrounds. Concentration, which occurs both in ghettos and suburban neighborhoods, can contribute to problems such as overcrowding or can have a benign impact on the community.
- Invasion: New groups moving into an area displace older, more established groups. This can be a gradual or a very rapid process. Sometimes longtime residents of the invaded neighborhood leave because they don't wish to live with their newly arrived neighbors. In other cases, a natural transition occurs as more established and financially secure residents move to the suburbs or to more desirable areas in the community. Parts of many cities have undergone periodic transitions as different ethnic groups or nationalities have moved in and others moved out. For example, in one neighborhood, the early Irish residents were followed by the Eastern Europeans including Slavic and Polish immigrants. These, in turn, were followed by African Americans from the southern United States who were eventually replaced by Puerto Rican immigrants. Still later, immigrants from southeast Asia took up residence in these neighborhoods.
- Succession: As invasion refers to the period when the new residents first move into the neighborhood, succession refers to the period when the new group has effectively "taken over" and the transition is complete.

- Gentrification: Older areas of a community (sometimes even its central business district) are rehabilitated or converted into housing for upscale families. An old building that has been divided into four small apartments is remodeled into a larger duplex. The new residents, usually middle-class or above, can afford the higher rents these units command. Or the second floor of a downtown business is converted to residential lofts for those who wish to live in the center of the city. This conversion process changes the nature of the neighborhood because it changes the income level of residents, reduces the supply of lower-income housing, and forces current tenants to seek housing in other neighborhoods. Like invasion, gentrification is followed by succession when the entire neighborhood has changed and one group has replaced the other.

Exercise 8.10: Identifying Changes

A.   *Centralization* occurs when certain businesses locate in a particular section of the community. What term describes groups of people choosing to locate in a particular neighborhood?

B.   How does *gentrification* differ from *invasion*?

C.   Think about your hometown or another community with which you are familiar. Is there evidence of *concentration* in that community? What might account for any concentration you identify?

Resource Systems in Communities
Social workers and community residents depend upon the availability of resource systems to meet a variety of needs. Most such systems can be classified as informal, formal, or societal.

Informal systems develop naturally and include family members, friends, and neighbors. The resources available from such a system might include emotional support, financial assistance, or both.

Formal resource systems (also called *membership systems*) are groups we have joined or of which we are members. They include service clubs (Junior League, Moose), unions (Teamsters, or American Federation of State, County, and Municipal Employees), professional organizations (Bar Association or NASW), and churches. Each of these resources can provide a variety of support and assistance to its members and sometimes to nonmembers. Any such group should be considered a possible source of help at the micro, mezzo, or macro levels.

Societal resources are the institutions, agencies, and organizations established to provide help to residents of the community. Among these are social service agencies (both public and private) in which most social workers are employed. While the resources of these societal systems may be great, it is often more appropriate to help clients (whether individuals, groups, or larger systems) use the other resource systems.

Exercise 8.11: Identifying Resource Systems

1.   List two people who are part of your own informal resource system. What kinds of assistance could they provide you in an emergency?

2.   Identify two formal resource systems of which you are a member. List the kinds of assistance you might expect from them if you were in desperate need.

3.   Identify at least three public and three private societal resource systems with which you are acquainted. These agencies can be drawn from any community.

The Demography of Communities

The demographics of a community include the age of the population, its range of income and education, and its ethnic composition. For example, a community with low educational and income levels, and composed largely of the elderly, is very different from one in which most residents are young, middle-class, and have college degrees. The resources, both human and financial, available to solve community problems are likely to differ, as are the problems themselves.

The size of a community is another important demographic characteristic. A large city may have different problems than a smaller community. Metropolitan communities (those with over 50,000 residents) are likely to have different challenges than rural communities of 5,000. Resources may also differ significantly.

The United States has undergone a number of trends that affect the demographic characteristics of cities. The early years of this century and the last half of the 1800s were characterized by urbanization, or movement from rural areas and small towns to the cities, because of the better paying jobs in factories and transportation systems. Often, this resulted in overcrowded housing and a host of social problems including child labor, poor sanitary conditions, and sweatshop employment conditions.

After 1950, the trend was significantly reversed as suburbanization drew millions away from the central cities. The suburbs were essentially bedroom communities that offered residents more space, lower taxes, and fewer social problems. Mass transit systems, the automobile, and a new interstate highway system made the cities accessible from these outlying areas. Since the majority of those making this movement away from the city were non-minorities, the term white flight has been used to describe the results of suburbanization.

Of course, nothing is forever. Gentrification is beginning to reverse this trend as middle- and upper-middle-class individuals seek housing in the central city. Renovation of old buildings and construction of higher quality housing increases property values in these areas, forcing earlier residents to seek less expensive housing. Naturally, this can and does produce overcrowding in more affordable neighborhoods which may already be struggling with high population densities and other social problems.

Exercise 8.12: Hometown Demographic Factors

Using your hometown as an example, identify the ways in which urbanization, suburbanization, white flight, and/or gentrification have impacted that community. Recognize that any community may be affected by one or more of these factors.

Rural Communities

Rural communities have been viewed from various perspectives at different times. Sometimes they are viewed as backwater towns offering little in the way of culture, job opportunities, or quality of life. At other times, they are portrayed as idyllic settings in which to raise children away from the hubbub of the city. They generally offer lower crime rates, lower taxes, and a more relaxed pace of living. Nevertheless, once former city dwellers move to rural areas, they often want the same types of services and amenities they had in the city. To achieve this, they may sacrifice those lower taxes and invite new social problems. On the other hand, rural communities do appear to provide an environment in which people know and care about one another and help in times of need. For the rural social worker, this can be a real benefit in terms of helping people use informal resources. Those resources must, however, make up for the lack of societal resource systems that might be available in larger communities.

Exercise 8.13: Costs and Benefits of Rural Communities

A friend of yours is a social worker considering whether to practice in a rural community of 12,000 or in a nearby large city of one million residents. Help your friend decide by identifying at least three advantages of practicing in each type of community.

Social Stratification

Another important variable in understanding neighborhoods and communities is social stratification—categorizing people, neighborhoods, and communities by social class or economic level. Stratification can be used to delineate the types of employment available in a community. For example, a community with no factories or large companies might rely largely on service occupations for employment. These tend to pay less than industrial or factory jobs and offer fewer benefits. Similarly, stratifying a community on the basis of the age of its population can be helpful. On the positive side, social stratification is a simple shorthand description of a community. On the negative side, however, it may be used to discriminate against certain groups. For example, a bank may redline a portion of the community where the income level is very low and the quality of housing is poor. The bank will then refuse to lend money for housing in this area. (Redlining is illegal, but is still covertly practiced in certain places.)

Socioeconomic class is one of the most common types of social stratification. It is based on the income and educational level of residents. Because the decision about where to draw the lines between one class and another are subjective, you will often encounter different class descriptions. Thus, one document may refer to lower, middle, and upper classes while another breaks each of these classes into several subcategories. What is most important is to recognize that social stratification is simply a tool.

Exercise 8.14: Hometown Stratification

Using your hometown as an example, identify two ways of stratifying or categorizing the community that would help an outsider better understand it.

Community Economic Systems

Producing, distributing, and using services and products are characteristic functions of all communities. All of us play some role in the economic systems of our communities as producers, consumers, or both. A healthy economic system is important for a healthy community so that people can earn money and spend it to support businesses and community functions.

Communities that lose businesses for whatever reason almost always suffer, and those that rely on a single large employer are always at risk of losing that employer. The absence of large businesses in a community affects employment possibilities for residents and places a larger property tax burden on homeowners. Of course, work remains a primary means of self-identity and economic mobility. Problems in a community's economic structure can impact both of these issues. At the same time, economic systems in any community are affected by many variables. Federal, state, and community laws and regulations affect businesses and industries. Competition, foreign subsidization of a particular industry, and changing tastes of consumers all affect what happens in your hometown. Many communities work very hard to retain and attract new industries and businesses by providing free land, offering tax incentives, and devising other inducements. These actions underscore the importance of a solid economic system to the well-being of a community and its residents. At the same time, we must remember that any economic system produces casualties. Loss of jobs, downsizing, and pay cuts are normal risks associated with our economic system. It is therefore critical that while we understand the importance of our economic system we also recognize its consequences for some members of our society.

Exercise 8.15: Hometown Economic System

Describe your hometown in terms of it success or lack of success in providing jobs to residents of the community.

Community Political Systems

Many decisions affecting social work and social welfare are political in nature. That means that governmental units at some level have a major role in deciding what programs get funded, which social problems should have greatest priority, and how much money can be spent to deal with a particular problem. It also means that many people have important input in making these decisions. Every community's political system includes both formal and informal political processes. For example, each community has some type of formal elected power structure charged with making decisions and spending tax money on identified problems. Of course, many decisions affecting social work are also made at the state or national level. At the same time, many decisions are made informally by individuals and groups who represent the informal political power structure but are not elected by voters. Their power and influence derive from their own resources (money, businesses, political involvement, academic credentials, etc.), relationships they have with others, or appointed positions they hold. This same pattern also operates at the state and federal levels.

Sometimes those with influence work so far behind the scenes that they are virtually unknown to the general public. At other times they may be prominent citizens one would expect to have political influence. Understanding the responsibilities and involvement of different levels of government is important to the generalist social worker. For example, if you are concerned about the enforcement of local health codes, you don't call your United States Senator to complain about the situation. On the other hand, a change in federal laws that reduce a community's eligibility for funding for low-income housing *does* require intervention on the national level. The federal government concerns itself with certain responsibilities and the city or county with certain others. Police protection is generally a local responsibility while many social service programs are state operated and funded. In some areas, there is significant overlap between local, state, and national government roles. For example, the federal government may provide special funding to combat street crime, drug-related violence, and gang activity. This funding may be provided to local communities through grants or other means. At the same time, some programs involve multiple levels of government working together. For example, the federal government provides money and sets guidelines for operating various social service programs which are then carried out by state and local governments.

Exercise 8.16: Hometown Political Systems

Briefly discuss your hometown community in terms of how local, state, and federal governments affect it. Identify functions or services performed by each level of government.

Community Power Systems

Power is the ability to get things done or to prevent others from doing things you don't want them to do. Power is either actual or potential. *Potential power* is the ability to influence others. *Actual power* is power in use. Sometimes there is no need to exercise actual power because others recognize and defer to an individual or group's potential power. For instance, the voting power of the elderly in our society is so significant that few political figures ever suggest cutting Social Security. To do so would likely result in an exercise of actual power: The elderly would vote against officeholders who supported such a plan.

Sources of power vary. Money has always been an important source of power in our society, but status, or position, also confers power. You can discover who the powerful people in a community are in one of three ways:

- The reputational approach relies on asking various people who, in their opinion, has power in the community. Popular people, respected and often talked about, are likely to be powerful.
- The issues approach examines critical concerns in the community and learns who is active on both sides of those issues. Those most involved in making decisions on these issues are considered powerful.
- The positional approach looks at the official positions people hold and assumes that the commissioners, the mayor, and the city council or county board representatives have power.

Each of these approaches is useful at certain times, but none is foolproof. You won't always recognize those who operate behind the scenes to influence those in official positions. What's more, power shifts from situation to situation. A powerful person in one arena or on a single issue might have no influence whatever in another situation.

Exercise 8.17: Power in My Community

Consider your hometown again. Identify at least two people who hold formal positions of power in the community.

List two other people who you believe are powerful, but who hold no formal positions.

The Neighborhood

Most of us grew up in something we referred to as a neighborhood, a common reference point for individuals and families. The term neighborhood usually refers to an area of land or a section of a community. Its boundaries are based on the perceptions of its residents rather than on any geographical marker. For example, a street separating two political districts in a city may have no bearing on one's sense of neighborhood. At the same time, a single political district or ward may be composed of several neighborhoods. The boundaries become most important when there is a threat to the neighborhood (as might happen when a nearby company wishes to expand its operation or a developer wants to build a shopping mall on the edges of the neighborhood). Boundaries can also become important when children are bused to schools outside their neighborhoods. Such boundary crossing activities are likely to arouse negative reactions from neighborhood residents.

Neighborhood Functions

Every neighborhood performs several functions for its residents. *Socially*, they provide status and friendships, and they are a potential resource in crises because of the relationships that exist among residents. *Institutional* functions—such as providing employment, education, or churches—are also commonly associated with one's neighborhood.

The *political* function of neighborhoods allows residents to become involved in the political process through seeking elective office or becoming active in neighborhood organizations. A neighborhood association fostering preservation and maintenance of the area can give residents considerable political influence. Finally, *economic* functions include such things as providing housing and shopping opportunities. The economic function of neighborhoods is always at risk as technology, changes in the business environment, and other factors influence events. As large malls replace neighborhood shopping centers and the corner grocery gives way to megastores located outside the area, the economic viability of the neighborhood is threatened. Redlining and gentrification can also affect the economic function of a neighborhood.

Neighborhood Types

Some neighborhoods are characterized by transiency—frequent turnover of residents—which can reduce cohesion and the sense of participation among those there. A high degree of transiency may result in feelings of social disorganization, reducing the social connection between residents.

Neighborhoods can also be understood by the names we apply to them. We refer to run down or deteriorated neighborhoods as slums, or we use the term ghetto to refer to an area in which a specific ethnic or racial group lives. Unfortunately, these terms tell us very little else about the area.

We can also characterize a neighborhood on the basis of the help it provides to residents. Neighbors can comprise a primary resource for other residents. Every neighborhood has some natural helpers on whom others rely for assistance, friendship, and support. Neighborhood organizations can help new residents feel welcome, protect the common interests of all residents, and encourage cooperation among residents. Because of the wide variety of functions served by such organizations, social workers should be aware of the existence of such organizations in the areas we serve. Conversely, the absence of a neighborhood organization may suggest a possible resource to be developed with the help of a social worker.

Neighborhood residents, particularly new ones, may be unaware of the large number of community resources available for dealing with a neighborhood problem. For everything from abandoned buildings to weed infested yards, the community itself often has resources to assist neighborhoods. Typically these functions are performed by some branch of city government, and it's a good idea to develop a list of such resources to assist residents with specific problems.

Exercise 8.18: Understanding Your Neighborhood

Describe the neighborhood in which you were raised. Discuss how well institutional functions and social functions were performed by the neighborhood. Identify any opportunities for residents to become involved in the political functions of the area. Briefly describe businesses or other organizations serving an economic function in your neighborhood. Finally, mention the degree of transiency of residents.

Assessing Communities and Neighborhoods

A more formal understanding of a community or neighborhood can be reached through the mechanism of a community assessment. An assessment is a detailed exploration of the community or neighborhood using a variety of data sources—census data, planning department records, newspapers, etc. It might also entail interviews with key residents of the area. An assessment might gather information on the location, population characteristics, social and economic influences, educational quality, and/or business and industrial climate in a community. It might also look at the history and attractiveness of a neighborhood along with such social amenities as parks, museums, and recreational opportunities. The availability of health and social service resources, income of residents, and distribution of power in the community may also be investigated. In the process of doing an assessment you might develop a database of the important people you met or learned about. The goal of an assessment is to achieve a better understanding of the community in which you work. It is a valuable tool for the generalist social worker.

Exercise 8.19: Assessment Tools

A.   If you wished to do an assessment of the community in which your college or university is located, what data sources would be relatively easy to locate?

B.   What kinds of data might be helpful to your assessment?

C.   Instructions for Students
Using your home community as an example, identify how well it carried out the functions of socialization, social control and mutual support.
1.   Socialization:
2.   Social Control:
3.   Mutual Support:
Identify how the functioning of your community could have been improved.

D.   Commentary
This exercise can be conducted in a large group with students reporting back to the entire group rather than to a smaller group.

Exercise 8.20: Involvement In Political Systems

A.   Brief Description
Students discuss the extent of their and their family's involvement in their hometown political system.

B.   Objectives
Students will:
1.   Recognize various mechanisms for involvement in the political process.
2.   Assess their own and their family's contribution to political decision-making.

C.   Procedure
1.   Review the ways in which social workers can participate in the political process.
2.   Ask students to look at their own level of political activity and that of their family with respect to their hometown.
1.   Have students share their observations with the entire class.
2.   After all students have shared, lead a discussion on why there are differences among the level of participation of different families/individuals.

D.   Instructions for Students
List and describe any involvement you or your family have had in your hometown political system. Please consider all possible levels of activity from voting to running for office.

E.   Commentary
This exercise can be done in small groups by asking the group to identity common themes explaining why some families/individuals are more politically involved than others.

I.   **Introduction**

II.   **Change in Communities**

      A.   Highlight 9.1: Community Change Activities

      B.   Highlight 9.2: Social Workers in the Community

      C.   A philosophical perspective on macro practice: Pursuit of social and economic justice

III.   **Perspectives on the Community**

      A.   The community is the context in which we practice

      B.   The community is the target of our change efforts

      C.   The community is the mechanism for change

      D.   Approaches to community change

            1.   Working with the power structure in a consensual, gradual way that focuses on service delivery

            2.   Focusing on conflict, mediation, and challenges to the power structure

            3.   Neighborhood maintenance, which combines a consensual, peer pressure system with legal action and political lobbying to improve property values, maintain neighborhoods, and deliver services

IV.   **Beginning the Change Process**

      A.   Engagement in the community

      B.   PREPARE: Assessing Potential for community change

            1.   Figure 9.1: PREPARE—An Assessment of Community Change Potential

            2.   Step 1: **PREPARE**—Identify **Problems** to address

                  a.   Identification by news media reports

                         1)   Sometimes the news media reports a sensational event that underscores the existence of a community problem

                         2)   Highlight 9.3: Gang Graffiti

                  b.   Identification by social service providers

<blockquote>

    c.   Identification by beneficiaries

    d.   Describe problems clearly

    e.   Research the problem carefully

</blockquote>

3.   Step 2: **PREPARE**—Assess your macro and personal **Reality**

<blockquote>

    a.   Force field analysis—a review of the barriers to accomplishing your goal and the factors likely to help you achieve it

    b.   Assessing target systems

    c.   Highlight 9.4: Geri's Force field Analysis

</blockquote>

4.   Step 3: PREPARE—**Establish** primary goals

5.   Step 4: PREPARE—Identify relevant **People** of influence

<blockquote>

    a.   Highlight 9.5: Identifying People of Influence

          1)   People who get things done

          2)   People to whom others look for guidance

          3)   People who will become leaders in your organization

          4)   People who can motivate their peers

          5)   People who have connections with other important people or resources

          6)   People who have particular skills

    b.   Highlight 9.6: Gathering People of Influence

</blockquote>

6.   Step 5: PREPARE—**Assess** potential financial costs and benefits

7.   Step 6: PREPARE—Review professional and personal **Risk**

8.   Step 7: PREPARE—**Evaluate** the potential success of a macro change process

<blockquote>

    a.   Collaborative approaches carry much less risk than conflict tactics, but they may not be as effective in getting you where you want to go

    b.   Highlight 9.7: Evaluating Potential Success

</blockquote>

C.   IMAGINE: A process for community change

    1.   Figure 9.2: IMAGINE—A Process for Initiating and Implementing Macro Change

    2.   IMAGINE: Start with an innovative **Idea**

        a.   The innovative idea you will begin with is the plan you identified for effecting change

        b.   Highlight 9.8: An Innovative Idea

    3.   IMAGINE: **Muster** support and formulate an action system

    4.   IMAGINE: Identify **Assets**

    5.   IMAGINE: Specify **Goals**, objectives, and action steps to attain them

        a.   Highlight 9.9: Goals, Objectives, and Action Steps: Reducing Gang Activity

        b.   Highlight 9.10: Getting Things Done

        c.   Highlight 9.11: Goal, Objective, and Action Step: Obtaining a Permanent Shelter

    6.   IMAGINE: **Implement** the plan

        a.   It is important to recognize the strengths of everyone involved in the implementation process

        b.   Holding meetings is one of the most frequent activities in the implementation phase

        c.   Highlight 9.12: Implementing the Plan

    7.   IMAGINE: **Neutralize** opposition

        a.   Highlight 9.13: Confronting a Bad Idea

        b.   Social action: Confrontation and conflict approaches

            1)   Clashes of position

                a)   Actions such as debate, legal disputes, written statements of intent, public speeches, and bargaining and negotiating

                b)   Highlight 9.14: Bargaining and Negotiating

            2)   Violations of normative behavior

        3)   Violations of legal norms

    c.   Choose goals wisely

8.   IMAGINE: **Evaluate** progress

    a.   Stabilizing change

    b.   Highlight 9.15: Evaluating Progress and a Follow-up

    c.   Termination and follow-up

Experiential Exercises and Classroom Simulations

Exercise 9.1: Community as Client, Target, Context or Mechanism of Change

A.   Brief Description
Students look at the community from several different perspectives.

B.   Objectives
1.   Students will:
2.   Recognize different perspectives on the community.
3.   Identify a particular perspective appropriate to a given community.

C.   Procedures
1.   Present an overview of the community as a potential client, target, context, or mechanism of change.
2.   Divide the class into groups of four to six.
3.   Ask each group to discuss the scenario shown in the box below and to arrive at a solution that most members agree with.
4.   Ask each group to report on their findings and their reasoning.

D.   Instructions for Students
Read the scenario shown in the box below. Share with members of your group your opinion about the appropriate answer and your reasoning.

> As the director of social services at a local hospital in Muddy Hills, you often use community services to help clients when they are discharged. These include programs such as Meals on Wheels, homemaking services, and chore services. Each service is designed to help clients who cannot take care of their own needs for food or household maintenance. Generally, the existing services are satisfactory, but they could be improved. You decide that the Meals on Wheels program in particular could be operated with greater sensitivity to the needs of Hispanic clients. You set up an appointment with the program's director to discuss your ideas. Do you consider Muddy Hills the context, target, client, or mechanism for your practice? Explain your reasons.

E.   Commentary
This activity can be done in the class as a whole rather than in small groups.

Exercise 9.2: People of Influence

A. Brief Description
Students discuss the concept of influence in a community.

B. Objectives
Students will:
1. Recognize their own potential for community influence.
2. Identify areas of the community where their influence can be exercised.

C. Procedure
1. Lead a discussion on the concept of influence in a community.
2. Ask students to identify people of influence known to them or to members of their family. Ask them to identify the sphere of influence that is evident.

D. Instructions for Students
1. Consider all the people of influence in your community that you know or that members of your family know.
2. Identify in which areas of the community they are most likely to have influence.
3. Share this information with the class

E. Commentary
This exercise may be done with small groups or with the entire class.

Exercise 9.3: An Innovative Idea

A. Brief Description
Students consider innovative ideas and possible obstacles.

B. Objectives
Students will:
1. Develop one innovative idea for community change.
2. Identify potential obstacles to achieving change.

C. Procedure
1. Ask students to look at their hometown and to identify one innovative idea that could improve the quality of life in the community.
2. Once this step is accomplished ask them to identify individuals, organizations, or groups who might oppose this idea.
3. Lead a discussion and help categorize the possible reasons for opposition to an innovative idea.

D. Instructions for Students
Look at your hometown and identify one innovative idea that could improve the quality of life in that community. Also identify any individuals, groups, or organizations that might oppose your idea. Why do you think this opposition might occur?

E. Commentary
This exercise can be done in small groups by asking the groups to categorize the reasons for opposition to an innovative idea.

Exercise 9.4: Community as Client, Target, Context, and Mechanism of Change

Match each of the following scenarios with the corresponding view of the community:

Scenario 1:   San Garcia is a community with many problems, primary among which is the absence of shelter for the homeless. The city council has repeatedly turned down a state grant that would help establish a homeless shelter. Julio Ruiz, the shelter's major opponent on the city council, is a very conservative individual who opposes all social programs. He faces reelection in a month and his opponent is a progressive former mayor of San Garcia, Miguel Gonzales. Mr. Gonzales has asked you to help him get elected because you are well known in the community, especially among the Spanish-speaking population. You both believe that residents will support a homeless shelter if for no other reason than to assure that the homeless will not begin sleeping on the streets of residential areas. If you decide to help in this campaign, would you consider the city of San Garcia the client, the target, the context, or the mechanism of change? Explain your answer.

Scenario 2: Franco City is a poor community on the edge of a mid-sized city, Beltville. Beltville has taken over most of the neighboring cities by annexation, a process of legally incorporating adjacent communities. A Franco City citizens' group is very concerned about this trend and wants the community to remain an independent community. At a community meeting they suggest that a task force be formed to plan a campaign against the loss of their independent status. You agree to serve on the task force. Is Franco City the target, client, context, or mechanism for change in this case? Defend your choice.

Scenario 3: Munchhausen Vale has been a wonderful community in which to live. Lately, several events have challenged the status quo in the town. The influx of immigrants from Southeast Asia has created tensions among many residents who have no experience with the benefits of community diversity. Residents have begun to lose the sense of community that once made living in "the Vale" so attractive. You live in the community and serve as an at-large member of the city council. The council decides to hold a series of community meetings to which all residents will be invited. The meeting will look at ways of recreating the positive feeling that previously characterized citizens' views of their town. You will serve as the convener for several of these meetings. Do you think that Munchhausen Vale is the mechanism, target, client, or context for your practice? Why?

Scenario 4: As the director of social services at a local hospital in Muddy Hills, you often use community services to help clients when they are discharged. These include programs such as Meals on Wheels, homemaking services, and chore services. Each service is designed to help clients who cannot take care of their own needs for food or household maintenance. Generally, the existing services are satisfactory, but they could be improved. You decide that the Meals on Wheels program in particular could be operated with greater sensitivity to the needs of Hispanic clients. You set up an appointment with the program's director to discuss your ideas. Do you consider Muddy Hills the context, target, client, or mechanism for your practice? Explain your reasons.

Undertaking Change in Communities

Any planned change must begin a purposeful set of activities. In the PREPARE model described in chapter 5, we follow a process for assessing the potential for change:

Identify Problems *to Address*

Problems are relatively common in any community. They may be pointed out by news media, by victims, by social service providers, by politicians, etc. But not all changes focus on a problem. Sometimes you will seek to *prevent* a problem because you recognize a situation that could deteriorate and want to keep that from happening. Once a potential problem or opportunity has been identified it must be described clearly in sufficient detail that others can understand the issues involved. It is not sufficient to simply say that the community has a problem with homelessness. We need to know the extent of the problem, the characteristics of the homeless, and any other information that will assist us in bringing about change.

Exercise 9.5: Problem Identification

Consult a newspaper for your hometown or another community. Identify one problem affecting the community that is reported in the paper. From the information in the newspaper story, provide a succinct description of the problem and its extent, the characteristics of those affected by the problem, and any other appropriate information. What information is missing that might help you decide whether this problem is of sufficient importance to pursue an intervention?

1. Identification of Problem

2. Description of Problem

3. Extent of Problem

4. Characteristics of Those Affected by Problem

5. Other Pertinent Information

6. Missing Information

Assess Your Macro and Personal Reality

Look first at the potential target. How powerful is it? Can it afford the changes you are pursuing? Next, find out whether the target itself shares your values and goals. If it does, it will be easier for you to "sell" your idea. Third, consider the consequences your projected change will have for the target. Is this target heavily invested in the status quo? Assess your own power to foster change. Finally, outline the general characteristics of the target: Is it susceptible to outside pressure? How will your change affect its sense of identity? Is it generally effective at achieving its own goals?

Exercise 9.6: Reality Check—A Force Field Analysis

Your social work program is considering raising the grade point average needed at the time of graduation from a 2.5 to a 3.5 because some faculty members believe that grade inflation has made the 2.5 meaningless. The social work program is your community. You spend considerable time in social work classes, many of your friends are in social work, and the social work program has become the context of your sense of who you are. You have a field placement set up for next fall, and you know that your own GPA of 3.1 will probably keep you from graduating if this new change is made. (The remaining exercises in this chapter will also focus on this example.)

As a social work student in this community, do a force field analysis. Review those variables that may help or impede your attempts to stop the implementation of this proposal. Answer the following questions:

1.   Who is likely to oppose this proposal?

2.   Who is likely to benefit from it?

3.   Who is unlikely to see the proposed change as a problem?

4.   Assess the power and influence of those who support the proposal.

5.   Assess the power and influence of those who oppose the proposal.

6.   Who is the potential target in this situation?

7.   Do you think the target shares your aspirations, values, and goals? Why?

8.   How susceptible is the target to outside pressure?

Establish *Primary Goals*

Once the force field analysis or assessment is completed, it is time to establish your primary goals. The goals are derived from the problem or change opportunity you have identified. If there are multiple goals, prioritize them because you can't usually do everything at once. Be sure that your goals are clear, easily understood, and capable of motivating people. It is much easier to get people behind a project or change effort if the goals sound attractive and if they will make a major difference in the quality of life in the community.

Exercise 9.7: What Is Your Primary Goal?
---

1.   In the situation concerning raising the grade point requirement (in exercise 9.6), what is your primary goal?

2.   Do you have any other goals? If so, describe them.

Identify Relevant **People** *of Influence*

In this step you pinpoint those individuals who are (1) likely to agree with your goals, (2) capable of influencing others, and (3) willing to participate in the change effort. You also try to identify those who are likely to hurt your cause (such as someone who always achieves his goals, but only after bruising the egos of everyone else involved). Do you need someone who can address the city council or the state legislature? Then avoid anyone who gets tongue-tied in front of groups. But maybe that person would be effective as a grant writer. Your goals influence your choice of actors.

Exercise 9.8: Who Will Help?
---

1.   Referring back to exercise 9.6, list the individuals who are likely to agree with your goals.

2.   Identify anyone who is capable of influencing others to stop this proposed change.

3.   Who might help you stop the proposed change? Why?

Assess *Potential Financial Costs and Benefits*

Consider the various costs and benefits of your proposed effort. Benefits are usually clear—a new playground for children, bus service for the frail elderly, or some other worthy goal—so benefit assessment is relatively easy. Recipients of benefits can include specific client groups (such as gay men and lesbian women) or broader groups (such as a whole community benefiting from decreased gang violence).

On the downside, new programs cost money and must frequently compete with existing programs for resources. Tactics also cost you. You can offend coworkers, force people into uncomfortable positions, and lose friends. There is also a negative cost for failure. It is demoralizing to attempt a macro change effort and fail.

Exercise 9.9: What Are the Costs and Benefits?

Identify at least two financial costs and benefits the proposed change would bring to your social work program. (Remember, in many real-life situations this step will either convince you and others to pursue the change or convince you to stop your efforts immediately.)

1. Financial Benefits of Proposal

2. Financial Costs of Proposal

3. Are there any financial implications to the *tactics* you are considering? If so, try to estimate that cost.

Evaluate *Professional and Personal* Risk

Life is a risk. The goal of this step is not to scare you or discourage you from undertaking a change effort. It is silly and dangerous, however, not to consider the risks you face when pursuing macro-level change. You're not very likely to lose your job because you undertake to change something in a community, but you may very well become unpopular with target system members. You may be perceived as unprofessional if you select tactics that make others uncomfortable. Some people may wonder why you should make it your business to try to change the world (or the piece of it that you occupy). Your colleagues may think you're biting off more than you can chew, and your supervisors may wish you'd spend more time keeping your case records up-to-date instead of taking on city hall. In many cases the risk factor is negligible compared to the potential benefits, but consideration of risk is still a necessary step in the process.

Exercise 9.10: Determine the Risk

1. What possible personal risks are entailed in undertaking this change effort to halt the proposed grade point requirement?

2. Do you see any professional risks inherent in trying to stop this proposal? If so, describe them.

3. Do you consider the risks high in relation to the good to be achieved? Explain.

Evaluate *the Potential Success of a Macro Change Process*

Remember, you have still not committed yourself to pursue this change. The last step is to honestly reflect on the potential for success. You may conclude that success is more likely if you can shift tactically from a conflict approach to a more collaborative approach. Or you may decide that only a conflict approach will work because everything else has been tried. You already know the potential benefits and costs of trying to change something, so you might decide that the goal is so desirable that even a small chance of success is sufficient reason to move ahead. At this point, you can still decide to drop the idea entirely or postpone it until a more propitious time. Your final decision should be reasoned and unemotional, the result of critical thinking, not gut instinct or personal hubris.

Exercise 9.11: Will It Be Successful?

1. Working toward the goal you described in exercise 9.6, list all the reasons this macro change effort is likely to succeed.

2. List all the reasons this change effort is *not* likely to succeed.

3. Is there sufficient potential for success to justify proceeding with the planned change? Why or why not?

Once a decision is made, you have more or less completed the planning process. We say *more or less* because new data can always come in—even during the implementation phase. Keep this in mind. You are now ready to consider the next phase and use the IMAGINE model as your guide through the implementation phase.

IMAGINE: A Process of Community Change

There are seven steps in this phase of the problem solving process. All were discussed in chapter 6 and are briefly summarized below.

Start with an Innovative Idea

You may actually have *several related ideas* that you intend to implement, either simultaneously or over time as the IMAGINE process unfolds.

Exercise 9.12: Restate Your Idea

Restate your *idea* regarding the grade point requirement.

Muster *Support and Formulate an Action System*

You muster support and establish an action system because you always need the help of others to achieve large-scale goals. You have probably already identified likely allies, but it is important to get their unambiguous support. To increase the action system's potential influence, ask members to identify others in their immediate environment whom they could influence to support your project or idea. If your action system members are sufficiently influential, these significant others will increase the strength of your intervention. If you discover that collectively your action system has few influential contacts, take another look at your approach and the likelihood of success. Once your action system is in place, use a PERT chart or some other guideline to assign specific tasks.

Exercise 9.13: Mustering Support and an Action System

1. Describe the steps you would take to muster support for your change effort.

2. Which of your potential action system members has the greatest influence and why?

3. Which of your potential action system members seems least committed to your effort and why?

Identify Assets

Assets are resources that can assist you in the change effort. They include everything from money to people to time. The members of your action system are one of your largest assets, especially if they are committed to the goals you have identified. In macro change activities, people are usually your most readily available asset. Money is another important asset, though it is often less available. Other assets may include office space, use of a telephone, copier, computer, and similar resources. Substantial available assets can encourage members of the action system. A lack of assets makes your work that much harder.

Exercise 9.14: Asset Identification

Identify the following types of assets available to you:

1.   Finances

2.   People

3.   Time

4.   Other

Specify Goals *and Objectives*

Your primary goal already emerged from the PREPARE process but now it will need further refinement. Goals are general statements of intent which are made up of subgoals or objectives. Essentially, we are separating major goals into their component parts. For example, your goal is to prevent any increase in the grade point average needed for graduation. You objectify this goal by stating that "we will marshal all of the objections to and evidence against changing the grade point average." If the original goal is broad enough, we can identify several objectives needed to achieve the goal.

Of course, marshaling evidence against changing the grade point average for graduation requires taking certain steps. These activities, called *action steps*, move you toward the objective. For example, making an appointment with the Program Director or meeting with the faculty could be steps in the process of achieving this goal. Each action step should be allotted a specified time frame and identified as the responsibility of a single person. Without such specificity, the steps are far less likely to be taken effectively.

Exercise 9.15: Spelling Out Goals, Objectives, and Action Steps

1.   List one primary goal of maintaining the current grade-point requirement:

2.   List two objectives that further specify the goal:

Objective one:

Objective two:

3.   List at least two action steps for objective number one:

Action Step:

Action Step:

Implement *the Plan*

Carrying out the plan requires careful use of all resources. If the plan includes such things as petitioning door-to-door, holding public meetings, or other steps that require meeting the public, assign such tasks to people who are comfortable with this type of responsibility. The quiet person who prefers to remain behind the scenes developing a computer database of potential supporters (or donors) is equally valuable in that role. Build on and use the strengths of your action system and assets. Keep on top of the action steps by meeting regularly with everyone to monitor progress and evaluate success. Give people something to do as soon as possible. Otherwise your human resources will lose their motivation and wander off into other projects. Keep them busy.

Exercise 9.16: Implementation

Indicate who will carry out each of the action steps listed above. Give your reason for assigning this step to this particular person.

1.   Action Step Implementer:

Reason:

2.   Action Step Implementer

Reason:

Neutralize *Opposition*

Neutralizing opposition means overcoming or outwitting those who oppose your goals and objectives. If the stakes—financial or otherwise—are large, you may face significant opposition. Sometimes the opposition turns out to be minor—or at least less substantial than you expected. Neutralizing tactics include bargaining, negotiating, mediating, persuading, and/or educating opponents. Most political decisions involve such trade-offs, and negotiating can be a lengthy process. This is a drawback if your action system members lose interest or your goals get so watered down that you really accomplish very little.

Remember that collaboration is less polarizing than confrontation or conflict. On the other hand less confrontational approaches are not always effective. The effort required to neutralize opposition depends on your opponents' power, resources, and degree of intransigence, and on the influence of your action system.

While less confrontational approaches are often desirable, they are not always effective. Sometimes other approaches are needed, including lobbying, boycotts, marches, rallies, strikes, picketing, and lawsuits.

Exercise 9.17: Neutralize 'Em

This may sound like hitting someone with a phaser, but neutralizing the opposition is really benign.

1.   In the space below describe the actions you would take to neutralize opposition to your change efforts. This might include bargaining, negotiating, educating, or persuading opponents, as well as other collaborative and conflictual approaches.

2.   Briefly indicate why you selected these tactics.

Evaluate *Progress*

Clearly stated goals and objectives are readily evaluated. Well-articulated action steps can be monitored to ensure that each is completed in a timely manner. If the agreed-upon steps are not followed, the final goal may not be achieved. However, monitoring is concerned only with the *process*, not with the goal itself. Evaluation, on the other hand, focuses on whether we achieved identified goals and objectives and lets us know what is still needed to ensure that progress will continue. Sometimes called *stabilization of change*, it keeps our objectives from being lost after the change effort is completed. Changes in laws, policies, and regulations are often used to ensure stabilization of change.

Negative consequences may also be revealed by evaluation. Unintended consequences may force us to work for additional changes. For example, a neighborhood complained bitterly to the city because its streets were in such poor repair. Large potholes the size of cows pocked the streets in the area until the city finally repaved them. Then traffic on the street increased, as did the speed of cars. Now the residents complain about this new nuisance. Sometimes you just can't win.

Termination of a change effort is usually the last step after objectives have been achieved. We may have to end our efforts short of complete success if it is clear that we can't achieve the goal or if the unintended consequences are too damaging.

Finally, follow-up ensures that the changes we attempted to stabilize remain in place. Promises made in the midst of negotiating can be forgotten or ignored after things have settled down. Organizations and people may return to their old ways of doing things when no one is watching. Follow-up helps reduce this possibility.

Exercise 9.18: Evaluate

1. Describe how you would monitor your proposed change effort to ensure that it stays on course.

2. Describe how you would evaluate the success of your change effort.

Chapter 10
Evaluating Macro Practice

I.   Introduction

II.   Overview of Evaluation

    A.   Evaluation research has a rich history at the macro level

    B.   Two perspectives of evaluation of macro practice

        1.   Determining effectiveness of specific programs (program evaluation)

        2.   Evaluation of success as macro-level change agents

III. Purposes of Program Evaluation: A Summary

    A.   Help us save time and money or avoid wasting precious resources on approaches that cither don't work or don't work very well

    B.   Allow us to spend our resources on unmet needs as we discover gaps among those being served

    C.   Allow us to change our programs to make them more effective, identifying areas of strength and weakness

    D.   Assure us that planned programs provide the services we intended

    E.   Build support for continuing effective programs

    F.   Distinguish which services produce the more favorable outcomes

    G.   Identify side effects that were not intended or planned for

    H.   Help us gain personal satisfaction from knowing that our programs work and work well

IV.   Key Concepts in Evaluations

    A.   Control group—the group used for comparison purposes that is not receiving the intervention

    B.   Experimental group—the group that receives an intervention

    C.   Dependent variable—that which we are most interested in understanding, measuring, or predicting

    D.   Independent variable—that which we believe is likely to influence, cause, or contribute to a particular phenomenon

    E.   Sampling—a sample or subset of the total group rather than the entire group

F.	Random sample—one in which every element in a population has an equal chance of being selected for inclusion in the sample

G.	Experimental design—involves attempts to manipulate the intervention to determine whether change occurs in a target group. Experimental designs cannot be followed in practice because we are not able to randomly assign clients to groups

H.	Quasi-experimental design—use some, but not all, elements found in the typical experimental design

I.	Baseline—tells us how often a problem or behavior occurred either at a specific point in time or during a specified period

	1.	Retrospective baseline—used when there is no data about something because no records were kept and is composed of data collected after the fact from people's memories

	2.	Concurrent baseline—used when there is no data about something because no records were kept and is data gathering simultaneously with the intervention

J.	Mean—an arithmetical average derived from adding all the entries and dividing by the number of entries

K.	Median—the centermost figure in a distribution of figures listed from highest to lowest or vice versa

L.	Mode—the most frequently observed score in a group of scores

M.	Standard deviation—a measure of the amount of variability of observations around a mean

N.	Reliability—the likelihood that a measurement will yield the same results at subsequent times

O.	Validity—the ability of an instrument to measure what it is supposed to measure

	1.	Face validity—means that a common-sense view of the instrument suggests that it measures what it's supposed to measure

	2.	Predictive validity—a measure of validity based upon the ability of an instrument to predict future performance

P.	Descriptive statistics—statistics that describe a phenomenon

Q.	Inferential statistics—any set of statistics used to make an inference (or draw a conclusion) about a population based upon a sample of that population

R.	Outcome—a quality-of-life change resulting from social work interventions

S.   Statistical significance—a measure of the risk that exists when we generalize from a sample to the population

T.   Chi-square test—a statistical procedure to compare the expected frequencies in a study to observed frequencies

      1.   Expected frequencies—the outcomes that are expected to occur

      2.   Observed frequencies—the actual results you get from your study

V.   Problems and Barriers in Program Evaluation

A.   Failure to plan for evaluation—without a built-in plan for evaluation, including decisions on what information to gather and for what purposes, evaluators are at a loss for ways to proceed

B.   Lack of program stability—it is likely that the program you started evaluating several years ago is not quite the same program now

C.   Relationships between evaluators and practitioners—practitioners are usually concerned primarily with delivering a service; evaluators are interested in measuring the effectiveness of that service

      1.   Practitioners may feel like their worth is under examination. Administrators need to involve practitioners in designing the evaluation, use measures that don't place undue record-keeping burdens on staff, and reduce disruptions in service

      2.   Give practitioners feedback during the process so that they see the importance of the evaluation to their practice

D.   When evaluation results are unclear—when well-planned evaluation produces equivocal or unclear results, perhaps the most logical solution is to conduct multiple evaluations so that no one explanation can rule out all your findings

E.   When evaluation results are not accepted—sometimes evaluations demonstrate things that the people involved do not or cannot accept

F.   When evaluation is not worth the effort—a special event that occurs only once does not necessarily merit evaluation

VI.   Kinds of Evaluation

A.   Formative (or monitoring) evaluations

      1.   Focus more on the process than on the outcome of an intervention

      2.   Occur during the implementation stage and are designed to improve the change effort

3. Focus on describing what the program does and what is happening during the service delivery process

4. Data to assist with monitoring is usually available through treatment manuals, minutes of board or committee meetings, monthly and annual reports, and case records

B. Summative evaluations

1. They are sometimes called impact evaluations, and they measure the consequences of services provided

2. They are normally conducted following an intervention and focus on changes occurring in the target population

C. Effectiveness and efficiency evaluations

1. To be effective, an intervention should produce a desirable end product

2. Efficiency evaluations are concerned with whether a program achieves outcomes in the least expensive manner

VII. **Evaluative Approaches**

A. Quantitative methods

1. Use objective (numerical) criteria (such as scores on a test, number of arrests, or frequency of temper tantrums) to learn whether change has taken place following an intervention

2. Meta-analysis—the combining of the results of several smaller studies, and statistically analyzing the overall findings

B. Qualitative methods

1. Designed to seek to understand human experiences from the perspective of those who experience them

2. Typically involve in-depth review of a small number of cases, and their goal is to describe or explore the experiences of clients or others involved in the process

3. Tend to focus more on the human experience and to provide substantial amounts of information that is then categorized, sorted, and analyzed to determine patterns

C. One group post-test designs—evaluations that look at a single target group, focusing only on changes that have occurred following intervention. They are sometimes called A-B designs

D. Pre-test/post-test designs—sometimes called A-B designs, they are more useful than post-test-only designs because they allow us to show changes over time

E. Client satisfaction surveys

    1. Client or consumer satisfaction inventories or surveys measure general satisfaction with a service or with achievement of specific goals

    2. One of the major drawbacks to client satisfaction surveys is that the results are almost invariably positive, regardless of the client population, services provided, or other variables

    3. Figure 10.1 Client Satisfaction Survey

F. Goal attainment scaling

    1. Design used to monitor the progress of individual clients and then to aggregate the data on a weekly, monthly, or yearly basis

    2. It is often, but not always, a qualitative design and is very flexible

    3. It generally has good face validity and usually does not interfere with the intervention

G. Target problem scaling

    1. A method of monitoring changes in a client's behavior, is primarily a qualitative design used in simple evaluations

    2. Figure 10.2: Target Problem Change Scale

    3. Advantages are that you can use it to assess changes in a macro-level problem in a single area or neighborhood, and you can also combine it with ratings from other neighborhoods to provide a more comprehensive view of residents' opinions

H. Case studies

    1. Qualitative measurement designs allowing the use of a single case or a small group of cases

    2. Allows the use of unstructured interviews and asking whatever questions that may help understand a situation

I. Group comparisons

    1. Compares outcomes between two or more groups—one of which is the treatment group and the other the control group

    2. Quasi-experimental designs use comparison rather than control groups

J.   Quality assurance reviews

1.   Involve determining compliance with an established set of standards and using the findings to correct shortcomings or deficiencies

2.   Focus on finding defects in service and enhancing uniform quality of service

3.   Figure 10.3 Quality Assurance Review

K.   Summary of evaluation designs

VIII.   **Stages in Evaluation**

A.   Stage 1: Conceptualization and goal setting

1.   Begins with agreement upon the goals to be achieved and the indicators of goal achievement to be employed

2.   Goal—a statement of observable effects that are expected from a set of actions

3.   One common problem involves goals that are so poorly defined they cannot be measured

3.   Feedback systems—methods employed to help us know whether goals were achieved

4.   Benchmarks—short-term indicators of progress that show how things are going

5.   Highlight 10.1: Guidelines for Planning an Evaluation

B.   Stage 2: Measurement

1.   In this stage you refine the measures you will use to learn whether the stated goals have been accomplished

2.   The more objective the measures, the higher the agreement rate about what they mean

3.   Quantitative evaluations offer certain kinds of information, and qualitative measures gather other information

4.   Unanticipated consequences have been well documented in the research and can have a very negative impact on clients

C. Stage 3: Sampling

    1. The stage where we decide whether to gather data from all participants or sample part of the population

    2 Systematic random sampling—simply divides the population by the desired sample size

    3. Stratified random sampling—used to ensure that clients are proportionately represented in the sample. You assign numbers using a table of random numbers (a table of random numbers is a list of numbers produced by a computer and is used for selection of random sample members)

D. Stage 4: Design

    1. Concerned with selecting an appropriate design and eliminating other possible explanations for the observed outcomes

    2. Creaming—selecting the "cream of the crop" for evaluation

    3. Maturation—an internal process in which time itself affects the client

    4 Highlight 10.2: Three Common Evaluation Designs

        a. Pre-experimental designs

            1) One-group post-test only design—involves a single group in which progress is measured only at the end of the intervention

            2) Post-test only design with non-equivalent groups—employs a comparison group that we hope will be similar to our experimental group

            3) One-group pre-test/post-test design—assesses change over time using the same test, or a variation of the same test, at two points

        b. Quasi-experimental designs

            1) Nonequivalent control group designs—use two groups, both of which are given pre-tests and post-tests. The groups are similar on important variables, but there is no random assignment

            2) Time series designs—use a series of observations before and after an intervention to gather longitudinal data to help spot patterns occurring over time

            3) Multiple time series designs—are essentially the time series design with an added control group

      c.   Experimental designs—an ideal model, most are difficult to use in actual practice. They require both random assignment of subjects and a control group that receives no (or different) treatment to compare with the treatment group

E.   Stage 5: Data gathering

      1.   Data gathered for evaluating, whether goals are achieved or not, can come from several sources

      2   Figure 10.4: Sources of Data

      3   Instruments, tests, and scales

            a.   Evaluating a program's effectiveness is often facilitated when the agency already uses standardized instruments for the quantitative analysis of clients' progress

            b.   Figure 10.5: Sources of Measurement Instruments and Tests

            c.   Important factors in instrument selection—validity, reliability, the sensitivity of the instrument to any changes caused by the intervention, length of the instrument, difficulty level for the client, and ease of use

            d.   CES-D Scale

                  1)   Developed to help measure depression and its symptoms

                  2)   Figure 10.6: CES-D Scale

            e.   Rosenberg Self-Esteem Scale

                  1)   A normed instrument that allows comparisons of those who complete it with a broader population

                  2)   Figure 10.7: Rosenberg Self-Esteem Scale

F.   Stage 6: Data analysis

      1.   Data analysis is the actual process of assessing the nature and significance of the results obtained

      1.   Univariate analysis—used if you are only interested in explaining single variables and descriptive statistics

      2.   Bivariate analysis—used to determine the degree of association between two variables

3. Multivariate analysis—used when examining three or more variables in relation to one another

    a. Multivariate analysis generally requires use of a computer and statistical software designed specifically for this level of analysis

    b. Regression analysis—a statistical procedure to determine how much of a change is due to the event under your control (independent variables) and how much to other factors

G. Stage 7: Presentation of data—must communicate clearly to your intended audience the evaluation's results. A final evaluation report will likely contain six sections

  1. Part 1: Introduction

    a. The introductory section reviews the situation that prompted the evaluation in the first place

    b. Here you describe the research questions you want answered

  2. Part 2: Literature review

    a. The literature review should provide a thorough summary of existing research on the topic under consideration

    b. Because of the potential wealth of material available, you may have to be very specific about what ends up in your literature review

    c. If relatively little information is available on a topic, that point should be included in your literature review

  3. Part 3: Methodology

    a. The methodology section describes the evaluation design and the data collection methods used

    b. Discuss the data analysis system selected

  4. Part 4: Results

    a. The results component describes your findings with appropriate graphics (charts, graphs) and reports on the findings' importance

    b. Figure 10.8: Pie Charts

    c. Figure 10.9: Line Graph, Bar Chart, and a Three-Dimensional Bar Chart

5. Part 5: Discussion

    a. The discussion section briefly summarizes your findings, describes any unexpected findings, and describes any practice implications

    b. Describe any limitations of the research

6. Part 6: References and appendices

    a. References include any sources (books, journal articles, and similar items) you consulted in preparing and conducting your evaluation .

    b. Appendices might include any documents too large to fit into the study itself

7. Summary of data presentation

    a. Always present data as clearly as possible

    b. Use headings, titles and numbers to delineate data

    c. Public presentation of data requires more use of graphics than might be required for a written report

IX. Ethics and Values in Evaluation

A. Whenever you contemplate using subjects as part of the evaluation (such as when interviewing or testing), those subjects must be volunteers, and they should know the risks associated with participation

B. The privacy of participants should be zealously protected

C. NASW Code of Ethics

D. Human subjects committees now routinely review research proposals that may expose people to emotional or physical danger

E. Clients must give permission before audio- or videotaping contact with them or before letting a third party observe sessions

F. Sometimes values can become a barrier to effective action following an evaluation

G. Perhaps the most important ethical consideration for doing evaluation is our obligation to clients

Exercise 10.1: Evaluating Your Practice

A.   Brief Description
Students will identify primary reasons for evaluation of practice.

B.   Objectives
Students will:
1.   Identify primary reasons for evaluating their own practice.

C.   Procedure
1.   Divide the class into groups of four to six students.
2.   Ask each group to identify as many possible reasons for evaluating their own practice as possible.
3.   Have each group list their reasons on the board.
4.   Discuss any reasons that students have not touched on.

D.   Instructions for Students
With other members of your group, list as many reasons as you can for evaluating your own practice as a social worker.

E.   Commentary
The exercise can be done in a larger class.

Exercise 10.2: Measures of Central Tendency

A.   Brief Description
Students practice calculating measures of central tendency.

B.   Objectives
Students will:
1.   Calculate the mean, median, and mode of a group of scores.
2.   Recognize the advantages of one measure over another.

C.   Procedure
1.   Have each person in the class write down their age on a piece of paper, fold it in half, and pass it to the front of the class.
2.   List all age figures on the board in order from lowest to highest.
3.   Ask students to calculate the mean, median, and mode for the age figures.
4.   Lead a discussion about which measure of central tendency would be most useful in describing this class of students.

D.   Instructions for Students
Write your age on a piece of paper, fold the paper and pass it to the instructor. After the instructor has placed all age figures on the board, calculate the mean, median, and mode for the ages listed.

E.   Commentary
Any set of figures can be used for this exercise including income.

A. Brief Description
    Students will become more familiar with various key concepts from the chapter.

B. Objectives
    Students will:
    1. Recognize the difference between descriptive and inferential statistics.
    2. Become sensitive to the concept of statistical significance.
    3. Identify characteristics of random sampling.

C. Procedure
    1. Divide class into small groups of four to six.
    2. Give the class the three problems listed in the box below and ask them to answer each question posed.
    3. Have each group report back to the larger group.

D. Instructions for Students
    In small groups, read the questions contained in the box and answer each question. Discuss answers within the group until you arrive at a consensus.

Questions to Consider

A recent report said that the average age of residents in a small nursing home was 72 and most residents were women. Are the statistics used here likely to be descriptive or inferential? Why?

The community of Plantwart has an average per capita income of $15,000 while the neighboring community of Nosegay has a per capita income of $16,000. A friend says there is a real difference of $1000 between the two communities but the difference is not statistically significant. What does she mean by this?

A polling organization is using sampling to gather opinions about voting preferences from members of your community. If every person in your community has an equal chance of being selected to participate in the study, what type of sampling is being used?

E. Commentary
    This exercise may be accomplished in the larger class or with any other set of questions from the chapter.

Exercise: 10.4: Evaluation of Practice

A. Brief Description
    Students will consider ways to improve objectives to enhance evaluation.

B. Objectives
    Students will:
    1. Recognize problematic program objectives.
    2. Identify ways to improve the evaluation of program objectives.

C.   Procedure
       1.   Divide the class into small groups of four to six.
       2.   Assign all groups the task of responding to the questions shown in the box below.
       3.   Ask each group to report back on their answers.

D.   Instructions for Students
       In your small group, discuss the questions posed in the box below. Come up with as many possible responses as possible.

Program Objectives

1.   Your field agency has a stated objective of helping each client improve his or her life. What potential problems might the agency have in evaluating its effectiveness in meeting this objective?

2.   How would you improve the objective?

E.   Commentary
       This exercise can be done with either large or small groups using these or similar questions from the chapter.

Exercise 10.5: Calculate It Yourself

Using the following ages of students in a social work class, calculate the mean, median, and modal ages.

Marcia	20	Alicia	26	Fred	26	Sam	56	Chou	41
Andrew	30	Miguel	34	Noel	35	Maria	38	Nathan	26
Louis	23	Martin	24	Jose	26	Xavier	31	Kay	33

Mean age: _____

Median age: _____

Modal age: _____

Another commonly used statistical measure is the *standard deviation*. This measure is based on the mean and measures how much the scores or observations vary above or below the mean. Standard deviations are usually derived using computers or calculators. (When I was a child we did it by hand using an abacus.)

Suppose we are interested in the grade-point averages of students in our after-school tutoring program. The mean GPA for these at-risk adolescents is 1.89. The standard deviation is .03 which means that most of the students have grades very close to the 1.89 GPA. In other words, there is very little variability in this group. A larger standard deviation would mean just the opposite—that several students had much higher or much lower GPAs.

Reliability is the extent to which a given measurement will produce the same results at different times. We want to know if our Legal Education Group (LEG) is helping delinquent youngsters better understand the law and the consequences of criminal behavior. Unfortunately, while developing the test we find that the youngsters in our test groups score very differently on the exam. Scores seem to go up or down without apparent reason. If the test were reliable, the only thing that would affect scores would be new knowledge covered in the LEG program. Clearly, our testing system is not reliable, so we must find or devise new tests.

Validity is an instrument's ability to measure what it is intended to measure. If your policy instructor gives you a test on the most effective interviewing approaches to use with resistant or involuntary clients, you will wonder what is going on. That test will not be a useful indicator of your knowledge of social welfare policy. There are many different kinds of validity. A certain degree of validity is assumed if an instrument appears to measure the right stuff. A social welfare history quiz covering the Elizabethan Poor Laws or the War on Poverty has *face* validity because it covers logical content from the course. The licensing examination for social workers in most states also has face validity because it measures what social workers should know about practice. Whether a high score on such exams means you will be a good social worker, however, is less certain. If an instrument can predict future behavior or performance, we say that it has *predictive validity,* a higher level of validity than simple face validity and one that requires more elaboration and testing to achieve.

Statistical significance is a measure of the relationship between two variables. For example, we might like to know whether the sample of neighborhood residents we used to study neighborhood attitudes toward crime is actually similar to the neighborhood population as a whole. If it is, we can have more confidence that the opinions we gathered truly reflect those of all neighborhood residents. We also use statistical significance to find out whether two variables are related to one another. For example, you have decided to explore whether grade point average was affected when adolescents completed an after-school peer tutoring program. If you discover that grade point averages were noticeably higher for students who completed the program, you can use this information to continue or expand the program. If your findings are challenged by opponents of the program, you can use statistical analysis to show that there is only 1 chance in 100 that the results obtained by students completing the program (i.e., improved grade point averages) could be due to chance. This bolsters confidence in the program because it shows that the results you obtained were statistically significant.

One of the most frequently used tests of statistical significance is the *chi-square*. The chi-square procedure allows us to compare expected frequencies with observed frequencies. Put slightly differently, the chi-square is a means of testing whether two observations are related. Let's say our new anti-violence program seems to be working. We notice that arrests for violence in our target neighborhood have dropped considerably. However, a report from the police department on violence-related arrests in the target neighborhoods indicates that the police have been arresting a larger number of people of color. That's curious because the neighborhood is very heterogeneous. You can't accuse the police department of uneven enforcement without some additional evidence, so you use the chi-square test to compare the actual numbers of people of color arrested to the expected number based upon the overall make-up of the community. For instance, people of color comprise 45 percent of the population in this neighborhood and in the community at large. All things being equal, we would expect to find about 45 percent of those arrested for violent crimes to be people of color. Instead, it appears that fully 90 percent of the arrests are of people of color. The chi-square test can help us verify statistically what our own common sense tells us, namely that something is rotten in Denmark.

In the following exercise match each concept with its corresponding definition. (No cheating—don't look back.)

1. Baseline	_____	11. Median	_____
2. Control Group	_____	12. Mode	_____
3. Experimental Group	_____	13. Standard Deviation	_____
4. Dependent Variable	_____	14. Reliability	_____
5. Independent Variable	_____	15. Validity	_____
6. Sampling	_____	16. Descriptive Statistics	_____
7. Random Sample	_____	17. Inferential Statistics	_____
8. Experimental Design	_____	18. Outcome	_____
9. Quasi-Experimental Design	_____	19. Statistical Significance	_____
10. Mean	_____	20. Chi-Square Test	_____

A. A statistical procedure for comparing expected and observed frequencies.
B. The most frequently observed score in a group of scores.
C. A group used for comparison purposes.
D. Using a subset of all clients seen by an agency rather than surveying the entire group.
E. The group receiving an intervention.
F. A design using control and experimental groups but not random assignment.
G. The original amount or occurrence of a behavior or event.
H. The behavior intervention is intended to change.
I. The ability of an instrument to measure what it is supposed to measure.
J. The arithmetic average of a group of numbers.
K. A measure of the variability of a group of scores around a mean.
L. A quality of life change resulting from social work intervention.
M. The risk involved generalizing from a sample to the population as a whole.
N. Statistics used to draw a conclusion about a population based on a sample of that population.
O. The middle figure in a distribution of figures listed from highest to lowest or vice versa.
P. The likelihood that a measurement will yield the same results at subsequent times.
Q. The average age of a group of delinquent youth, for example.
R. A social work intervention is an example of this type of variable.
S. A subset chosen so that all members of the population have an equal chance of being selected.
T. An elaborate method for evaluating an intervention; includes control groups, experimental groups, and random assignment of clients to one group or the other.

Why Evaluations Don't Always Work

Many potential problems can arise before, during, and/or after a program evaluation, so it helps to be alert to the more common difficulties.

- First, program developers often fail to plan for evaluation at the time they begin their efforts. Later, then, when evaluation becomes necessary, there is insufficient data (lack of a baseline, for instance) and no efficient system for data gathering.

- Lack of program stability is another potential problem. Nothing is static in social work practice. Any program undergoes changes as personnel become more sophisticated and learn new approaches, and as the clientele changes. Evaluations, however, work best when the program is stable. Instability leaves evaluators in a quandary: Are they evaluating the original program or some modified version of it? The longer the program goes on before evaluation occurs, the greater the risk that such changes will confound the results. To overcome this difficulty, evaluators can focus on specific portions of the program that have *not* changed significantly or conduct the evaluation over a shorter time period. Nevertheless, all programs change and this problem cannot be entirely eliminated.

- The relationship between evaluators and practitioners can also create difficulties. As a social work practitioner, you probably prefer providing service to clients to attending to paperwork. The evaluator, on the other hand, is concerned with assessing program effectiveness, so records and data are of considerable consequence.

- There is also the implicit threat that an evaluation might prove that you aren't accomplishing your objectives or that your program should be eliminated or restructured. This scrutiny, although uncomfortable for you, is the evaluator's primary task.

- Evaluators are interested in such things as random assignment of clients, accuracy of records, and other details that may seem unimportant to the practitioner. Workers often rely on practice wisdom—the day-to-day knowledge and experience we gain by routinely doing our jobs—to assess whether progress is being made. This practice wisdom includes observations, assumptions, and intuition, but evaluators want hard data. How do we balance these two sets of priorities? We can focus the evaluation on the theory or approach that underlies the program rather than on the program itself. Practitioners feel less threatened when the focus of the evaluation is not on their performance. Also, evaluators can offer feedback to workers in such a manner that the worker is given an opportunity to improve practice, not simply criticized.

- Evaluation results are often unclear. For example, what if the results of a peer-tutoring program show only a very modest improvement in the school performance of participants? Do we discontinue the program, change it in some unspecified way, or argue that any improvement is better than the status quo? What if results show that an improvement occurred but its effects disappeared after a year or two? What do we do? Can we conduct another study to determine why the results were not longer lasting?

- Sometimes evaluation results are not accepted. This can occur when evaluations support ideas and programs that influential people find unacceptable. A popular program can be threatened because results don't bear out its effectiveness. An unpopular program works but is anathema to the public or to policymakers. For example, a pilot program that gives high school students ready access to birth control information and devices may reduce the number of young women who drop out of school because they had babies, but giving condoms to adolescents is not a popular practice. We must keep in mind that we live and practice in a political and social context which can have profound effects on what we seek to do. We can attempt to convince policymakers that the program produces solid results, but we may lose the battle.

- In some cases, a proposed evaluation is not worth the effort. Some people want to measure everything, but one-time or short-term projects are unlikely to benefit from evaluation. By definition, they are not going to be repeated. If evaluation results won't be used to enhance the program, why bother? If the cost of doing the evaluation outweighs the potential benefits, why put your time and energy into the process?

Exercise 10.7: Name That Barrier

John Moses, Director of the Community Action Center, has asked you as a new staff member to evaluate the low-income weatherization program the agency began five years ago. A new regulation requires that all agencies receiving federal funding prepare a detailed evaluation of the program's success. The program provides low-income residents with assistance in weatherizing their homes to reduce energy costs. The program began by providing residents with insulation, expanded to include storm windows and doors, and has grown substantially since its inception. Full-time employees have replaced the part-timers who helped launch the program during its first year.

Identify and explain the possible barriers and problems you would anticipate in attempting to carry out your assignment.

Exercise 10.8: Which Interventions Should You Evaluate?

You will often have the opportunity to evaluate, but you may decide that some efforts simply are not necessary. Look at the following four vignettes, then decide which you would evaluate and explain why or why not.

Vignette 1: Nathan House Renovation

Nathan House is a shelter for runaways that is operated by your agency. A local service organization has offered to renovate Nathan House over a six-month period. Renovations will include paint, new carpeting and furniture, and new lighting. Would you evaluate this intervention? Explain your answer.

Vignette 2: Nathan House Legal Education Program

Runaways at Nathan House are expected to participate in a legal education program designed to make them aware of their rights and obligations under the law. The program is founded on the idea that residents will be less likely to get into further trouble if they understand the law. Should you attempt to evaluate this program? Why or why not?

Vignette 3: Drug Abuse Community Education Program

Nathan House is one of several agencies offering all residents an opportunity to learn about drugs and thus to help reduce the levels of drug abuse in the community. The program is based on a national model in use in other states and will begin in about six weeks. Would you recommend evaluating this program? Give your reasons.

Vignette 4: Council of Agency Executives Group

Your agency director is part of a new group composed of executives of all agencies serving adolescents in the community. The group meets once a month to share information and discuss community-wide problems. The director asks you if you think this group should be evaluated. *Should* this group's efforts be evaluated? Discuss your reasons.

Types of Evaluations

Two types of evaluations are commonly used in social work. One type—the *formative* or *monitoring* evaluation—is done during the implementation phase of a program. These evaluations keep track of such things as the *output* (as opposed to the *outcome*) of the program—such things as the number of clients seen, the number of hours of service given, or the opinions of clients and workers about the change process. This evaluation might also ask clients whether they received prompt service from the agency and whether they were treated with respect. These are additional characteristics of output. Obviously, such a focus will not help us learn whether the program is worthy of continuance, but it will reveal problems in the process itself.

To help evaluate the data gathered in the monitoring process, we can compare the number of hours clients are seen with some national, state, or professional standard or guideline. We can also measure our output in relation to the target established when the program was begun. Maybe we are seeing more clients than we expected. By looking at data on age, gender, or presenting problem, monitoring can also show whether we are reaching the population we intended. As always, we must determine what data is needed. Finding out after the fact that you never kept records on client ethnicity or race may stymie you in monitoring this aspect of your program.

The second category of evaluation is called *summative*. Summative or *impact* evaluations are concerned with outcomes. What are the consequences of the program in terms of quality-of-life changes experienced by participants? Typical program evaluations are summative, concerned not with whether clients were seen promptly or treated well, but with whether the program produced the results intended. Ultimately, summative evaluations are the ones funding bodies care about.

Like many summative evaluations, *effectiveness evaluations* focus on determining whether an intervention worked, but they also aim to discover whether the change was achieved as efficiently as possible. It is entirely possible for two programs to produce the same outcome at very different costs or over significantly different time periods. Was the intervention conducted in accordance with proper procedures? If an intervention failed to warn the client system of possible negative consequences, it would be unethical. For instance, if a worker failed to inform her clients engaged in a rent strike that the landlord could legally evict them, she would not fulfill her ethical obligations. This failure compromises the efficiency of the intervention and could also have implications for its effectiveness.

Exercise 10.9: Summative and Formative Evaluations

Describe the primary difference in purpose between summative and formative evaluations, and discuss how each might be used in a social service agency.

Evaluation Designs

Selecting the right design to evaluate a macro level intervention is as important as choosing the most appropriate change strategy. For example, you would not use an intrapersonal intervention such as cognitive restructuring to help clients adjust to substandard housing. You should be familiar with several different evaluation designs, including quantitative and qualitative designs, post-test and pre/post test designs, client satisfaction surveys, goal attainment and target problem scaling, case studies, group comparisons and quality assurance reviews.

Quantitative designs use objective and numerical criteria to measure change following an intervention. These designs typically use baselines, require a high degree of specificity, and focus on readily observable indices of change, such as a reduction in the number of reported burglaries to determine the effectiveness of a neighborhood watch program or the number of clients receiving public assistance who found employment following completion of a job training program. The use of such specific measurement devices makes it easier to identify whether change has occurred.

Qualitative designs do not usually use numeric indicators. Instead, they often rely on in-depth review of a small number of cases. For example, to learn about resident's concerns about housing, we might interview a sample drawn from target neighborhoods. Our open-ended interview would let respondents answer in their own words instead of giving them a list of problems to check off. The results of this survey would be subjected to a content analysis to find common themes in the responses. (A content analysis looks for patterns among responses, then counts the most frequently occurring responses.) Qualitative designs can also show how a program affected participants and what recommendations they might have for future interventions. These designs—which rely on interviews, logs, or journals kept by participants—can be used in conjunction with quantitative designs to get a fuller evaluation of a program. We might use a formal survey to ask residents of a public housing project about their perceptions of changes in drug and gang problems following an increase in police patrols. This quantitative measure could be combined with a qualitative study of residents' experiences with the police to learn whether the added police involvement produced any new problems.

The reference above to "changes" in perceptions suggests that we already have baseline data on residents' perceptions before the intervention took place. The ability to compare changes following an intervention is characteristic of a *Pre-test/Post-test design*. The "test" might actually be any baseline data such as police reports, attitude surveys, or any other information that allows a comparison over time. Frequently, this is termed an A-B design because it assesses change from time A (pre-intervention) to time B (post-intervention).

Without a baseline, the most common evaluation approach is a *One-group, Post-test design*. As the name implies, we are dealing with a single group and have no baseline available. We have to measure the impact of an intervention with very limited information about the situation prior to intervention. For example, we might want to know whether the new after-school recreation program for boys has helped them stay out of neighborhood gangs. We can show that fully 90 percent of the boys who participated never became involved in gangs, clearly a positive figure. But without a baseline to show the percentage of boys who became involved with gangs before the program was initiated, we cannot say with certainty that the recreation program worked. This design is often called a "B" design since we have only the post-intervention data from which to draw our conclusions.

Sometimes, we simply want to know program participants' perceptions. One of the most frequently used evaluation designs for this purpose is the *Client Satisfaction Survey*. These surveys gather opinions of those who used a service to determine clients' degree of satisfaction about such things as accessibility of services, fairness of policies and procedures, and what components of a program are viewed most favorably. A primary drawback of this design is that it measures only perceptions rather than actual changes in behavior. The fact that clients liked a program does not, ipso facto, mean that it was effective. The surveys can be used, however, to compare changes in perception over time if a baseline of previous survey results is available. Thus, the surveys can be used in both A-B and B designs.

Goal Attainment Scaling attempts to monitor progress in a client system to determine whether attainable and desirable goals were achieved. This design allows clients and workers to see actual case progress and to assess both the type and percentage of goals that were achieved. Goal attainment scales are considered qualitative designs since the goals and their achievement are specified and assessed by the client and worker. Generally, this design has good face validity and good reliability, and it can be combined with other designs when appropriate. The principle value of this measure at the macro level is the ability to combine the results of multiple goal attainment evaluations to get an overall picture of program effectiveness across all clients served. Figure 10.4 shows a goal attainment scale used to evaluate the success of a neighborhood watch program.

Figure 10.4: Goal Attainment Scaling

Levels of Predicted Outcome	Primary Objective
Least favorable outcome	No reduction in home burglaries
Less than expected outcome	Reduction in home burglaries is below 33%
Expected level of success	Reduction in home burglaries is 33%-40%
More-than-expected level of success	Reduction in home burglaries 41%-50%
Most favorable outcome	Reduction in home burglaries above 51%

Another qualitative design is *Target Problem Scaling*. The principle behind this design is that a problem is carefully identified, intervention occurs, and the existence and degree of the problem are measured over some time period. By using repeated measurements, the worker is able to determine what changes are taking place with respect to the identified target problem. For example, if the problem is lack of park facilities in a community, the results of a community-wide drive to develop parks could be assessed across several months or years.

We use *case studies* when we want to know a great deal about a single case or a small group. Using the earlier example, we might want to know, for example, why the 10 percent of boys who ended up in gangs did not benefit from our after-school recreation program. We would probably use unstructured interviews to find out what factors made the program less effective for this group. Depending upon the participants' answers, we might need to ask additional follow-up questions. The case study might also consider such demographic data as age, race, or other factors.

Group comparisons are designs that compare two or more groups (such as a "treatment" and a "control" group). It can also be used to compare different interventions used on different groups. Group comparisons may be either of the post-only or pre-post design. We might like to measure how two groups of at-risk children differ in terms of drug usage. One group may have received an education-focused intervention while the other participated in an activity program designed to strengthen their involvement with their parents. With quasi-experimental designs such as group comparisons, we never know for certain that the intervention produced the observed change. The absence of random assignment of members to the intervention group cannot rule out other explanations for the outcome.

Quality Assurance Reviews focus on ensuring a uniform quality of service in an agency or organization. The quality assurance review is typically a comparison of actual agency operation to a standard of performance. For example, an agency policy may require that each referral be followed up within 24 hours. A quality assurance review will verify whether this standard of service is being maintained. Similarly, regulations or policies may require that each case file contain a plan for service and a record of worker contacts. These items can be assessed during a quality assurance review. This type of evaluation design can be done on an ongoing basis or when problems arise. As noted, the purpose of the review is to help the organization determine if its own standards are being maintained.

As you can see, each of the evaluation designs described above helps us monitor and evaluate our interventions. Some are focused on process and others on outcomes. Each differs in its degree of rigor and selection is based upon the purpose and capabilities of the design.

Exercise 10.10: Designing an Evaluation Program

For each of the scenarios described below, discuss how you would evaluate the program.

A: *Evaluating Hospital Discharge Planning:* You are the Director of Social Services at Our Lady of Perpetual Misery Hospital. Your unit is primarily involved in doing discharge planning, with three BSW social workers assigned to this function. Discharge planning involves working with the hospital medical staff to facilitate patients' transition following discharge. Typically, your unit helps clients return to their own homes, go to nursing homes for temporary care or on a permanent basis, or go to live with relatives. Your unit uses a variety of community services including transportation, medical equipment for use in the home, visiting nurses, home health care, and similar services. The hospital administrator has asked all directors to begin to consider how they might evaluate the effectiveness of their units. You want to develop an evaluation program that can be done with existing staff, does not intrude on your work with patients, and is relatively simple to implement. Explain the methods you will use to evaluate your unit's effectiveness.

B: *Evaluation of a Hospice Care Program:* Your hospice program has been funded by the county for its first year of operation. As a condition of continued funding, you must develop an evaluation component that will allow the funding source to determine whether to continue your program next year. Patients come to you from area hospitals, nursing homes, and from their own homes. All are suffering from terminal illnesses ranging from AIDS to cancer to other life-ending diseases. Your hospice provides services to in-patients and to people in their own homes. Your evaluation plan should provide the county with data to justify your continued funding.

C: *Evaluating an Assertiveness Training Group:* Your agency operates assertiveness training groups for women who are survivors of domestic violence. Each group lasts four weeks and consists of 6-8 women per group. You lead this group and are curious about whether members really become more assertive after leaving the group. Design an evaluation system that would help you answer this question.

D: *Evaluating a Neighborhood Watch Program:* You have helped the Green Oak neighborhood develop a neighborhood watch program to combat the many burglaries and auto thefts suffered by area residents. The police department was very cooperative in helping you establish this program, but your agency director isn't convinced that these kinds of programs are worthwhile. He questions why you spend your time on such activities. How would you design an evaluation program to show whether this type of program is effective in reducing crime?

Stages in Evaluation

Like the problem-solving process, conducting an evaluation consists of specific steps. The most rigorous evaluations require you to think about what will be needed before you begin the intervention or program. Finding out afterward that you should have kept certain records can doom you to a substandard evaluation.

The first stage in evaluation is *conceptualization* and *goal setting*. You would not begin an intervention until you had considered where you were going and what you hoped to accomplish. The same is true in an evaluation. A goal is an observable outcome that will occur as a result of our efforts. If an agency's goal is to serve ten new low-income clients each month, the outcome is easily measured. If the goal is to develop a transition facility to house families moving from the homeless shelter to independent living, evaluation is easy. Either the facility has been developed or it has not. The more clearly specified and articulated the goals, the more readily they can be assessed. Ideally, some sort of feedback or management information system will be in place to record data on goal achievement. Let's say we wanted to determine what percentage of clients successfully completed the agency's outpatient drug treatment program. Agency records should give us this information, but if those records are not kept or are not accurate, we'll have a problem. If records don't detail each worker contact with a client, we can't determine whether the agency's goal of prompt service is being achieved.

The second stage of evaluation is *measurement*—identifying the measures to be used in the evaluation, such as worker records, other agency or organization data, results of surveys undertaken specifically for this evaluation, etc. We might want to measure the number of clients seen by a worker, the number of arrests in a neighborhood for gang activity, or the number of homes receiving energy reduction treatments such as insulation and storm windows. We must decide what data to collect and how to collect it. It is critical that the data we collect be appropriate to the research question we want to answer. Program records provide some information, but other data must be acquired elsewhere—through case studies or client interviews, for instance.

In the next stage, *sampling*, we must decide whether to include the total client population or create a subset (sample). Gathering data for an entire population can be expensive and unnecessary if the population is sufficiently large and rigorous sampling procedures are followed. The size of the sample we use is generally a function of the size of the population: A large population may allow a sample size as low as 10 percent while a smaller population may require a 50 percent sample. Once the decision is made to use a subset of the population, several types of sampling are available. We have already discussed random sampling, in which every member of the population has an equal chance of being included. A modification of the random sample, the systematic random sample, allows us to simply divide the population by the desired sample size and select every *n*th client for inclusion in the research. Absent any naturally occurring bias (such as every tenth person just happening to be a woman), this approach offers most of the benefits of a random sample. Sometimes, however, random samples can cause problems. If your agency wants to know whether outcomes for gay men and lesbian women served by the agency are different from those of straight men and women receiving the same help, a typical random sample of clients served might not include any gay men or lesbian women at all because they constitute a very small portion of the entire client pool. The solution is the *stratified random sample*. Using this method, you divide your population into two groups, gays and straights, and assign numbers to all members of each group. If 5 percent of your population is composed of gay men and lesbian women, you select 5 percent of your sample from this group and 95 percent from the other group. Random sampling will predict with some accuracy whether the results found in the sample are typical for the population.

The fourth stage of the evaluation process is *design*. The goals of this stage are to select an appropriate design and to rule out other possible explanations for our findings. For example, without a comparison group or control group, we might erroneously conclude that our new first offender diversion program is ineffective because only 50 percent of the participants stayed out of trouble. With a control group, we might discover that our 50 percent success rate is twice that of first offenders not receiving the intervention. The design stage also helps us eliminate other problems. Research results can be called into question when the success of a program appears to be the result of factors such as the developmental maturation of participants or the fact that only the most promising clients were selected for inclusion.

The fifth stage of the research process is *data gathering*. Sources of data can include observations by the worker, client, or others in the environment; written survey results; official records (such as census or agency records); and case notes. Data may include opinions, test scores, and ratings completed by workers, clients, or others.

The sixth stage is *data analysis,* the process of reviewing the nature and significance of the data you have gathered. If the goal is to determine how many clients' files are marked, "closed, improved," simply count them. Data analysis can be simple if we report only means or modes (such as the average income of clients before and after receiving job training services). Other levels of analysis involve two or more variables. Computers are frequently needed to analyze such findings.

The final stage in designing an evaluation is *presentation of the data*. Data analysis provides results, but they are only as useful as the presentation method employed. The intended audience for your evaluation determines how your report is constructed. Clarity is critical. A single-page executive summary of the results should be included identifying the most important findings, though the report itself typically contains several sections including an introduction, literature review, methodology, results, discussion, references, and appendices.

Exercise 10.11: Sample or Population?

Read the following case example and propose a sampling method:

Your dispute resolution agency helps community residents involved in disagreements by providing a mediator to help work out their differences. The agency has assisted in this manner with custody disputes, landlord-tenant issues, and employer-employee disagreements. You serve about 250 people per year, including members of the community's small Latino population. You wish to learn the opinions of those who have used your service during the past year and are especially interested in how Latinos see your agency. You decide to use a client satisfaction survey to gather this information. Indicate whether you would select a sample of your potential population or survey everyone who used your service. Give your reasons for this decision.

Exercise 10.12: Selecting the Right Stage

Next to each evaluation stage listed below, write the letter of the activity that belongs at that stage:

Stage	Activity
1. Conceptualization/goal setting	a. Preparation of written report on findings
2. Measurement	b. Collecting information on outcomes from client records
3. Sampling	c. Specification of outcome
4. Design	d. Reviewing the nature and significance of information acquired from various sources
5. Data gathering	e. Deciding how information will be gathered
6. Data analysis	f. Deciding whether to include all clients or a subset of them
7. Presentation of data	

The principles of ethical research suggest several general rules:

- First, participants must have the right of self-determination and the right not to participate.
- Second, risks to participants should be described honestly. No harm must come to participants who participate or choose not to participate.
- Third, confidentiality is maintained as scrupulously as in practice.
- Finally, recognize that there may be clashes between the implications of our research findings and our desire to help others. If the results of our research show that a program is not efficient and/or effective we must accept the fact and move on. A generalist social worker should not fail to be guided by research.

Exercise 10.13: Ethical Research

You are part of a community-school task force focused on identifying adolescents at risk of dropping out of school. To get a better estimate of the incidence of behaviors which might place adolescents at greater risk of dropping out, Horace, a member of the task force, proposes that the group survey all junior high students. He suggests that the surveys be coded in such a way that the task force can later identify the most at-risk respondents. With this information in hand, school social workers, guidance counselors, and others can begin to work with each of these youngsters. Evaluate this proposal, then state and explain your reactions.

Chapter 11
Advocacy and Social Action with Populations-at-Risk

I. **Introduction**

II. **Defining Advocacy, Social Action, Empowerment, and Populations-at-Risk**

    A.   Highlight 11.1: Key Terms

        1.   Advocacy—representing, championing, or defending the rights of others

        2.   Case advocacy—work on behalf of individuals and families

        3.   Cause advocacy—work on behalf of groups of people

        4.   Discrimination—negative treatment of individuals, often based upon their membership in some group (such as women) or upon some characteristic they share with others (such as a disability)

        5.   Empowerment—ensuring that others have the right to power, ability, and authority to achieve self-determination

        6.   Oppressed populations—refers to groups that experience serious limitations because others in power exploit them

        7.   Populations-at-risk—those groups in society most likely to suffer the consequences of, or be at risk for, discrimination, economic hardship, and oppression

        8.   Social action—a coordinated effort to achieve institutional change to meet a need, solve a social problem, correct an injustice, or enhance the quality of human life

        9.   Social and economic justice—exists when every individual has opportunities, rights, and responsibilities equal to those of all other members of a society

    B.   Defining advocacy

        1.   Advocacy—representing, championing, or defending the rights of others

        2.   Macro practice, in particular, often involves cause advocacy, which is work on behalf of groups of people who lack the ability to advocate for themselves

        3.   You are likely to pursue case advocacy in micro and mezzo practice with individuals and families

        4.   Social workers have a rich history of cause advocacy, including working for civil rights legislation and fighting for the rights of people with physical and emotional disabilities and for other populations-at-risk

        5.   Highlight 11.2: Advocacy Produces System Change

C. Defining social action

    1. Social action is a method of practice designed to place demands on a community to obtain needed resources, attain social and economic justice, enhance quality of life, and address social problems affecting disenfranchised and disadvantaged populations

    2. Highlight 11.3: Coordinated Social Action Efforts

D. Defining empowerment

    1. Empowerment is the use of strategies that increase the personal, interpersonal, or political power of people so that they can improve their own life situations

    2. It assumes that people have the right to power, ability, and authority to achieve self-determination

    3. Highlight 11.4: Caveats in Empowerment

E. Defining populations-at-risk

    1. Populations-at-risk are those groups in society most likely to experience and suffer the consequences of discrimination, economic hardship, and oppression

    2. Historically, among the groups most frequently experiencing these societal influences are women, lesbian and gay people, and persons of color

    3. Also includes elderly persons with physical, emotional, or developmental disabilities and those holding religious views significantly different from those of the rest of society

III. Populations-at-Risk

A. Factors contributing to populations being at-risk

    1. Physical differences

    2. Values and beliefs that differ from those of the dominant or more powerful segment of a society

    3. Preconceptions about the ability or competence of members of a group

    4. A result of our economic system

    5. Values are often behind other instances of discrimination and oppression

    6. Others in society may define a group as economically or socially insignificant

    7. When businesses decide to move away from communities where wages are considered too high

B.   Examples of populations-at-risk

    1.   African Americans

    2.   Hispanic Americans

    3.   Native Americans and Alaskan Natives

    4.   Asians and Pacific Islanders

    5.   Women

    6.   Lesbian and gay persons

    7.   Clients receiving public assistance

    8.   Other at-risk populations

        a.   Homeless

        b.   People with physical and mental disabilities

        c.   Teenagers who have no plans for college

        d.   Teens who have planned, or unplanned/unwanted pregnancies

C.   The role of social workers with populations-at-risk

    1.   Social workers are in an excellent position to help prevent populations from being placed at risk

    2.   Social workers must be vigilant regarding how their agencies and other societal institutions interact with high-risk populations

    3.   Social workers must alert themselves to the community's treatment of populations-at-risk

    4.   Social workers will face some practical and ethical considerations with working to assist populations-at-risk

        a.   Clients have the general right to self-determination

        b.   Clients have the right to fail as well as to succeed

IV.   **Advocacy**

A.   Concerns about the use of advocacy

1.   Workers may be afraid of controversy, which is a natural consequence of advocating for an oppressed group or population-at-risk

2.   Workers may be unable to determine the outcomes of advocacy

3.   Workers may fear what will happen if they advocate for a change and the change actually occurs

B.   The value and limitations of advocacy

1.   The National Association of Social Workers' (NASW) and the Canadian Association of Social Workers' (CASW) ethical codes make it a worker's duty to engage in advocacy

2.   A major benefit of macro-level advocacy is that it can attack core problems rather than merely treat crisis situations

3.   Apathy is perhaps the most dangerous threat to progress in combating oppression and pursuing social and economic justice

C.   Agency commitment to advocacy

1.   Some agencies actively pursue outreach efforts to ensure that their services are available to populations-at-risk and groups underserved by existing agencies

2.   Some agencies do not see advocacy as an important part of their mission

D.   Opportunities for macro-level advocacy

1.   Highlight 11.5: Advocacy for Change—Thinking Big about Child Care

2.   Efforts to change policies and laws at the institutional, community, or other level

3.   Homophobia—irrational fear and loathing of homosexuals

E.   Principles of macro-level advocacy

1.   Advocates should work to increase accessibility of social services to clients

2.   Advocates must promote service delivery that does not detract from the dignity of the groups they serve

3.   Advocates should work to ensure equal access to all who are eligible

F.   Guidelines for macro-level advocacy

    1.   Be reasonable in what you undertake

    2.   Teamwork often produces better outcomes

    3.   Being an advocate sometimes requires being assertive

    4.   Flexibility is a strength, not a weakness

    5.   Accept that sometimes you win—sometimes you lose

    6.   Be prepared to use a variety of strategies

G.   Advocacy tactics

    1.   Persuasion

        a.   Inductive questioning—asking the target system a series of questions designed to make them think about their original conclusion

        b.   Provide arguments on both sides of an issue—involves stating not only your opinions and facts, but also acknowledging the opinions, concerns, and facts of the other side

        c.   Persistence—most people give up when they meet resistance

        d.   Highlight 11.6: Advocacy in Action

    2.   Fair hearings, grievances, and complaints— administrative procedures designed to ensure that clients or client groups, who have been denied benefits or rights to which they are entitled, get equitable treatment

        a.   Fair hearings—an outside person (usually a state employee) is appointed to hear both sides of the argument

        b.   Grievances—are usually a part of an agency's own policies

        c.   Complaints—are similar to grievances but are provided for in certain laws

    3.   Embarrassing the target of change

        a.   Highlight 11.7: Embarrassing the Target

        b.   Letters to the local newspaper, sit-ins, and demonstrations are tactics designed to embarrass (and inconvenience) the target

    4.   Political pressure—public (tax-supported) organizations are more likely to be sensitive to the concerns of political figures who control them

5.   Petitioning

       a.   Petitioning is the act of collecting signatures on a piece of paper that asks an organization or agency to act in a specified manner

       b.   Highlight 11.8: A Petition Form

V.   Legislative Advocacy

A.   Legislative advocacy—a macro-level intervention like other types of cause advocacy, specifically involves efforts to change legislation to benefit some category of clients

    1.   Responsibility for legislative advocacy is part of being a social worker because so many decisions affecting social work programs, social workers, and clients are made in the legislative arena

    2.   Realistic barriers reduce the likelihood of getting new legislation passed

    3.   Even bills that seem to benefit everyone may not become law

    4.   Even a legislator's agreement to support a bill may prove meaningless

B.   Factors affecting legislative advocacy

    1.   Financial or fiscal implications of a bill

    2.   A bill's popularity

C.   Steps in legislative advocacy

    1.   Highlight 11.9: Steps in the Legislative Process

    2.   Step 1: Developing and revising the draft bill

       a.   Most ideas for laws are sent to an already established unit (sometimes called a legislative reference bureau)

       b.   Because legislative reference bureaus work for the legislative body, it is difficult for social workers to have much direct impact on their work

       c.   In the process of pursuing a macro intervention in the legislative arena, you will have to become something of an expert on the bill(s) in which you have an interest

    3.   Step 2: Identifying, obtaining and maintaining the bill's supporters

       a.   Every bill has some natural supporters

       b.   It is equally important to predict who will be neutral or opposed to a bill

      c.   In many cases it is wise to meet with both supporters and opponents and go over actual copies of the draft bill

      d.   State and federal agencies are more likely to be successful in getting bills they support approved

4.   Step 3: Arrange for sponsorship of the bill

      a.   It is essential to identify legislators willing to introduce and work for passage of a bill

      b.   Legislators who easily win election or re-election (safe legislators) can often take riskier positions than those who worry that they may lose the next election

      c.   Whenever feasible, seek support from legislators in the majority party

5.   Step 4: Introducing the bill

      a.   Early bills give you more opportunity for lobbying and, if necessary, amending the bill to attract supporters

      b.   Lobbying—involves seeking direct access to lawmakers in order to influence legislation and public policy

6.   Step 5: Work with interest groups to broaden support for a bill

7.   Step 6: Educate the public

8.   Step 7: Influence legislative committee consideration

      a.   The specific committees that consider given bills are a potential focus of lobbying efforts

      b.   Suggestions for presenting testimony at public hearings

          1)   Identify those who will speak, in what order, and what they will say

          2)   Don't use professional terms that only those in your field will understand

          3)   It is permissible to use case examples to illustrate the impact of a specific bill

          4)   Use humor very carefully

          5)   Avoid hostility and focus testimony on the proposed legislation

6)   Practice what you will say and dress professionally

7)   Having the ability to get up in front of a group, describe a problem, propose a solution, and ask others to support the position is an important skill to macro practitioners

     9.   Step 8: Influencing action on the floor

         a.   Most bills are modified by legislators once they reach the floor of the House or Senate

         b.   If at all possible, you and your supporters should be present for the debate on a bill

         c.   Do not become discouraged when a bill is amended

   D.   Other ways to get involved

     1.   An appropriate macro-level intervention is working for the election of candidates favorable to social work positions and issues

     2.   Political Action for Candidate Election (PACE)—established by NASW to work for candidates who support social work values and ideals

     3.   Highlight 11.10: Communicating with Elected Officials

     4.   Some of the skills that social workers already possess, such as the ability to compromise and bargain, are particularly useful in the political arena

   E.   Other political activities

     1.   Registering voters

     2.   Running for nonpartisan political office and seeking appointment to boards and commissions in their area of interest

     3.   Becoming involved in local, state, and national campaigns as long as the activities take place outside the workplace

VI.   Social Action

   A.   Alinsky's social action approach

     1.   Power is essential to change the status quo

     2.   Power is not the sum of what you actually have, but rather the sum of the appearance of what you have

     3.   Power is not given to you; you acquire power by taking it from those who have it

     4.   Use methods that are familiar to you (or the action system) and unfamiliar to the target system

5.   All organizations have rules that they say they can live by

6.   People should be organized around issues that are vital to them

7.   Most people in power respond to political pressure

8.   Successfully attacking a target requires a clear demarcation between good and evil, or haves and have-nots

9.   Turn negatives into positives

10.   Prepare yourself to propose an alternative

B.   Concerns about social action

1.   Zippay argues that some of Alinsky's principles may be less useful today

   a.   Enemies are harder to identify and the high-tech world of today makes the role of the media much more influential in affecting ideas, perceptions, and actions

   b.   We need to connect people to existing sources of power both inside and outside the community

   c.   Skills needed today are much more collaborative approaches than Alinsky advocates

2.   Gelman argues that social workers who violate rules and regulations end up putting themselves, their clients, and the profession at risk

3.   To be effective generalists, social workers must be flexible

4.   Highlight 11.11: Social Action on Behalf of the Homeless: Some Considerations

C.   Legal action

1.   *Roe v. Wade* (1973)—women's right to an abortion

2.   *Brown v. Board of Education* (1954)—separate but equal school systems struck down

3.   First Nations Peoples—Court decisions have returned lands or required restitution to the plaintiff tribes

4.   The Americans with Disabilities Act has provided a means for courts to force an end to discrimination against people with disabilities

5.   Class action suits argue that an entire group has been hurt and needs the courts' help to remedy the problem

6.   Finding that the courts will help is an empowering experience for those long used to having no power

7.   Courts tend to be more immune to the political process

8.   Lawsuits can seemingly take forever to run their course, leaving you and your group waiting

9.   When you decide to use legal action to pursue your claim, others may brand you as a troublemaker

10.   Court injunctions are sought when immediate steps are needed to stop an impending action that, if allowed to proceed, could not be undone

VII.   Empowerment

A.   Inherent in both social and legal action is a commitment to the principle of empowerment

B.   Oppression, exploitation, and the absence of alternatives all lower the opportunity to self-determine and can result in social and economic injustice

C.   Sharing power with clients may mean giving clients more role in deciding how agency resources are spent, organizing clients of the agency as a collective and dealing with them as a group, or creating alternative programs

D.   Your expert knowledge is a form of power that can further distance you from clients

E.   Demystifying what you do can empower clients

F.   Another source of power is the legitimate authority vested in you by the state

G.   The strengths perspective, so important to generalist practice, assumes that power resides in people and we should seek it through such things as refusing to label clients, avoiding paternalistic treatment of clients, and trusting clients to make appropriate decisions

Experiential Exercises and Classroom Simulations

Exercise 11.1: Populations-At-Risk

A.   Brief Description
Students discuss what places a population at risk.

B.   Objectives
Students will:
1.   Recognize factors that place a population at risk.
2.   Identify populations that are at risk.

C. Procedure
    1.   Divide class into small groups of 4-6.
    2.   Ask the groups to respond to two questions: Identify at least 5 populations-at-risk served by social workers and what places the population at risk.
    3.   Have each group report back to the larger group and list their responses on the board.

D. Instructions for Students
In groups of 4-6, answer the following two questions:
    1.   Identify at least 5 populations at risk served by social workers.
    2.   What places these populations at risk?
    3.   Report your responses back to the larger group.

E. Commentary
This exercise can be done with any size group including using the entire class as a group.

Exercise 11.2: Advocacy

A. Brief Description
Students discuss various aspects of advocacy.

B. Objectives
Students will:
    1.   Recognize the role of advocacy in improving services to clients.
    2.   Examine advantages and disadvantages of certain forms of advocacy.

C. Procedure
    1.   Divide the class into three groups.
    2.   Assign each group one of the following questions to discuss and decide.
    3.   Ask each group to report their results to the rest of the class.

D. Instructions for Students
Discuss one of the three questions below as assigned by the instructor. Be prepared to report your response back to the entire class.

Advocacy Questions

1. What does it mean to say that advocacy should be designed to increase the accessibility of services for clients?

2. Discuss the advantages and disadvantages of the following two advocacy tactics: persuasion and embarrassing the target.

3. Under what circumstances would political pressure be an appropriate advocacy tactic?

E. Commentary
This exercise can be used with any number of small groups by adding more questions. It can also be used as a discussion starter with the entire class.

Miguel Gonzales is a social worker with A Family Affair, a counseling service for couples and families. During one of his sessions with the Chou Vang family, recent immigrants from Southeast Asia, he learns that the Vang children have been prevented from using the community swimming pool. According to Mrs. Vang, one of the lifeguards has called her children names and said they should go back to their own country. Miguel offers to help the family deal with this situation and agrees to talk to the city's recreation director who oversees the pool. Using the information given you, answer each of the following queries.

1.   Is Miguel engaged in cause advocacy or case advocacy as he seeks to help the Vang family? Explain your answer.

Miguel discovers that the director of recreation believes that the Vang children and other Hmong refugees should not be using the pool because they are not yet U.S. citizens. Miguel decides to challenge the director's decision by enlisting the help of the local Urban League. Together, they picket the swimming pool and invite the media to cover the event.

2.   Does Miguel's strategy fall under the classification of social action? Why or why not?

3.   What would be needed to empower the Vang family to solve this problem by themselves?

4.   Do you consider the Vang family a population-at-risk? Explain your answer.

What Puts a Population at Risk?

Factors which help put a population at risk include physical differences, values and beliefs at variance with other dominant groups in society, and economic conditions. Some populations are at risk because they look, act, or believe differently from the majority, and this difference makes the majority uncomfortable or fearful. This reaction may be based on ignorance or on lack of experience with the at-risk group, so it can often be ameliorated by increasing contact between groups.

When a population is at risk because its members do not hold the same beliefs as the rest of society, the situation can be more difficult to remedy. People who misquote or misuse the bible to define homosexuality as sinful justify their discrimination toward and oppression of gay men and lesbian women. Unrealistic fears about homosexuals in the armed forces are also based on views that highlight differences rather than commonalities.

A group's economic condition also can place it at risk. People of marginal economic standing tend to be less valued in a capitalist society, but economic marginality may be created by institutional behaviors. For example, both government policy and economic goals led to such atrocities as the banishment of Native Americans from their lands and efforts to exterminate tribes and their traditions. The land was considered more valuable than its owners. African Americans were enslaved for economic purposes. Asian Americans were prevented from owning land and discouraged from immigrating here for both social and economic reasons. Finally, women were denied the right to vote and otherwise participate in the political process in part because they were not an economic force in society.

Today, clients receiving public assistance are similarly perceived as economically insignificant except as a drain on tax dollars. This places them at risk. When employers hire two part-time workers rather than one full-time employee to avoid paying such mandatory benefits as health insurance or retirement pensions, they increase the risk to these individuals.

Common Populations-at-Risk

According to Ginsberg, (1992) the groups described below are some of the most-at-risk.

African Americans, for example, have infant mortality rates 80 percent higher than whites. Black males are seven times as likely to die from homicide as white males. Blacks are arrested more frequently for criminal behavior and comprise about one-half of the U.S. prison population, well beyond their representation in the general population. They routinely experience discrimination in employment, education, and other areas of opportunity, nondiscrimination laws and affirmative action policies notwithstanding.

Hispanics are also at risk. They comprise over 25 percent of those in federal prisons, and Hispanic juveniles are being incarcerated at a greater rate than youngsters from other ethnic groups. Trends indicate that Hispanics are moving increasingly to one-parent household status and are less likely to have completed college than either African Americans or whites. Recent efforts to reduce or eliminate welfare benefits for immigrant groups are also affecting Hispanics disproportionately.

Some of the most serious social and health problems in the United States are faced by *Native Americans* and *Alaskan Natives*. Both groups suffer a higher than average incidence of death from causes ranging from cancer to accidents. In fact, deaths from alcoholism and tuberculosis are five to seven times as high among these groups as among whites.

Asian Americans have often been called the model minority because many of them have made great strides in pursuing education and economic success. However, what is true of many Chinese and Japanese is not true for other groups from Southeast Asia. Those who came to the United States after the end of the Vietnam War arrived with few language skills, an agrarian background, and values and behaviors at odds with those of Western society. Their customs sometimes clash with those of whites or African Americans, and they may be seen as rivals for certain types of employment.

Women have always experienced conditions that place them at risk. Early debates about whether women should be able to vote have been supplanted by arguments over a woman's right to control her own body. Women are the primary victims of sexual harassment in the workplace and domestic violence in the home. They receive lower pay for the same jobs, discrimination in certain types of employment, and stereotypes about their performance on the job.

Gay men and lesbians constitute another group at risk. Legal barriers to certain jobs, discrimination in areas as diverse as insurance coverage and child custody, and homophobia constitute just some of the problems facing this group. The anti-homosexual religious and political agendas of some groups represent a major threat to the ability of gay men and lesbians to enjoy the same rights and opportunities available to the rest of our society.

Exercise 11.4: Populations-at-Risk

1. Think about the place where you grew up. List any groups living in your community that you would classify as at-risk and give a brief explanation of why you listed them.

2. Now think about where you are living today. List any groups in your present community that you would classify as at-risk. Again, give your reasons.

3. Is every member of these groups at risk? Explain your answer.

What Is the Role of Social Workers with Populations-at-Risk?

The social work profession is both aware of and well placed to help populations-at-risk. Social workers are likely to witness the devastation caused by prejudice and discrimination. Social workers are aware that institutions such as social agencies can be guilty of insensitivity, poor planning, and outright discrimination against these groups. Agencies purporting to serve an entire community, for example, should be evaluated based on this claim. If an agency fails to live up to its claim, its own workers should pursue remedial action. A community that fails to address problems facing a particular group can also be the target of an appropriate intervention.

Social workers have the skills to help bring about macro system change by preventing conditions that place populations at risk and by advocating on their behalf. This can be done by closely monitoring what goes on in your agency, community, and state—keeping your eyes and ears open, reading the newspaper, attending community forums and public meetings, and looking for evidence of problems. Of course, you don't have to wait for a problem to arise. If you see a change opportunity that will improve the quality of life of populations-at-risk, determine how you might intervene.

Social workers, as described in chapter 10, learn to evaluate programs to determine whether they are effective in achieving their objectives.

Social workers also have mezzo-level skills (highlighted in chapter 3), particularly those associated with teamwork.

Exercise 11.5: Keeping Your Eyes Open

1. Read your local newspaper for three days. Look for examples of populations-at-risk and the problems they are experiencing. Describe the groups you found in the paper and briefly summarize their problems.

2. Look in your community newspaper for an interesting article about a human service-related program. In what ways, if any, does the article discuss the program's services to populations-at-risk? What services are provided?

Advocacy

Social workers have long used advocacy to bring about large-scale change in organizations and communities. Advocacy is clearly consistent with the values of the profession, especially those that support the basic worth and dignity of people and their rights to make their own decisions. In fact, advocacy has been the primary road to achieving civil rights for people of color, those with mental illness, and others with various physical and mental disabilities. Advocacy won minorities and women the right to vote, and it is needed today to ensure that those who have this right exercise it. Of course, advocacy is difficult when economic times are tough. New and expensive programs are usually viewed with skepticism when money is tight.

Exercise 11.6: Assessing Your Experience as an Advocate

In the past you've probably come across situations when it was necessary to advocate for yourself or others. Describe such situation you encountered and list the actions you took. If you took no action, what considerations led you to decide *not* to act? What was the eventual outcome? Looking back, what do you think you should have done to increase your effectiveness?

Agency Commitment to Advocacy

Not every social work agency is committed to advocacy. Shelters for domestic abuse victims are often at the forefront of efforts to protect and enhance the lives of their clients, but other types of agencies have little or no such commitment. Some organizations engage in modest efforts to expand their services to underserved populations, but others do not even inform existing clients about available services.

Without an agency commitment to change, it is very difficult—though not impossible—for an individual worker to undertake large-scale efforts. In such cases, your sanction and motivation for advocacy must stem from your own professional values rather than from agency support.

Exercise 11.7: Organizational Commitment to Advocacy

Identify one organization with which you are familiar that appears committed to advocacy. What does this organization do that makes you believe it supports advocacy?

Identifying Opportunities for Macro-level Advocacy

Opportunities for advocacy are virtually endless. They include extending services to underserved populations, placing clients on the agency's board of directors, hiring staff from populations-at-risk, or changing agency policies that do not support social work values. Public information and education can help combat stereotypes and overcome irrational fears (such as the fear that talking about sex or homosexuality will actually produce sexually active teens or gay men and lesbians). Legal advocacy may be appropriate when legislation is needed to enhance or protect the rights of groups victimized by discrimination.

Exercise 11.8: Macro-level Advocacy Opportunities

Think of one situation which you perceive as an opportunity for macro-level advocacy. Explain why you think this situation represents (1) a problem and (2) an opportunity for advocacy.

Principles of Macro-level Advocacy

The first principle of macro-level advocacy is that it should be designed to increase the accessibility of services to clients. This requires that we look not only at *whether* we serve a population but at *how well* we do so. Offering services that are physically inaccessible, tangled in red tape, or beyond the client's capability to pay denies access.

A second principle is that we advocate for services that enhance and do not detract from people's dignity. Many clients find the conditions and treatment they experience in seeking help humiliating and degrading. Lack of privacy, insensitive treatment by staff, and similar problems undercut efforts to help.

The third principle of advocacy is that it should be aimed at developing services that are available to all who are eligible. Services that assist only one group or that ignore or downplay others' needs should be eliminated.

Exercise 11.9: Applying Principles of Macro-level Advocacy

---

1.   What kinds of conditions or treatment do you define as humiliating, degrading, or damaging to a person's dignity?

2.   Can you think of an experience in which *you* were treated this way? Describe the situation and how you felt at the time.

Guidelines for Macro-level Advocacy

The principles above provide useful direction but they are insufficient to guide the pursuit of macro-level advocacy. Several guidelines can help improve your chances of success in macro advocacy.

- First, be reasonable in what you undertake. Changing an organization often means challenging the beliefs, values, assumptions, or behaviors of those who make up the organization. This can be daunting especially when there is much that needs to be changed. It is usually best to focus on the most achievable objectives and postpone the greater challenges. For example, if you advocate that the agency stay open one evening a week to serve clients who work during the day, you are less likely to meet resistance than if you suggest the agency should stay open until 10:00 p.m. Monday through Friday.

- Second, use teamwork whenever possible. Working in teams takes advantage of the expertise and energies of different groups and agencies, thus maximizing the resources directed at a problem. One person working alone can achieve great things, but a group can usually advocate more effectively than a single person.

- Third, recognize that advocacy sometimes requires that you not be nice. This can be unpleasant, because most of us want to be liked. Constant niceness, however, may require us to ignore very real problems. Being cooperative and ready to compromise may seem a sign of weakness in certain situations. Standing up for those without power is not likely to be popular, especially when you are asking people to change their behavior or to expend resources.

- Fourth, see flexibility as a strength, not a weakness. Sometimes it's best to accept half a loaf if that's all we can get this time around. Advocates must know when they have achieved the maximum benefit from an approach and be willing to change direction as needed.

- Fifth, remember that you win some and you lose some. Even the best advocates sometimes encounter too many barriers or decide that a given end does not justify the means needed to achieve it. Know when to "fold 'em."

- Finally, use a variety of strategies whenever possible. Have both adversarial and cooperative approaches at your disposal, and use them simultaneously or sequentially. If possible, use collaborative strategies first in order to achieve a win-win outcome for both parties. Be prepared, however, to use other advocacy approaches as needed.

Exercise 11.10: Understanding the Guidelines for Advocacy

Select any three of the six guidelines discussed in the section above. For each guideline, describe at least one situation in which it would be helpful in your advocacy efforts.

Advocacy Tactics

Advocacy can include a number of approaches in the repertoire of the generalist social worker—persuasion, fair hearings, grievances and complaints, embarrassing the target, political pressure, and petitioning.

Persuasion is a matter of getting the target system to alter its decisions and/or actions in a way that reflects your goals. This can be accomplished in some cases simply by providing information, especially if the information is new to the target. You can also persuade by questioning your adversaries in a way that forces them to rethink previous positions or decisions. Persuasion is quite effective if you can articulate the arguments on both sides of an issue, because that forces you to anticipate an opponent's arguments and prepare appropriate counterarguments. Persuasion is enhanced by persistence: Persistent people don't forget promises that were made. They follow up to see that what was promised was delivered. What's more, they don't give up when confronted with a setback or when an issue is not quickly resolved.

Fair hearings are administrative procedures available to those who believe they have been denied a benefit or right. Most agencies that receive federal or state money have fair hearing processes in place to consider the appeals of those who have been refused assistance. An outside evaluator (fair hearing examiner) is brought in to hear arguments on both sides. The examiner's decision can uphold either the agency decision or the petitioner's position.

Grievances and *complaints* also challenge decisions made by administrators and others. Grievance and complaint procedures may be outlined in agency policies, union contracts, or laws governing the organization. For example, denial of either civil rights or rights of people with physical disabilities can be met with a complaint filed with state or federal agencies. Sometimes the mere threat of filing such a complaint will force decision-makers to reconsider their positions.

Embarrassing the target is another effective tactic. An advocate can point out in a public forum that the decision-maker's actions are not consistent with previously expressed intentions. In effect, the advocate holds the target up to public ridicule, sometimes by calling media attention to a problem. Letters to newspapers, picket lines, and press releases can all embarrass a target.

Political pressure can also force necessary changes, especially if the advocate is dealing with tax-supported (public) organizations and/or people in political office. In some cases, political office holders themselves can be persuaded to intervene and pressure a public agency to change its policy or practice. Since public organizations draw most of their support from tax money, such an approach of collecting signatures on a form asking an organization, agency, or individual to act in some specified manner may be helpful. Petitions have been used by city residents to oppose massage parlors, request changes in the way property taxes are computed, and demand better police protection. Signatures on petitions can be gathered by going door-to-door or by soliciting them in public spaces such as shopping centers. While petitions are relatively easy to use, their impact on the target system may be less noticeable. To enhance their effectiveness, petitions should be presented to the target at a public meeting where the action is a matter of record.

Exercise 11.11: Using Advocacy Tactics

Five advocacy tactics are described above. Based on the information given in each of the scenarios below, indicate which of the tactics might be most appropriate.

Scenario 1: The state legislature is taking up the issue of property tax reform and is considering shifting financial responsibility for certain public assistance programs from the local community to the state. This would result in lower property taxes for everyone in the community but higher income taxes. You believe this would make the method of paying for welfare fairer and more progressive. Select the advocacy tactic that seems most appropriate for this situation and explain your choice.

Scenario 2: Neighbors in the Elm Terrace section of your community are upset by a proposal to widen their street to allow larger trucks into the area. Many residents are elderly, low-income, and politically inexperienced. Select the advocacy tactic you would use to oppose this proposal. Explain why you chose this tactic.

Scenario 3: Your agency director has been asked to hire at least one new Spanish-speaking worker to work with the growing Hispanic population served by your organization. He isn't convinced that there is sufficient justification for such a hire. As his assistant director, he has kicked the issue down to you for input. Assuming you support this proposal, what tactic would be most appropriate and why?

Scenario 4: Rosa Daniels has been suspended from school because she came to class wearing her hair in the braided fashion popular in Jamaica. Other teenagers are free to wear their hair in the latest fashion. However, the school's principal believes Rosa's hairdo is a sign of gang affiliation. If you were to advise the Daniels family, which advocacy tactic would you suggest and why?

Social Action

Social action, as defined earlier, typically involves more difficult, complex, and confrontational approaches to problem solving. It may be used in combination with advocacy or when more collaborative efforts fail. Because of its more confrontational aspects, social action raises ethical issues and differences of opinion.

One of the more militant approaches to social action was formulated by Saul Alinsky (1971). Alinsky believed deeply in the concept of power as a key to social change. Only those with power are in a position to control their environment. Power may come from money or from people (because when enough people support an idea, they have power). Alinsky's strategy was to acquire power by organizing people in their own interests. He also argued that sometimes the illusion of power is enough, since it is the appearance of power that matters. Thus, it can be important for others to think that you have more power than you actually do.

According to Alinsky, power is not given to people but is acquired when they take it from those who have it. He believed that people with power do not give it up willingly, and therefore the more confrontational aspects of social action are necessary. Alinsky observed that all organizations have rules—policies, laws, or other regulations—by which they *say* they abide. He taught that by making organizations operate in accordance with their own rules, an activist could ensure fairness and improve the quality of services provided. He achieved his goal by embarrassing the target—by showing that people were not following their own rules. Another Alinsky rule was to organize around issues that are vital to people. If an issue is not considered very important, it is not a suitable cause for social action. He also firmly believed in using political pressure to create change.

Perhaps the most controversial Alinksy rule was to paint the issues as a conflict between good and evil, or the haves and the have-nots, thus positioning yourself as moral and good and suggesting that your opponent is immoral and bad. The final Alinsky suggestion is to propose an alternative. It is not sufficient to simply complain—you must suggest a better way of doing things.

Concerns about Social Action

More recent writers have suggested that Alinsky's ideas are somewhat dated (Zippay, 1994). Zippay notes that enemies are harder to identify today, situations are more complex, and technology and media are more influential than they were 30 years ago. Community problems can rarely be solved solely by local resources. External resources are needed in many situations because cash-strapped communities lack the ability to create massive programs. Zippay urges working collaboratively with business and civic leaders to bring about change. Skills such as fund-raising, lobbying, legislative advocacy, and the ability to work with local groups are the route to successful social action.

Exercise 11.12: Understanding Alinsky

---

1. Saul Alinsky believed that power and the appearance of power are critical elements to the success of social action. Do you agree or disagree with his perspective? Give your reasons.

2. Another Alinsky rule was that you always paint issues as a conflict between good and evil or the haves and have-nots. Do you agree with this argument in a current context? Give your reasons.

Legal Action

Legal action involves using the court system to resolve issues or to force changes that otherwise would not occur. Recent history shows the influence of legal action on a number of issues from a woman's right to an abortion to the now discredited "separate but equal" school system. Similarly, Native Americans have used the court system to force restoration of tribal lands stolen many years ago. Courts are also the place where those who refuse to obey the law are called to task. For example, those who discriminate against protected classes or people with disabilities may find themselves in court. Courts are used to force obedience to specific laws, to requirements of the U.S. Constitution (such as due process), or to settle disputes of a contractual nature. The civil courts provide an alternative to criminal courts in some cases, and the class action suit is a frequently used tool in civil court. This type of suit argues that an entire group of people has been harmed. For example, women paid lower wages by an employer may file suit charging sex discrimination and naming all women employees (past and present) as part of the class seeking the court's help. Courts can also be used to challenge a law that you believe is unconstitutional or overly vague (and therefore unenforceable).

Sometimes, courts are used to force organizations to obey their own rules and policies. For example, an agency might be taken to court for firing a worker without letting him know why. If the agency policies require that workers be given the opportunity to correct poor performance, the court may find that the organization has failed to live up to its own rules.

Even the threat of using the courts to settle disputes or create change can prove effective. The expense, bother, and embarrassment of going to court are often sufficient to bring the other side to the bargaining table. Finding that the courts can be used to help achieve group goals can be very empowering. Generally speaking, courts are less susceptible to the political process than are other elected officials, so they are unlikely to be swayed by phone calls, letters, contributions, and other means that might persuade other political leaders. This can be both an advantage and a disadvantage. On the one hand, the decision of the court will be based as much as possible on legal issues, and your opponent will be less able to use political clout. On the other hand, you also lose the ability to influence the judge.

A very real disadvantage to using the courts is the time involved. Court decisions may not come for several months or years. Of course, if your group benefits from the delay the time issue may be moot. You may be able to use the time to get a law changed or to force your opponent to expend more resources. Residents of the City of Yarg were opposed to the newly proposed nuclear power plant to be built on the edge of the community. Not only would it consume a sizeable chunk of lakefront property known for its scenic beauty, but many residents were opposed to nuclear power for environmental reasons and out of ordinary fear. Residents and environmentalists together went to court to block construction of the power plant citing several federal laws as the basis for their lawsuit. The court case took so long to resolve that the electric power company scrapped the project. The time delay had added unacceptable costs to the project and the company suffered a black eye in public opinion because of all the publicity. In addition, new regulations on nuclear power had been developed while the case dragged on and greater attention was focused on the problem of disposing of nuclear waste.

Another potential disadvantage to using the courts is the cost. Attorney fees can mount up quickly for both sides, and it is not always possible to get attorneys who will work pro bono (free). On the other hand, your opponent is also going to have to pay for an attorney.

Using the courts is very confrontational and can label you a troublemaker, but if you are certain this is the most effective means at your disposal, don't be intimidated.

Exercise 11.13: Taking Legal Action

1.   Identify at least one social issue that has been affected by court decisions in your lifetime. What is your opinion about each decision?

2.   Assess the advantages and disadvantages of using the legal system to bring about social change.

Empowerment

We indicated earlier that using the court system can be an empowering experience, especially for those who are typically powerless in society. Empowerment, as Hartman (1993, p. 365) notes, is "the right to power, ability, and authority to achieve self-determination." Although empowerment is supported by social work values, practitioners cannot always achieve it in work with client systems. Those with less power in society are often the most in need of being empowered. There are many ways to empower clients. We can demystify what we do by explaining precisely how our agency works and what needs to be done, and by encouraging the client system to carry out tasks rather than doing it for them. Allowing client systems to make their own choices and keeping them informed of their options and their progress will increase their sense of power.

Group approaches to problem solving that emphasize collaboration are also potentially very empowering. Participating in a group creates a sense of connection, and finding that other people share one's problems and concerns lessens the sense of isolation. It also multiplies the energy, time, and other resources directed at a problem. Effective empowerment unlocks the natural ability of client systems to solve their own problems, use their unique skills and abilities, and make their own decisions.

Sam Woodson, a worker in your agency has just come back from a workshop on empowerment. Grousing about the new emphasis on empowerment, he says, "It's really crazy, you know? There are *no ways* to empower our clients. For crying out loud, this is a *nursing home* and now the Director of Social Services wants us to empower our clients." You disagree with Sam. Offer at least two arguments and two examples of how it is possible to empower nursing home residents:

1.   Argument:

      Example:

2.   Argument:

      Example:

Legislative Advocacy

Previous sections of this chapter covered case and cause advocacy. Legislative advocacy is an effort to change legislation to benefit some particular category of clients. In this sense, it is a form of cause advocacy, focused—at its most basic level—on getting legislators to pass laws you want enacted. (The term *legislator* in this section refers to both federal and state lawmakers.)

Passing new laws, of course, is not the only form of legislative advocacy. We can, for example, work to defeat proposed bills or eliminate existing laws that we think are harmful. We can also seek increased funding for existing programs or attempt to get portions of a law modified in some way. For instance, social workers in several states worked diligently to establish certification and licensing laws for those practicing social work.

There is nothing magical about legislative advocacy. Legislators are responsible to those who elected them and must stand for election on a regular basis. Thus, they are interested in the views of those they represent. At the same time, legislators often have inadequate information on which to base their decisions. If they never hear from their constituents and the only views expressed to them come from professional lobbyists, who is to blame if we disapprove of their votes? (Many lobbyists work for organizations whose agendas we agree with and even support, but they may nevertheless be unaware of their legislation's effects on our clients.) Bills are sometimes so complex that even legislators don't understand all aspects of a proposed law. The need to supply legislators with important information is a major point of access for social workers. It is well known that legislators are often influenced by a handful of letters about a bill. Some legislators are reputed to count the letters they receive on each side of an issue and use this information to determine how to vote. Let your legislator know what you think about a bill. Enlist colleagues or clients to share their opinions. Clients, the ones directly affected by a bill, are too often the last ones to know about it and are unlikely to contact lawmakers. Don't ignore this potential source of support.

Skills needed for legislative advocacy include sensitivity and awareness of the factors that affect the legislative process: What will it cost to implement a bill? How popular is it with the public? Bills that benefit obscure groups or are expensive are less likely to find legislative support. A bill that requires authorities to notify neighbors if a convicted child sex offender moves into the neighborhood is more likely to pass than one that provides expensive treatment for the offender.

Once a bill has been drafted, become an expert on it. Find out who has taken or is likely to take a stand on the bill, how much implementation of the bill will cost, and what advantages or disadvantages passage will have for your clients. Identifying, obtaining, and maintaining sponsors for a bill is the next step, and you need to know whom to contact for support.

List those supporting your bill, those opposed, and those who are neutral to the idea. Both neutral legislators and opponents can be persuaded, so don't ignore them. Recognize that support for a bill may come from outside the legislature. Professional organizations such as NASW, social service providers, and other community groups may support (or oppose) a given piece of legislation, and these groups may employ lobbyists who are familiar with both the process and the legislators. In addition, the governor or president and the various federal or state agencies affected by the bill may be actively working for or against its passage.

Lobbying for passage of the bill can include writing, telephoning, e-mailing, telegraphing, or speaking directly to legislators or their staffs. Try to work with other interest groups who support the law.

Educating the public is another facet of legislative advocacy. While the public is not interested in many bills, the perspectives of the average citizen should not be ignored. Opposition to certain bills can be increased, especially when the general public has strong views that are not being heeded by their legislators. Public support for bills can be garnered if people know about a proposed law and are helped to express their opinions. For example, a social worker could stimulate public awareness of a bill by writing letters to the newspapers, holding public meetings to discuss a topic, and, if appropriate, going door-to-door with leaflets that provide additional information. One social worker who was concerned about proposed welfare reform legislation pending in the state legislature, spoke on the topic at the public library. He and his colleagues advertised the meeting by word of mouth and by posting flyers in area churches and restaurants. Those who attended learned much more about the welfare reform proposals, had an opportunity to share their views, and left with additional written information including the names, addresses, and phone numbers of their elected representatives.

Influencing legislative committees is crucial. These bodies discuss, often modify, and hopefully act on the bill. A favorable decision by the committee or subcommittee means that a bill will be sent to the entire body for a debate and a vote. Of course, a committee can decide to kill a bill by voting against it or by simply not getting around to discussing it.

If you write to your legislators, use the correct form and address for such letters. Some common addresses and the accompanying salutations appear below:

Letters to the president:
> The President
> The White House
> 1600 Pennsylvania Ave., NW
> Washington, DC 20500

Salutation: Dear Mr./Ms. President:

Letters to U.S. Senators:
> The Honorable (insert full name)
> United States Senate
> Washington, DC 20510

Salutation: Dear Senator (insert last name):

Letters to members of the House of Representatives:
> The Honorable (insert full name)
> U.S. House of Representatives
> Washington, DC 20515

Salutation: Dear Representative (insert last name):

A current list of your elected representatives at all levels from local to national can be found at most public libraries or by checking with city hall. If possible, open your letter by telling the officials that you are pleased with some action they have taken. Starting on a positive note is more persuasive than berating the person for disappointing you. State your purpose clearly and explain precisely what you would like the recipient to do. Give reasons for your position and request. Be polite and respectful of the person's position even if you disagree 100 percent with all of that person's decisions. Always thank legislators or executives for considering your views and invite them to share with you their perspectives.

Exercise 11.15: Advocating with Legislators

1. Give two reasons why legislators are interested in the views of their constituents.

2. Respond to Jack, another social worker, who says that the proposed new licensing bill for social workers is so well written that there is no need for any amendments. He argues that your coalition of social work groups should convey this message to the bill's sponsor. How would you respond to Jack?

3. Your friend Melanie is very unhappy about the new welfare bill going through your state legislature. She confides to you that she is writing a letter to the President really blasting this bill. What would you say to Melanie?

4. Write a letter to your U.S. Senator Mortimer Snerd asking him to support changes to the welfare bill that would provide two full years of child care for every client going off public assistance and taking a job that pays less than $9 per hour. Senator Snerd is an influential member of the senate public welfare committee currently considering the bill. Suggest changes and present your arguments. Keep your letter under one page in length.

Chapter 12
Ethics and Ethical Dilemmas in Macro Practice

I. **Introduction**

II. **Professional Values and Ethics in Macro Contexts**

    A.   Values are what you consider good or desirable

    B.   Ethics are sets of principles that guide the behavior of professionals

    C.   Five dimensions of ethical decision making (Cournoyer)

        1.   Understand those legal duties that apply to all professional helpers

        2.   Be familiar with the state, local, and federal laws and regulations that affect the profession and practice of social work in your locale

        3.   Thoroughly comprehend the core social work values and be extremely familiar with the social work code of ethics

        4.   Be able to identify those ethical principles and legal duties that pertain to specific social work practice situations

        5.   When several competing obligations apply, you need to be able to decide which take precedence

    D.   Ethical dilemmas

III. **The NASW Code of Ethics**

    A.   Highlight 12.1: A Summary of the Ethical Standards in the NASW Code of Ethics

    B.   The social workers' ethical responsibilities to clients

        1.   1.01: Commitment to clients—the client should come first

        2.   1.02: Self-determination—requires that clients know what the resources and choices are and the consequences of selecting any of them

        3.   1.03: Informed consent—means that clients know the risks of social work services or other interventions, limitations imposed by managed care, costs of service, alternatives that are available, and their right to refuse to participate

        4.   1.04: Competence—you must use interventions for which you have appropriate training or education

5.   1.05: Cultural competence and social diversity—strive to identify and appreciate the strengths inherent in any particular culture and recognize differences among cultures

      a.   Highlight 12.2: Ethical Boundaries and Spirituality

            1)   Religion—involves people's spiritual beliefs concerning the origin, character, and reason for being, usually based on the existence of some higher power or powers. These beliefs often include designated rituals and provide direction for what is considered moral or right

            2)   Spirituality—the individual search for meaning, purpose, and values that typically rises above everyday physical limitations and connects one to something greater than oneself

            3)   Social workers must develop sensitivity and competence in dealing with spiritual diversity, just as in dealing with cultural diversity

6.   1.06: Conflicts of interest—situations where the client's benefit is actually or potentially compromised by an action of the social worker

      a.   Dual or multiple relationships—occur when professionals assume two or more roles at the same time or sequentially with a client (such as blending a professional and nonprofessional relationship)

      b.   Examples of dual relationships include providing counseling to a relative or a friend's relative, socializing with clients, becoming emotionally or sexually involved with a client or former client

      c.   One of the more problematic areas of dual relationships is when a social worker is providing services to multiple people who have relationships with each other

7.   1.07: Privacy and confidentiality

      a.   Privacy—people's right to be free from other people's intrusion in their personal affairs

            1)   Information a social worker seeks should be clearly related to providing service, not information sought out of pure curiosity

            2)   Information learned from a client must be maintained in confidence

      b.   Confidentiality—the ethical principle that workers should not share information provided by or about a client unless that worker has the client's explicit permission to do so. This confidentiality is not absolute

    c.   New NASW Code of Ethics' references concerning how clients should be reported under certain circumstances: *"However, social workers' responsibility to the larger society or specific legal obligations may on limited occasions supersede the loyalty owed clients, and clients should be so advised. (Examples include when a social worker is required by law to report that a client has abused a child or has threatened to harm self or others) (NASW, 1999, 1.01)"*

    d.   The use of computers for maintaining records has opened up other possibilities for breaching confidentiality

8.   1.08: Access to records—clients should have reasonable access to records that concern them

9.   1.09: Sexual relationships—explicitly prohibits sexual activities or contact between current or former clients and workers, regardless of whether it is consensual. The prohibition extends to client's relatives or others with whom the client has a close relationship. It is also inappropriate to provide professional services to a client with whom one has had a prior sexual relationship

10.   1.10: Physical contact—it is prohibited; appropriate "culturally sensitive" physical contact is permitted as long as the worker sets clear boundaries for such contact

11.   1.11: Sexual harassment—explicitly prohibited and includes such actions as solicitation for sexual favors, verbal or physical sexually tinged contact, and advances

12.   1.12: Derogatory language—social workers are not to use derogatory language in any of their communication about or with clients

13.   1.13: Payment for services—social workers are responsible for establishing fair and reasonable fees that reflect accurately the services provided

14.   1.14: Clients who lack decision-making capacity—when you must act on behalf of clients with diminished capacities, it is critical that you take all reasonable actions to protect the clients' interests

15.   1.15: Interruption of services—continuity of service is an obligation of the worker that requires that appropriate efforts be made to ensure clients get services they need

16.   1.16: Termination of services—should occur when the professional relationship is no longer necessary or when it no longer is beneficial

C.   Social workers' ethical responsibilities to colleagues

1.   2.01: Respect—required to treat colleagues with respect and never to misrepresent the competence and views of their coworkers

2.   2.02: Confidentiality—obligated to maintain in confidence information provided by colleagues in their professional capacity

3.   2.03: Interdisciplinary collaboration—the well-being of clients is the primary basis for collaboration among professionals on an interdisciplinary team

4.   2.04: Disputes involving colleagues—never take advantage of a dispute involving colleagues and their employers for their own interests nor exploit clients in disputes with colleagues

5.   2.05: Consultation—the act of seeking help from someone with expertise in a subject to devise a plan or solve a problem, should involve only a colleague, administrator, or another person who has the appropriate competence or experience

6.   2.06: Referral for services—requires that the worker take steps to ensure an effective referral including, with clients' permission, providing all appropriate information

7.   2.07: Sexual relationships—between supervisors and supervisees are prohibited, as are such activities between students and field supervisors or in any other situation where one worker exercises authority over another. Sexual relationships between colleagues in other situations that may create a conflict of interest should be avoided

8.   2.08: Sexual harassment—workers are not to engage in sexual harassment of supervisees, students, or colleagues

9.   2.09: Impairment of colleagues—if you are aware of a colleague's impairment or incompetence, you must consult with that individual (if possible) and help the person seek help

10.   2.10: Incompetence of colleagues—if you are aware of a colleague's impairment or incompetence, you must consult with that individual (if possible) and help the person seek help

11.   2.11: Unethical conduct of colleagues—whenever possible you are obligated to prevent, expose, or otherwise discourage the unethical behavior of colleagues

D.   Social workers' ethical responsibilities in practice settings

1.   3.01: Supervision and consultation—no one should purport to provide either without the requisite knowledge and skill, and both consultants and supervisors should operate only within their specific areas of knowledge and competence

2.   3.02: Education and training—teachers, trainers, and field instructors are required to base their instruction on the most up-to-date information available, and only operate within their areas of competence

3.   3.03: Performance evaluation—evaluators are obliged to conduct their evaluations in a fair manner, based upon clear performance criteria, and in a way that is considerate of the person being evaluated

4. 3.04: Client records—ensure that documentation in records is accurate and clearly identifies the services given

5. 3.05: Billing—ensure accurate representation of the type and extent of services provided and clearly identify the service provider

6. 3.06: Client transfer—prior to accepting a client for service, the social worker should determine whether the client has an on-going professional relationship with another service provider

7. 3.07: Administration—social work administrators are responsible for advocating for sufficient resources to meet client needs, and to ensure adequate staff supervision, and that the employing environment supports compliance with the code

8. 3.08: Continuing education and staff development—both administrators and supervisors are responsible for providing or arranging continuing education and staff development for those they supervise

9. 3.09: Commitment to employers—adhere to commitments to employing organizations and to do our best to improve agency policy, procedures, and services provided to clients

    a. Help make employers aware of our obligations under the code of ethics and of the code's impact on social work practice

    b. When there is a conflict between policies and the code, the worker is obliged to seek changes in the former

    c. It is the social worker's responsibility to prevent or end discrimination in employment practices or work assignments

    d. The social worker is expected to make appropriate use of agency resources, conserve funds when possible, and never to employ funds for unintended purposes

10. 3.10: Labor-management disputes—the code of ethics specifically allows social workers to participate in labor unions to improve both services to clients and working conditions

E. Social workers' ethical responsibilities as professionals

1. 4.01: Competence—it is imperative that we accept employment or professional responsibilities only when we have the ability to perform those duties satisfactorily

2. 4.02: Discrimination

    a. Social workers are expressly forbidden to engage in any form of discrimination based upon race, ethnicity, religion, age, sex, disability, marital status, national origin, color, sexual orientation, or political belief

b. Highlight 12.3 Combating Your Own Stereotypes and Prejudices

    1) Carefully observe and monitor your thoughts when interacting with anyone belonging to a group with characteristics significantly different from your own

    2) Identify exactly how you treat this person differently

    3) Gradually change your behavior toward the identified person, bringing it more in line with your behavior toward "nondifferent" people

    4) Monitor your progress in combating your stereotypes and prejudices

    5) Maintain a perspective that appreciates and respects both individual and cultural differences

3. 4.03: Private conduct—social workers must not allow their private conduct to interfere with their professional responsibilities

4. 4.04: Dishonesty, fraud, and deception—have no place in the practice of social work

5. 4.05: Impairment—must not let these difficulties interfere with their professional performance or harm those to whom they have a professional obligation

6. 4.06: Misrepresentation—must be careful to not allow statements or actions as private citizens to be misconstrued as representing the social work profession or one's employing agency

7. 4.07: Solicitations—should not solicit clients in any way that takes advantage of their vulnerability nor should you ask clients to provide testimonials of your service to them

8. 4.08: Acknowledging credit—claiming credit for work that you have not done or submitting as your own work done by others is a violation of the code

F. Social workers' ethical responsibilities to the social work profession

1. 5.01: Integrity of the profession—seek to promote and maintain the highest practice standards

2. 5.02: Evaluation and research—ensure that your own practice reflects the best practices of your profession

G. Social workers' ethical responsibilities to the broader society

   1. 6.01: Social welfare—social workers are expected to act to benefit the general welfare of society at all levels

   2. 6.02: Public participation—social workers should encourage the public's involvement in the development and improvement of public policy

   3. 6.03: Public emergencies—social workers should offer their professional services to the extent possible and with consideration of the needs of the public

   4. 6.04: Social and political action—the goals of providing people equal access to all critical societal resources require that social workers pursue appropriate political and social action

IV. **Personal Values**

   A. It is important to separate your personal values from professional, objective judgments in the macro context

   B. When confronted with any macro situation, you must carefully identify your personal values and distinguish them from what is in your client system's best interest from that system's own perspective

V. **Types of Ethical Issues Confronting Agency Workers**

VI. **Ethical Absolutism versus Ethical Relativism**

   A. Ethical absolutism—assumes that moral laws exist to govern ethical decision making in virtually any situation

   B. Ethical relativism—requires the evaluation of any particular action on the basis of its potential consequences. The emphasis is on *results* rather than on *principles*

VII. **Ethical Dilemmas**

   A. Ethical dilemmas—problematic situations whose possible solutions all offer imperfect and unsatisfactory answers

   B. In an ethical dilemma, we are faced with a situation in which a decision must be made under circumstances that set two or more ethical principles in conflict

VIII. **Facing an Ethical Dilemma: Decision-Making Steps**

   A. Figure 12.1: Conceptualizing an Ethical Dilemma

   B. Step 1: Recognize the problem

   C. Step 2: Investigate the variables

   D. Step 3: Get feedback from others

E.   Step 4: Appraise the values that apply to the dilemma

F.   Step 5: Evaluate the dilemma

G.   Step 6: Identify and think about possible alternatives

H.   Step 7: Weigh the pros and cons of each alternative

I.   Step 8: Make your decision

IX.   Ranking Ethical Principles

A.   Reamer's guide to ethical decision-making

1.   Rules about basic survival supersede rules governing lesser actions

2.   One person's right to well-being supersedes another person's right to self-determination

3.   One person's right to self-determination supersedes that same person's right to well-being

4.   Obeying rules you have agreed to support supersedes the right to freely break these rules

5.   People's right to well-being supersedes adherence to rules you have agreed to support

6.   Preventing harm and fulfilling basic needs supersedes withholding your own property

7.   Postscript

B.   Dolgoff, Loewenberg, and Harrington's "Ethical Principles Screen"

1.   Figure 12.2: A Hierarchy of Ethical Rights: ETHICS for U

a.   **E—Exist** with their basic needs met (Life)

b.   **T—Treatment** that is fair and equal (Equality)

c.   **H—Have** free choice and freedom (Autonomy)

d.   **I—Injury** that is minimal or nonexistent (Least harm)

e.   **C—Cultivate** a good quality of life (Quality of life)

f.   **S—Secure** their privacy and confidentiality (Privacy)

g.   **U—Understand** the truth and receive available information (Truthfulness)

262

2.	Principle 1: People have the right to *Exist* with their basic needs met (life)

3.	Principle 2: People have the right to *Treatment* that is fair and equal (equality)

4.	Principle 3: People have the right to *Have* free choice and freedom (autonomy)

5.	Principle 4: People have the right to *Injury* that is minimal or nonexistent (least harm)

6.	Principle 5: People have a right to *Cultivate* a good quality of life (quality of life)

7.	Principle 6: People have the right to *Secure* their privacy and confidentiality (privacy)

8.	Principle 7: People have the right to *Understand* the truth and receive available information (truthfulness)

## X.	Ethical Dilemmas in Macro Contexts

A.	Distributing limited resources (four variables to consider when trying to make the right distribution of scarce resources, Reamer, 1995)

1.	Equality

2.	Need

3.	Compensation

4.	Contribution

B.	Community support (or the lack thereof) for service provision

C.	Relationships with colleagues

1.	Choices when dealing with colleagues' unethical behavior (Dolgoff, et al., 2005)

a.	You can simply ignore the behavior, the "out of sight, out of mind" attitude

b.	Approach the colleague yourself and share your concerns with him or her informally

c.	You can inform your supervisor about the situation

d.	In the event that the colleague is an NASW member, you can bring the unethical behavior to the attention of the local NASW chapter for censure

e.	You can bring it to the attention of the state licensing board for professional social workers

f.	Consider whistle-blowing

263

2.   Highlight 12.4: Whistle Blowing

      a.   Whistle-blowing—the act of informing on another or making public an individual's, group's, or organization's corrupt, wrong, illegal, inefficient, or hazardous behavior

      b.   The choice of whether to blow the whistle should be based upon the seriousness and the harm involved, the quality of the evidence of wrongdoing, the impact on both the agency and the perpetrator, the motivation of the whistle-blower and other options available

      c.   Before blowing the whistle on agency or colleagues, consider four questions

          1)   How great is the threat to the potential victims?

          2)   What type and quality of proof do you have available that the wrongdoing has occurred or is going on?

          3)   Will less severe alternative measures remedy the problem?

          4)   Can you assume the burden of risk?

      d.   Recommendations to consider before blowing the whistle

          1)   Be certain that you clearly define the variables and issues involved

          2)   Know what your rights are

          3)   Be prepared for the consequences

          4)   Follow the chain of command

          5)   Establish a clearly defined plan of action

D.   Engaging in sexual activities with clients

E.   Neglecting child maltreatment

F.   Highlight 12.5: Negative Responsibility

      1.   Positive responsibility—responsibility for your own behavior

      2.   Negative responsibility—you are also responsible for those actions you choose *not* to take

G.   Incompetence due to personal problems

H.   Conforming to agency policy

I. Highlight 12.6: Agency Policy and Ethics in a Multicultural Context

    1. Recommendations for applying ethical principles in multicultural contexts (Pack-Brown & Williams, 2003)

        a. Anticipate potential conflict

        b. Assess the cultural sensitivity of your ethical code

        c. Balance culture and the ethical code

    2. Cultural encapsulation—the perspective characterized by defining reality according to one set of cultural assumptions, insensitivity to cultural variations, irrational adherence to one's own beliefs as being the only right ones, and an overly simplified view of both reality and problem resolution

    3. Ten conditions that tend to characterize cultural encapsulation in agencies and their staffs (Pedersen, 2000, 2002)

        a. All persons are measured according to the same hypothetical "normal" standards of behavior, irrespective of their culturally different contexts

        b. Individualism is presumed to be more appropriate than a collectivist perspective in all settings

        c. Professional boundaries are narrowly defined, and interdisciplinary cooperation is discouraged

        d. Psychological health is described primarily in abstractions [using technical jargon and vague labels], with little or no attention to [how people effectively function in their unique] cultural context

        e. Dependency [on others including family or community members] is always considered to be an undesirable or even a neurotic condition

        f. A person's support system is not normally considered relevant to any analysis of the person's psychological health

        g. Only linear, "cause-effect" thinking is accepted as scientific and appropriate

        h. The individual is usually or always expected to adjust to fit the system

        i. The historical roots of a person's background are disregarded or minimalized

        j. The [social worker] presumes her- or himself to be free of racism and cultural bias

J.   Breaching confidentiality in a macro context

    1.   Absolute confidentiality—the clients' confidence will not be broken no matter what

    2.   Relative confidentiality—professional practitioners may have to break confidentiality under compelling circumstances

    3.   Eight common reasons for breaking confidentiality

        a.   When a court appoints a social worker to evaluate a person, that worker is obligated to provide the court with information about the client

        b.   In the event that a worker determines that a client is a potential suicide risk, that worker should inform the appropriate helping body

        c.   When a client sues a social worker, such as for malpractice, the worker may have to share information about the client

        d.   When a client introduces "mental condition" as a claim or defense in a court action, the worker may be forced to respond to this claim

        e.   Workers must report confidential information in the event that a minor is being maltreated

        f.   A worker must report information and get help for a client who the worker suspects has such a severe mental condition that she requires hospitalization

        g.   When otherwise confidential information is made an issue in court, a worker must respond

        h.   Social workers must report to the appropriate authorities when a client reveals that she is going to harm someone else

    4.   Communication with other professionals

    5.   Administrative record-keeping

    6.   Insurance company requirements

    7.   Police concerns

K.   Co-optation versus cooperation

    1.   Co-optation—refers to eliminating opposition to a cause, plan, or organization by assimilating opponents into the group favoring the cause, plan, or organization

    2.   Cooperation—involves different factions working together to achieve some mutually agreed-upon goal without either faction losing its own identity

L.   Conflict of interest

M.   Potential harm to participants

N.   Stigmatization tactics

    1.   Stigmatization—identifying or describing someone or something in disgraceful, contemptuous, or reproachful terms

    2.   Recognize realistically that there are few permanent friends, allies, or enemies in a professional context

O.   Furthering ethical practice in agency settings

Experiential Exercises and Classroom Simulations

Exercise 12.1:NASW Code of Ethics

A.   Brief Description
Students discuss core values of the Code of Ethics and relate the Loewenberg and Dolgoff hierarchy of ethical principles to the Code.

B.   Objectives
Students will:
1.   Recognize core values undergirding the NASW Code of Ethics.
2.   Relate the work of Loewenberg and Dolgoff to the Code

C.   Procedure
1.   Use this exercise with the entire class as a discussion starter.
2.   Ask students to identify each of the six core values underpinning the Code of Ethics.
3.   Place these core values on the board and ask the students to define each of them using their own words.
4.   Ask students how the Loewenberg and Dolgoff hierarchy of ethical principles can be used by a social worker adhering to the Code of Ethics.

D.   Instructions for Students
Not applicable.

E.   Commentary
This exercise can be done in six small groups, with each asked to define one of the values underlying the Code of Ethics, and identifying one way in which the Loewenberg and Dolgoff hierarchy of ethical principles can be employed to assist a social worker to abide by the Code of Ethics.

Exercise 12.2: Using an Ethical Screens

A. Brief Description
Students discuss the use of ethical screens for making appropriate practice decisions.

B. Objectives
Students will:
1. Utilize an ethical screen for making an appropriate practice decision.
2. Identify situations where organizational guidelines clash with ethical principles.

C. Procedure
1. Divide the class into groups of 4-6 students.
2. Give each group the scenario noted in the box below and ask them to decide as a group what action is appropriate.
3. Ask each group to report back to the entire class.

D. Instructions for Students
In your groups, review the case situation below. Discuss your response to the case and what you would advise Manny and his social worker to do.

Using Ethical Screens
Manny H. has told his social worker that he intends to hurt his ex-girlfriend who he says "dumped him" for another guy. According to Loewenberg and Dolgoff, a client has a right to autonomy and self-determination, confidentiality and privacy. Yet the social worker is concerned about possible harm to Manny's ex-girlfriend. What principles from the ethical screen would apply here? Manny's agency has a policy that attempts to ensure absolute confidentiality to clients and discourages workers from talking about cases with other agencies without a written release of information from the client. What should Manny and the social worker do?

E. Commentary
The exercise can be used with a large group to get discussion going. Additional scenarios can also be created by the instructor with a different one being given to each group of students.

Exercise 12.3: Making Decisions about Limited Resources

Resources are consistently limited, and they appear to be shrinking continuously (Reamer, 1987). Hard decisions must frequently be made regarding what is more necessary and what is less necessary. Choosing some things probably means giving up others. Read the following vignette and answer the questions that follow.

The family services agency where you work counseling survivors of domestic violence has suffered significant budget cuts. The agency administration has indicated that it will eliminate some services in order to stay afloat. Potentially targeted programs include day-care for working parents, sex education and contraception counseling for teens, or the thriving but expensive foreign adoptions program. The agency's other alternatives might include elimination of your own domestic violence program, decreasing staff for all programs including your own, or significantly cutting workers' salaries (including your own) across the board.

The community has depended on your agency's provision of its various services for many years. Thus, adequate alternate services do not exist in your community.

1.   Which principles in *ETHICS for U* might apply to this situation?

2.   How can you use the Ethical Principles Screen in deciding how best to cut expenses?

3.   As a social worker, what would *you* do in this situation?

**Exercise 12.4: Unethical Behavior on the Part of Colleagues—
Sexual Involvement with Clients**

On one hand, the NASW Code of Ethics dictates that professional social workers "should treat colleagues with respect" (NASW, 1996). On the other hand, it emphasizes that "the worker's primary responsibility is to promote the well-being of clients" in addition to strictly forbidding engagement "in sexual activities or sexual contact with current clients" (NASW, 1996).

Read the following vignette and answer the questions that follow.

You see a professional colleague engaging in what you consider unethical behavior. Twice you have seen him out in the community on dates with women you know to be his clients. It would be very uncomfortable for you to confront him about this behavior. Informing your supervisor seems like tattling.

1.   Which ethical principles in *ETHICS for U* might apply to this situation?

2.   How can you use the principles' ranking in deciding what to do in this situation?

3.   As a social worker, what would *you* do in this situation?

Exercise 12.5: To Blow the Whistle or Not to Blow the Whistle? That Is the Question

---

Whistle-blowing means "alerting those in positions of higher authority in an organization about the existence of practices that are illegal, wasteful, dangerous, or otherwise contrary to the organization's stated policies" (Barker, 1991, p. 250). It means taking the problem outside the organization and making it known to others, possibly the general public.

Whistle-blowing carries a degree of risk that varies in direct proportion to the seriousness of the allegations. Airing "dirty laundry" outside an agency can be very threatening to people who run the agency. All agencies have problems of one sort or another, just as all individuals have problems. People responsible for agency activity do not like the negative aspects of this activity to be displayed for all to see. Such exposure reflects badly on the agency and its administration because the implication—perhaps rightly—is that the administration is at fault. As a result, whistle-blowers have been fired, reassigned to insignificant responsibilities at remote locations, harassed into quitting, and even blacklisted as troublemakers in the professional community. In short, administrators and other people in power can make a whistle-blower's life extremely miserable.

Nevertheless, sometimes whistle-blowing is necessary, especially after other less extreme measures (such as discussing the problem with the agency administration) have already been tried and failed. It may be an ethical imperative "when the violations of policy or law seriously threaten the welfare of others" (Reamer, 1990, p. 219).

There are several factors to consider before blowing the whistle: How serious is the actual threat to potential victims? What type and quality of proof do you have that wrongdoing has occurred? Could the problem be addressed and solved in some other way? To what degree will whistle-blowing put you at risk of such negative consequences as ostracism by other staff or loss of your job (Reamer, 1990)? It is critical to weigh the pros and cons of each alternative to determine your most viable course of action.

If you do decide to blow the whistle:

1. Clearly define the variables: the proof of your allegations and the specific rules being breached.
2. Know your rights and the agency's grievance procedures.
3. Prepare yourself for possible consequences such as reprimands and ostracism.
4. Follow all steps specified by agency policy for raising issues and follow the chain of command.
5. Establish a clearly defined plan of action: whom you will tell, whom you will solicit as allies, and what you will say.

Read the following scenario and respond to the questions that follow:

You are a public assistance worker facing an ethical dilemma concerning whether or not to blow the whistle on a newly promoted supervisor (Reamer, 1990). You have worked at the agency for almost two years, and you are increasingly frustrated by the attitudes and work habits of a number of your immediate colleagues. They seem to spend as little time as possible with clients, even denying them necessary and appropriate assistance if the worker doesn't have time to complete all the necessary paperwork. In other cases, workers bend the rules to give clients benefits to which they are not entitled. For instance, many clients work as domestic help and are paid in cash, and workers do not always report all the clients' income. Workers simply make decisions according to their own discretion. Additionally, you note that workers consistently pad their travel expense accounts.

You are appalled by this behavior, and although you don't like the thought of "making waves," you finally confide your concerns to your friend and colleague Zenda. Zenda "pooh-poohs" your concerns condescendingly, remarking that such violations bend rules that aren't very good to begin with. She explains that such worker discretion is really an informal agency policy and adds that padding travel expense accounts is universally accepted as a means of increasing workers' relatively meager salaries. Zenda tries to soothe you and arrest your concerns, but it doesn't work. You decide that from now on you had best keep your concerns to yourself until you can figure out what to do about them.

Abruptly you find out that Zenda has been promoted and is your new unit supervisor. You are stunned. How can Zenda maintain order and help supervisees follow agency and other regulations when Zenda herself typically violates them?

What can you do? Ignore the whole situation? Confront your colleagues about their behavior? Confront Zenda again, even though it did no good the first time? Report your concerns to someone higher up in the administration? If you do and Zenda considers you a traitor, how miserable can Zenda make your life as an employee? Should you report the problem to NASW or the State Licensing Board? Should you blow the whistle to the press? How long do you think you'll keep your job if you take the problem outside established agency channels? Should you quit?

1. Discuss which principles in *ETHICS for U* might apply to this situation?

2. How can you use the principles' ranking to come to a decision?

3. As a social worker, what would *you* do in this situation?

Exercise 12.6: Unethical Behavior on the Part of Colleagues— Racist Individual and Organizational Behavior

In addition to dignity and worth of the person, the NASW Code of Ethics emphasizes social justice and the need for "cultural competence" in terms of understanding cultural and social diversity (1.05). It asserts the importance of workers acting to prevent and eliminate discrimination (6.04d) and stresses that "social workers should not use derogatory language in either written or verbal communications to or about clients" (1.12). It also states that "social workers should not practice, condone, facilitate, or collaborate with any form of discrimination on the basis of race, ethnicity, national origin, [or] color . . ." (4.02). Instead, they should "act to prevent and eliminate discrimination in the employing organization's work assignments and in its employment policies and practices" (3.09e).

The private social service agency you work for does not have a formal affirmative action policy for hiring personnel. You have heard the agency director make several lewd racial remarks and jokes. You cannot believe he has gotten away with it. You have only worked for the agency for three months of your six-month probationary period, so you could be dismissed in the blink of an eye. The agency has no minorities of color on staff though it has clients who are minorities of color.[1] You believe that recruiting staff who are minorities of color is essential to the agency's ability to perform its functions. You also think the staff and the agency director need feedback in order to change their prejudicial and discriminatory behavior.

What is your role? Should you look away and pretend you don't know anything is wrong? Should you charge into the Director's office like a bull in a china shop and complain? Can you talk to other staff to see what they think? Should you contact the agency's board of directors? Should you contact the press or some external regulatory agency and blow the whistle? Should you quit your job?

1.   Which principles in *ETHICS for U* might apply to this situation?

2.   How can you use the principles' ranking to come to a decision?

3.   As a social worker, what would *you* do in this situation?

Exercise 12.7: Initiating Community Action "Against the Flow"

We have established that the NASW Code of Ethics maintains that service, social justice, and dignity and worth of the person are core concepts in making ethical decisions. The Code also states that "social workers generally should adhere to commitments made to employers and employing organizations" (3.09a). Additionally, the Code provides guidelines for social and political action (6.04). It emphasizes that "social workers should engage in social and political action that seeks to ensure that all people have equal access to the resources, employment, services, and opportunities they require to meet their basic human needs and to develop fully" (6.04a). Social workers are responsible for expanding the "choice" and "opportunity" available to all people, especially those who are vulnerable and disadvantaged (6.04b). Read the vignette below and respond to the questions that follow.

---

[1]*Minority* is "one term for a group, or a member of a group, of people of a distinct racial, religious, ethnic, or political identity that is smaller or less powerful than the community's controlling group" (Barker, 1995, p. 236). The term *minorities of color* concerns "people who have minority status because their skin color differs from that of the community's predominant group. In the United States, the term usually refers to African Americans, Asian Americans, American Indians, and certain other minority groups" (Barker, 1995, p. 236).

The community in which you live and work provides no services for homeless people, despite the fact that their numbers are escalating. Every day on your way to and from work you pass at least a half dozen people roaming the urban streets. Many times you see children with them, dirty, probably hungry, and obviously not in school. Most people at your agency don't really want to talk about it. You get the feeling that colleagues, supervisors, and administrators think they have enough to do already. Work demands continue to increase while funding resources shrink.

1. Which ethical principles in *ETHICS for U* might apply to this situation?

2. How can you use the principles' ranking to come to a decision?

3. As a social worker, what would *you* do in this situation?

EXERCISE 12.8: Community Support (or Lack Thereof) for Service Provision

The NASW Code of Ethics maintains that social workers should "respect and promote the right of clients to self-determination" and help clients work toward the identification and clarification of their goals (1.02). Social workers should seek to educate themselves about social diversity including sexual orientation (1.05c). Furthermore, they should "engage in social and political action" aimed at providing all people with equal access to resources and opportunities (6.04). Finally, social workers should pursue the elimination of discrimination against any person or group based on sexual orientation (6.04d).

Read the following scenario and respond to the questions that follow.

You are a worker at a rural county social services agency. You, other colleagues, and agency administration have identified a significant lesbian and gay population in the area. You and the other professionals would like to implement a new program providing support groups for lesbian and gay people dealing with several issues, including single parenthood, legal difficulties such as housing discrimination, and other issues. Several relatively powerful members of the County Board get wind of your idea and react with almost violent frenzy. They band together with a number of citizens who adamantly refuse to allow expenditure of public resources on lesbian and gay people.

1. Which principles in *ETHICS for U* might apply to this situation?

2. How can you use the principles' ranking in coming to a decision?

3. As a social worker, what would you do in this situation?

272

Chapter 13
Working with the Courts

I.   **The Significance of the Legal System**

   A.   Social workers and others serving as advocates for those denied social and economic justice have repeatedly asked the court system to intervene

   B.   Seven areas basic to all social work practice and its relationship to the legal system

      1.   Confidentiality

      2.   Clients' consent to intervention

      3.   Legal rights of clients

      4.   Documentation of evidence in the case record

      5.   Legal authority for practice

      6.   Testimony in court

      7.   Legal duties implicit in professional practice

II.   **Functions of Professional Terminology**

   A.   To shorten communication and ensure shared meaning

   B.   To establish boundaries between users of such terms, such as the designated professional, and those who do not belong to these professions

III.   **Important Legal Terms**

   A.   Highlight 13.1: Legal Terminology in Your Area of Practice

   B.   Laws—those standards, principles, processes, and rules that are adopted, administered, and enforced by a governmental authority and that regulate behavior by setting forth what people may and may not do and how they may do what they can do

   C.   Criminal laws—those that govern the operation of the criminal justice systems within states and at the federal level

   D.   Civil laws—govern the behavior of individuals or organizations; however, they are materially different from criminal law in that it is usually private citizens who exercise the power to punish the person who has broken a civil law

E. Violations—offenses that involve the breaking of a law or rule. Violation and offense can be used interchangeably

    1. Criminal violations—offenses penalized by fine and/or imprisonment or probation

        a. Felonies—crimes considered serious enough to be punishable by imprisonment for a term of one or more years

        b. Misdemeanors—less serious crimes punishable by confinement in a city or county jail for a period of less than one year

    2. Civil offenses—the sole penalty is forfeiture of money or goods

    3. Ordinance offenses—violation of civil (noncriminal) laws enacted by a local unit of municipal government. Conviction for a noncriminal offense can draw a fine but not incarceration of the offender

F. Jurisdiction—authority to act

    1. Juvenile court has jurisdiction over most illegal acts committed by children (people under age 18); however, there are exceptions

        a. Delinquency—definitions typically include the following factors: age and the identified behavior, often defined as a behavior that would be a law violation if committed by an adult

        b. Children in need of services—is often defined using incorporation of status offenses (acts that if committed by an adult would not be illegal, such as truancy or curfew violations)

        c. Children referred to as dependent, neglected, or abused

    2. Initially established in the early 1900s as family courts, such legal arrangements were organized and run on a more informal, often paternalistic model, where there was legal recourse to appeal for rights similar to those of an adult

    3. Social workers involved in jurisdictional disputes over procedures are well advised to consult with their supervisors or corporation counsel

G. Allegation—the assertion of one side in a lawsuit setting out what that party expects to prove at the trial

H. Court process

    1. Adjudication—phase where facts are presented, and the charge is determined by a judge or a jury

    2. Disposition—occurs after adjudication and refers to the sentence determination

I.   Due process

      1.   The 14th Amendment to the U.S. Constitution mandates that courts must document that it guarantees the protection of a fair trial (innocent until proven guilty)

      2.   *In re Gault*, 1967—due process rights protect juveniles as well as adults

      3.   "Best interest of the child" concept—decision making by any authority figure should reflect the adult's judgment as to the best alternative for the child

J.   Stipulation—both parties agreeing on the point of information or fact

K.   Burden of proof—rests on the prosecution or plaintiff (the party making the complaint)

L.   Standards of proof—level or degree of certainty needed to prove an allegation in court

      1.   Beyond a reasonable doubt—used in criminal or delinquency cases (*In re Winship*, 1970). It necessitates evidence that is entirely convincing to a moral certainty (sometimes referred to as 90 percent sure)

      2.   Clear and convincing evidence—refers to approximately a 70 percent degree of certainty. Such a degree may be used in cases of child abuse or neglect

      3.   Preponderance of the evidence—51 percent minimum certainty; it is the standard of proof applied in civil (as opposed to criminal) cases; some states also use this standard for child abuse and neglect cases

M.   Evidence

      1.   Real evidence—consists of tangible objects, such as weapons or photographs

      2.   Documentary evidence—pertains to certified documents usually identified and authenticated by proper authorities

      3.   Testimony—refers to the actual interviewing of a witness by the defendant or, more typically, his or her attorney

      4.   Hearsay evidence—refers to testimony about a statement made outside the courtroom

      5.   Quality of evidence

            a.   The source must be competent (qualified) to make the observation

            b.   Information must be relevant; meaning is must bear on the proceeding at hand

            c.   Information must be material and thus have important consequences for the case

N. Witnesses

    1. Lay(factual)—refers to one who is limited in testimony to what she or he saw, heard, smelled, or touched

    2. Expert—is rendered "qualified" by the judge or give opinions in a particular area of expertise. Judges vary greatly in admissibility of social workers as expert witnesses

O. Guardian *Ad Litem*—appointed to represent that person's "best interests"; to be determined by the guardian *ad litem*, not by what the client might identify as his or her preferences

P. Confidentiality and privileged communication

    1. Confidentiality—refers to the principle that information shared between the client and social worker is intended to be kept private. As both a professional and a legal term it is seldom as pure as inexperienced social workers or clients might expect

    2. Privileged communication—refers to information shared between the client and another party that is protected by statute

    3. Contempt of court—refers to willful disobedience to or open disrespect for the rules of the court

    4. *Jaffee v. Redmond*, 518 U.S. 1 (1996) recognized that, like psychologists and psychiatrists, communications between clients and social workers should remain confidential and that this is essential to psychiatric treatment

Q. Subpoena—required to appear in court

    1. Often the subpoena requires that the professional bring any and all paperwork, files, reports, and informal notes as well

    2. The NASW's Code of Ethics notes that the professional maintains client confidences "except for compelling professional reasons"

    3. The social worker should keep a detailed record on what steps were taken to ensure compliance with the order but still protect the client as much as possible

    4. The area of subpoenaed documents often creates a potential conflict between legal requirements and professional ethics

IV.   **Differences Between Courtroom Protocol and Social Work Practice**

     A.   Figure 13.1: Social Work Practice versus Courtroom Protocol

     B.   Adversarial versus conjoint problem solving

          1.   For the duration of the proceedings in court, plaintiff and defendant become adversaries

          2.   Social work practice is much more likely to be based on a model of planned change that stresses a conjoint solution

          3.   Highlight 13.2: Court is Like a Stage

     C.   Formal versus informal atmosphere

          1.   A court of law is conducted according to historical precedents that dictate the setting, appearance of the participants, and rules of conduct

          2.   Practitioners are advised to prepare themselves for the differences in formality and to dress much more formally than usual for a court appearance

     D.   Legal due process versus client rights

          1.   In a court of law in this country, the defendant is assumed to be the one most in need of safeguards protecting his or her rights

          2.   Common client rights include foreknowledge of confidentiality and its constraint, self-determination, and informed consent for treatment

     E.   Outcome: Determination of the charge versus rehabilitation

          1.   The end result in the courtroom is clear and unambiguous

          2.   Social work practice is much more ambiguous in process and, often, in outcome

V.   **Presentation in Court**

     A.   Highlight 13.3: Summary: Your Role in Court

          1.   The primary mission of a professional social worker testifying in court is to inform or educate the finder of fact

          2.   Social workers are generally advised to present themselves as "friends of the court"

VI. Preparation for Testimony

    A. Documentation

        1. Often the credibility or believability of testimony is directly related to the amount and accuracy of detail the worker has put into the case record

        2. Documentation typically includes acknowledgment of all contacts the worker has had with the client and others involved in the case

        3. Avoid value-laden terms and use more neutral terms plus one or two behaviorally specific descriptions to enhance the record's and the worker's credibility

        4. Positive, as well as negative, observations should be included in the record

    B. Review of other documents

    C. Establishment of expert witness status

    D. Review of testimony with attorney

        1. Petition—essentially a complaint that specifies the reasons for a case being brought to court and usually identifies a remedy sought by the petitioner

        2. Highlight 13.4: A Court Petition

    E. Preparation of witnesses

VII. Phases in the Adjudication Process

    A. Direct examination of witnesses

        1. The purpose of direct testimony is to communicate as persuasively as possible the truthful facts pertinent to a case

        2. The social worker as a witness is allowed to use notes during testimony

        3. Language is more lively and forceful if the active voice is used

        4. Exhibits are tangible articles, such as weapons or copies of documents, that have been collected, identified, and made available to the court for a particular case

        5. Highlight 13.5 Questions for Direct Examination

    B. Cross-examination of witnesses

        1. Cross-examination is the step in the courtroom process that is most likely to show the adversarial nature of the proceedings

        2. Highlight 13.6 Cross-Examination

VIII. Strategies in Cross-Examination

    A. Attacking direct examination testimony

    B. Attacking credentials

    C. Attacking you as a person

    D. Attacking the profession

    E. Other confrontational tactics

    F. Suggestions for cross-examination testimony

        1. It is generally advisable not to answer questions that are ambiguous or unclear

        2. Use of listening skills

IX. Stages in the Juvenile Court Process

    A. Figure 13.2 The Temporary Custody Stage of the Juvenile Court Process

    B. Figure 13.3 The Jurisdictional Stage of the Juvenile Court Process

    C. Figure 13.4 The Dispositional Stage of the Juvenile Court Process

    D. Figure 13.5 The Post-Dispositional Stage of the Juvenile Court Process

X. Developing Issues in Social Work and the Law

    A. Social workers in hospitals and nursing homes must have a working knowledge of patient rights, advanced medical directives, and legal guidelines regarding the appointment of any interactions with guardians and protective payees

    B. Confidentiality and privacy of client information and the type of storage of documents relating to any given case are new and developing issues

    C. Many states, in an attempt to deal with an increase in the seriousness of juvenile crimes, have lowered the age at which a juvenile is automatically transferred into adult court

    D. Forensic social work will continue to expand as society asks the courts to decide complicated moral and ethical issues (National Organization of Forensic Social Work)

    E. In child abuse and neglect cases, an emerging issue is "fetal abuse": drug use by the mother and the resultant damage to the fetus

    F. The "recovered memory" controversy (adult client's onset of "remembered" alleged physical or sexual abuse) and the possible legal ramifications to the family may be adjudicated through the legal process

    G. Social workers are also working alone and with others in doing life history research for capital cases

Exercise 13.1: Understanding Court Terminology

A.   Brief Description
Students match various concepts of court terminology with their respective meanings.

B.   Objectives
Students will identify and discuss various concepts of court terminology.

C.   Procedure
1.   Provide students with copies of the matching exercise under "Instructions for Students."
2.   After allowing students a few minutes to complete the exercise, initiate a discussion with the class regarding the importance and relevance of each of these concepts.

D.   Instructions for Students
Match the following concepts concerning goals with their respective meanings.

1.	Criminal violation	_____
2.	Jurisdiction	_____
3.	Allegation	_____
4.	Disposition	_____
5.	Due process	_____
6.	Stipulation	_____
7.	Burden of proof	_____
8.	Standards of proof	_____
9.	Real evidence	_____
10.	Documentary evidence	_____
11.	Testimony	_____
12.	Hearsay evidence	_____
13.	Civil offense	_____
14.	Misdemeanor	_____
15.	Felony	_____
16.	Confidentiality	_____
17.	Privileged communication	_____
18.	Subpoena	_____

a.   An agreement by both parties on a point of information or fact that pertains to the proceedings or trial.
b.   The principle that information shared between the client and social worker is intended to be kept private.
c.   A legal writ ordering an individual to appear in court to testify regarding a client, often requiring that written documents be brought along as well.
d.   An offense penalized by fine and/or imprisonment.
e.   A violation for which the sole penalty is forfeiture of money or goods.
f.   A less serious crime considered serious enough to be punishable by imprisonment for a term of one or more years.
g.   Authority to act.

h.   The requirement that law in its regular course of administration must document that it guarantees the protection of a fair trial.
i.   Testimony about a statement made outside the courtroom.
j.   The condition that it is the responsibility of the party making the complaint to prove the allegations set out in the petition filed before the court.
k.   Information shared between the client and another party that is protected by state statute.
l.   The assertion of one side in a lawsuit setting out what that party expects to prove at the trial.
m.   Evidence consisting of tangible objects such as weapons or photographs.
n.   The second phase of the court process where the sentence is determined.
o.   The level or degree of certainty needed to prove an allegation in court.
p.   The actual interviewing of a witness by the defendant or, more typically, his or her attorney.
q.   Certified documents usually identified and authenticated by proper authorities.
r.   A crime considered serious enough to be punishable by imprisonment for a term or one or more years.

E.   Commentary
Answers are: 1d; 2f; 3l; 4n; 5h; 6a; 7j; 8o; 9m; 10q; 11p; 12i; 13e; 14f; 15r; 16b; 17k; 18c.
This exercise may also be conducted using the small group format described in earlier exercises.

Exercise 13.2: Courtroom Protocol and Social Work Practice

A.   Brief Description
Using a small group format, students appraise a vignette describing a social worker's behavior in court and make suggestions for improvement.

B.   Objectives
Students will:
1.   Appraise a vignette describing the behavior of a social worker in a courtroom setting.
2.   Identify inappropriate courtroom behavior.
3.   Compare and contrast behavior patterns commonly characterizing social work practice and those patterns deemed appropriate in court.
4.   Recommend improved behavior coinciding with formal courtroom protocol.

C.   Procedure
1.   Review the material on the differences between courtroom protocol and social work practice.
2.   Read the vignette presented below under "Instructions for Students" and initiate a discussion for each regarding which functions the vignettes indicate are being fulfilled and how.
3.   Divide the class into small groups of four to six.
4.   Ask the groups to discuss the first three steps of the IMAGINE process to begin program development in the vignette described below under "Instructions for Students." Instruct them to address the questions provided after the vignette. Indicate that they should select a group representative who should be prepared to report to the entire class the small group's findings.
5.   After about 10 minutes, ask the small groups to terminate their discussions and participate in a full class discussion regarding their findings.
6.   Ask the representative from each group to share her or his summary of the discussion. Encourage participation from all class members.

D.   Instructions for Students
        Read the following vignette and answer the subsequent questions.

> *Vignette:* Larry is a social worker at a residential treatment center for adolescents who have serious behavioral and emotional problems. He attends a courtroom proceeding to speak on the behalf of Archibald (nicknamed Archy), one of his clients at the center. Archy was caught shoplifting and faces a possible return to a juvenile correctional facility. Larry feels Archy has made significant progress at the center and hates the thought of Archy returning to "jail" and backsliding concerning the treatment progress he's made. Wearing blue jeans and an orange T-shirt, Larry is called to the stand.
>
> Larry is an outgoing person who tends to act in a friendly manner with most people with whom he comes into contact. On his way up to the stand, he smiles, waves, and says, "Hi, Judge." His intent is to develop rapport with the judge. As Larry answers questions, he leans towards the bench and the judge. He speaks using his most sincere tone. At times he raises his voice to make his point. He hopes he doesn't sound like he's whining, but is committed to helping Archy.
>
> When asked to make his recommendations regarding Archy's treatment for the next six months, Larry states, "It seems to me that Archy will be capable of making much more progress at the treatment center than in the residential facility." Larry is then asked to submit his progress reports for the judge's perusal. Larry indicates that he isn't quite finished with them yet, but will get them to court by tomorrow.

---

    1.   What behavior might be ineffective and inappropriate in a courtroom setting?
    2.   What are the differences between common behavior patterns in social work practice and
            the appropriate behavior patterns in a formal courtroom setting?
    3.   What are recommendations for improved courtroom protocol?

E.   Commentary
    1.   Note that some of the behavior described above may not be allowed in a real courtroom
            setting. It is presented here simply as fuel for discussion.
    2.   This exercise may also be conducted using a full class discussion format without
            breaking students into small groups.

Exercise 13.3: Sorting Out the Violations

Julian Wainwright is part of a social action group protesting at a nuclear power plant. He and other group members who chained themselves to the front gate of the plant were arrested for violating the law and face penalties including fines and up to six months in jail for trespassing. In addition, the city is charging them with loitering, which carries a possible fine of $100.

1.   How would you classify the violations facing Julian and his group in terms of the categories
        discussed above?

2.   How serious are the charges against them?

3.   If the power plant operator sues Julian and his group for lost income and the costs of providing
        extra plant security, what kind of violation would this entail?

Jurisdiction

Jurisdiction is the authority to act in a given situation. For example, a court in one state does not have jurisdiction to punish someone for a violation that occurred in another state. The issue of jurisdiction frequently arises when you are dealing with juveniles. Most states give jurisdiction over juvenile cases to a juvenile court. This means that a young person who commits a crime will not be tried in adult court. There are exceptions to this rule: Several states allow juveniles to be "waived" into adult court if they have committed particularly serious crimes.

Since laws sometimes vary greatly from one community or state to another, jurisdiction is an important concept. Determination of the proper jurisdiction is often left to the discretion of the prosecuting attorney.

Exercise 13.4: Who Has Jurisdiction?

Marian, a 15-year-old, is stopped in Georgia for driving her mother's car without permission. Marian and her mother live a few miles away near Tallahassee, Florida. The local Georgia newspaper, in a misguided effort to stamp out youthful crime, has suggested that teenagers like Marian should be flogged. The paper's editors call upon the local prosecutor to charge Marian with auto theft, treat her as an adult, and give her the maximum punishment.

As a social worker in the prosecutor's office you are asked to write a brief letter to the editor informing the paper and its readers about such cases. What would you say in the letter to deal with the jurisdictional issue?

Allegation

When one individual charges that another has committed a violation, this is called an *allegation*. (This should not be confused with the reptiles that frequent local swimming pools in Florida.) Courts refer to someone against whom an allegation has been made as an "alleged offender" because under our system of justice a person is innocent until proven guilty. Get in the habit of calling accused persons "alleged" offenders.

Court Process

What goes on in a court can be broken down into two phases, *adjudication* and *disposition*. In the first phase, a determination is made by a judge or jury following the presentation of evidence. Adjudication ends when the judge or jury arrives at a verdict. If the accused is found guilty, disposition begins. In this phase a decision is reached about what punishment or consequences are appropriate. Sometimes the law gives clear guidance: An adjudication of murder may require the death penalty or life imprisonment. In other situations, a judge or jury has considerable latitude. Several days or weeks may pass between adjudication and disposition. The judge may order a pre-sentence investigation prior to the dispositional hearing in order to get additional input and information.

Exercise 13.5: Explaining the Relationship

As a juvenile probation officer, you often give talks to the public about the juvenile court. At the local Rotary Club you are asked to talk about what happens in the courts to "those delinquents." Explain in a few words what you see as the relationship between an allegation of delinquency and the adjudication and disposition process in court.

Due Process

Due process is guaranteed by the Sixth Amendment in the Bill of Rights. It ensures that all proper procedures, rules, and opportunities permitted by law are guaranteed to all individuals before a legal judgment can deprive them of life, liberty, or property. Due process rights were extended to juveniles in 1967 under a Supreme Court decision known as *Gault*. Juvenile court had previously been governed by the principle that adults acted in the "best interest of the child." The extension of due process rights to juveniles was designed to protect them from arbitrary decision-making by courts and judges.

Exercise 13.6: What Is Due?

You are working with Malcolm and Jamal Washington, two brothers who are part of a boys' club. Last night, on the way home from the club, they were stopped by the police, their car was searched, and despite their protests they were detained for two hours at the police station. Their requests to speak to an attorney were ignored. They were later released without any charges being filed. The boys ask you if this seems fair and inquire whether their rights were violated. What would you tell them and why?

Stipulation

A *stipulation* is simply a statement that both sides in a court case agree on the accuracy of certain facts or information, thus eliminating unnecessary discussion of evidence that is not in dispute. For example, a stipulation might be used in a murder case involving domestic abuse. The defendant admits to committing the crime, but the defense argues that it was a justifiable response to physical abuse by the deceased. By stipulating to the killing itself, the defense removes the need for argument over opportunity, weapon, and motive.

Burden of Proof

The burden of proof is the obligation of the prosecution (in a criminal case) or the plaintiff (in a civil case) to prove their assertions. Neither a criminal nor a civil defendant is required to prove anything, so both can concentrate on refuting evidence offered by the prosecution or plaintiff.

Exercise 13.7: Defending the Burden of Proof

An editorial in your local newspaper asserts that too many "criminals" are avoiding punishment because courts find them not guilty when "everyone" knows they're guilty as sin. As a social worker working for the judge, you are asked to respond with a letter to the editor. Explain how you would defend the burden of proof principle.

Standards of Proof

In criminal and delinquency cases the prosecution must prove its case beyond a reasonable doubt. The level of certainty is referred to as the *standard of proof*. If it could be quantified, reasonable doubt might constitute about 90 percent certainty. Child abuse and neglect cases generally require a standard of proof referred to as "clear and convincing evidence," roughly a 70 percent degree of certainty. In most civil cases, the burden of proof requirement is "a preponderance of the evidence." This is simply the majority of the evidence, about a 51 percent certainty. The greater the potential punishment for the defendant, the higher the standard of proof.

1.   What is your opinion of these differing standards of proof?

2.   *Should* there be a different standard for different types of cases or situations? Explain.

3.   What if the courts adopted a single standard for all cases?

Evidence

Evidence is proof of the accuracy of an allegation, but not all evidence is equal in nature or importance. *Real evidence* consists of things, such as weapons, blood, and fingerprints. *Documentary evidence* is material identified and authenticated by proper authorities. An emergency room doctor, for example, might testify that the X-rays used in a trial are the same ones he took the night a person was admitted to the hospital. *Testimonial evidence* is actual testimony given in court under oath and is subject to legal regulation and to careful examination by opposing counsels. Mary, for example, cannot testify to what Sam said to her because that would be hearsay. Sam is not available to verify what he actually said, and Mary could have misheard or misunderstood him.

In addition, only statements made under oath are allowed in court.   Mary can testify to what she told Sam because she is now under oath, but Sam's statements (as related by Mary) were *not* made under oath. Also, the judge and jury can't see Sam or hear his inflection, so they cannot judge his demeanor based on what Mary reports. Think about it. If Sam said, "I'm going to kill Bob," that could be a serious threat. But what if Sam was laughing at the time? What if he was reacting to one of Bob's practical jokes? What if Sam was just blowing off steam. The statement itself is meaningless without this additional information. If the attorneys cannot bring Sam into court (via subpoena) to testify under oath, his words will be inadmissible.

Evidence presented in court must be competent, relevant, and material. Testimony from a person who was drunk or delusional is not competent. Neither is medical testimony from a baseball player or blood-spatter testimony from a chef. *Competent evidence* comes from qualified people. *Relevant evidence* is information with a direct bearing on the case. The ingredients of Aunt Hattie's apple pie are not relevant unless the pie contained arsenic and Uncle Fred was poisoned. *Material evidence* is more than relevant—it proves or refutes an essential fact. Therefore, if it's established that Uncle Fred was poisoned *with arsenic,* evidence of Aunt Hattie's whereabouts during the preparation of the poisoned pie would be material—that is, it would show that she was out of the house while the pie was baking or waiting to be baked (thus refuting the allegation that no one else could have administered the poison) or that she was in the kitchen all day long (thus proving that it would have been almost impossible for anyone else to have tampered with the pie). On the other hand, testimony that Boris has a crush on Natasha is probably not material to her trial for poisoning Rocky.

Exercise 13.9: Evidence, Evidence, Evidence

Match each example to the appropriate type of evidence.

1. Documentary _____   5. Relevant _____

2. Testimonial _____   6. Material _____

3. Real _____   7. Competent _____

4. Hearsay _____

A. Statements made to a witness by a person who is not present in the courtroom
B. Evidence considered consequential to the outcome of the trial
C. Evidence provided by a qualified witness
D. Testimony by a crime victim about his injuries
E. A gun used in a robbery
F. Testimony with a direct bearing on a case
G. Medical records authenticated by a hospital records clerk

Witnesses

Courts typically recognizes two types of witnesses: *Lay witnesses* can testify to things they experienced. They may be asked for opinions based on their experience, but those opinions can be challenged by opposing counsel since the witness has no particular expertise. Expert witnesses, on the other hand, are accepted as such based upon academic credentials, experience, and specialized training. Expert witnesses are given greater latitude in expressing their opinions about a case, but expert status is given on a case-by-case basis. Thus, one judge might consider you an expert while another views you as a lay witness. As a social worker you should be prepared to defend your qualifications.

Guardian ad Litem

Children and others judged not competent by a court may have a guardian *ad litem* appointed. This person is often, though not necessarily, an attorney and is charged with guarding the person's best interests. In many cases, the viewpoint of the guardian *ad litem* is different from that of either side in the dispute. For example, when two parents argue in court for custody of a child, a guardian *ad litem* may agree with one or the other, or may firmly believe that the only healthy caretaker for the child at this point is the maternal grandmother.

Confidentiality and Privileged Communication

Confidentiality and privileged communication have important implications for social workers and their clients. *Confidentiality* dictates that information shared by the worker and client is kept from others unless the client gives permission to share what has been said. It is a primary tenet of social work practice, but it is also a relative concept since absolute confidentiality is often impossible. For example, all agencies keep records, have supervisors, and are subject to control by legal authorities, so information must be available to agency supervisors, executives, secretaries, and others. Files and records may have to be turned over to the court to settle a related dispute.

Privileged communication has legal protections, usually in the form of state laws, and it is not subject to disclosure in court. Many states routinely grant this protection to the testimony and records of physicians, lawyers, psychologists, spouses, and sometimes social workers. Interestingly, the patient or client—*not* the doctor or lawyer—has the right to invoke privileged communication. Laws governing these matters are meant to protect clients, not professionals.

What are the primary differences and similarities between confidentiality and privileged communication?

Differences Between Courtroom Protocol and Social Work Practice

There are multiple differences between the structured world of the courtroom and the environment of the generalist social worker, but social workers are trained to work in a variety of arenas, ranging from the one-to-one interview to the legislative chamber. Most social workers, therefore, can successfully make the transition to this new environment. Recognizing and anticipating the differences will help them do so.

The atmosphere of most social work activities is informal. Staff refer to each other by first names, as do many clients. Dress is casual. Language and words used by social workers reflect opinions, are hedged by such phrases as "it seems," and emphasize flexibility. After all, the goal of social work intervention is to achieve client-identified goals, and to serve the client system. Mutual problem solving is the professionally approved means of handling disputes, disagreements, and difficulties. Professional social work values accord certain rights to clients (e.g., confidentiality and self-determination). This is the world of the social worker.

The courtroom is markedly different. The atmosphere is very formal, and participants refer to each other accordingly: Your Honor, Counselor, Ladies and Gentlemen of the Jury. Language is similarly formal, precise, and definitive, and dress in court is "business attire." There is an adversarial relationship between the opposing sides. The parties to a disagreement present their arguments, and the judge or jury makes the final decision. The goal of the court system is to determine the truthfulness of an allegation, and its values reflect this: the right to legal counsel, to refuse self-incrimination, and to face one's accuser, for example.

Many social workers feel uncomfortable in the courtroom. It's an unfamiliar place, and sometimes opposing attorneys go out of their way to make social workers look incompetent. To prepare for your courtroom experience, adopt the conservative appearance that is characteristic of the rest of the participants (attorneys, witnesses, etc.)—more or less what you would wear to a funeral. If you can, visit the courtroom when court is not in session or observe a trial as a visitor. Talk with others who have testified in court and are knowledgeable about the protocol. Don't go in cold.

Make a chart on which you briefly identify the primary differences between social work practice and courtroom protocol. Include degree of formality, dress, language, methods of settling disputes, values/rights, and collegial relationships, etc.

Preparation for Testimony

Some general rules will help you prepare for a court appearance.

- Offer documentation that enhances, rather than detracts from, your testimony. Case notes and records should be detailed and clear. Opinions and impressions that are undocumented or too broadly stated undermine the worker's credibility. Dates; descriptions of contacts between worker, client, and others; and impartial presentation of information all contribute to the social worker's air of professionalism. Descriptions of a client or situation should be as free as possible of any value-laden terms. Avoid references to "weird behavior" or "uncooperativeness." Instead, describe precisely what you observed in words that don't inflame or prejudice your listeners. Offer your impressions, but be sure they are clearly labeled as such.

- Review all appropriate documentation—prior court decisions in similar cases, agency records and policies, and appropriate state laws—before you appear in court. For example, if you are testifying about your work with a local anti-gang program, review your agency's policies and procedures for providing this service. The ability to cite the applicable section of a policy manual or state law greatly enhances your credibility. Your awareness of relevant court decisions or precedents is likely to win you greater recognition by the court.

- If an attorney is seeking to have you accepted as an expert witness, prepare for this additional responsibility. Expect to be asked about your education, professional experience, and past work with similar cases.

- One side or the other has requested your presence in court, so review with this attorney the nature of the questions you will be asked. If specific information will be sought, review your notes and the case file. You may suggest strategies that would be appropriate given your own experience, but remember that this is the attorney's world—so let the lawyer lead. He or she may also offer some guidance about questions the judge might raise. You will be better prepared if you can think about such questions beforehand. If necessary (though it should not be), press the attorney to meet with you prior to the trial.

- Help prepare anyone else who will be asked to testify. Perhaps you will need to orient your clients to the formalities of the court, the differences in language and terminology, and the importance of nonverbal communication. You may have colleagues who argue that you and your clients *should not* have to observe all these niceties, that judges and juries *should not* be influenced by factors like attire and whether nonverbal communication matches verbal testimony. Nonetheless, there is empirical evidence that these factors *do* affect a person's credibility. Failure to inform clients about these issues does them a disservice.

Exercise 13.12: Testifying

On Friday of next week your friend and colleague, Jane, is to appear in court as a witness in a child abuse case. It will be her first court case. What advice would you give her about how to prepare for this "experience"?

Phases in the Adjudication Process

The primary phases in the adjudication process are direct examination of witnesses and cross-examination. (These may be followed by redirect and recross-examination.) Direct examination aims to present an accurate and truthful recitation of the facts. Questions asked in this phase are generally straightforward, and you are permitted to use notes to help you recall information. This is advisable, especially if anxiety is high or your memory poor. Look over the case record before testifying, but don't attempt to memorize data. Stumbling over details reduces your credibility and makes your testimony look rehearsed.

In all phases, including direct examination, you must respond verbally. Nods and gestures cannot be recorded by the court reporter who is making a transcript of the trial. Be prepared to explain professional terms with which attorneys, judges, or jurors may be unfamiliar. Limit your comments to direct responses to the questions. The judge and attorneys may rebuke you for going into long explanations and making tangential remarks. Wait for each question to be asked, and pause, if necessary, to think briefly about the question. If you don't understand the question, ask the attorney to rephrase it. If you still don't understand, say so. Don't be intimidated into giving estimates or opinions with which you are uncomfortable. Feel free to say, "I don't know."

You don't have the option of refusing to answer a question, but if you remember to pause after each question, you give the opposing attorney time to object. If there are no objections, address your answer to the judge or jury. If the opposing counsel or the judge begins to speak, stop immediately. Wait for direction from the judge or the questioning attorney. Usually the judge will rule on any objections lodged by opposing counsel and then direct you to continue or tell the lawyer to move on to another question.

Cross-examination of witnesses is part of the adversary system. The goal of cross-examination is to reduce the credibility of the witnesses or the believability of their information. Expect probing and challenging questions worded in ways that can confuse witnesses or put them on the defensive: "Isn't it true that you really don't know much about this family?" Be prepared for very limited questions that do not let you amplify what you said or that seek yes or no answers to complex questions.

Exercise 13.13: Adjudication Processes

1.   What do you understand to be the primary purposes of direct examination of witnesses and cross-examination?

2.   Why is cross-examination likely to be more stressful for the witness?

Strategies Used in Cross-Examination

Four strategies are used in cross-examination to undermine the credibility of a witness:

- The first is an attack on testimony. Using this approach, an attorney points out discrepancies in the witness's statements, such as differences between direct and cross-examination testimony, or between testimony and records. Attorneys may attack your impartiality by suggesting you are motivated by animosity, prejudice, or other factors. They may also challenge your competence or experience. For example, a young worker might be challenged about her lack of personal child-raising experience.

- The second strategy is an attack on witnesses' credentials, and its goal is to challenge the professional education and experience of the worker. The questions may aim at undermining your academic degree, your continuing education courses, or other training.

- The third strategy, attacking the person, is employed when other methods have failed. Personal challenges can be directed at your opinions or at other aspects of your life that appear relevant: "You don't really *like* Mrs. Ortega, do you?" would be an attempt to discredit your observations about her.

- The fourth strategy, attacking the profession, attempts to undermine the credibility and expertise of your whole profession: "Isn't it true that just about anyone can be a social worker?" Don't let this upset you. Remain calm, and remember the joke that professional courtesy keeps sharks from eating attorneys.

Other methods of discrediting a witness include forcing yes/no answers to complex questions, bombarding the witness with questions in order to create confusion, and using an overly friendly or condescending attitude. The best response in these situations is to answer politely, pleasantly, and firmly. Don't become angry or upset. And don't think it's over until the fat lady sings. As a witness you can be brought back to the stand by either side. Redirect or recross-examination is always possible—usually when critical information is at stake and the trial's outcome may hinge on the presentation of certain testimony. Recognize that your testimony must be important or you would not be back on the stand.

Working in the court system can be exhilarating, frightening, and fun. The key to making it a reasonably enjoyable experience is to learn what to expect, prepare yourself accordingly, and remember that your knowledge and skills in this area will improve with time.

Exercise 13.14: Cross-Examination Strategies

Julio Stalking Wolf, a social worker with the Astewaubanon County Community Action Agency (ACCAA), is testifying in a civil court case. His agency received a grant that another agency had applied for, but did not receive. The other agency sued both the ACCAA and the foundation that provided the grant. The opposing attorney has asked a series of questions suggesting that Julio is "just a social worker" with a BSW degree who lacks the experience to manage this grant. She says that Julio's agency got the grant only because his wife works at the foundation. Shaken by his experience, Julio talks with you about what happened in court.

How would you explain what the opposing counsel was trying to do and why she used these strategies?

Chapter 14
Developing and Managing Agency Resources

I. **Introduction**

II. **Working with the Media**

    A.   Highlight 14.1 The Media's Influence

    B.   General guidelines for using the media

          1.   Maintain ongoing relationships with media personnel

          2.   Nurture a variety of contacts within the media

          3.   If you happen to be a local expert on a subject, let the media know this

          4.   Make sure you have sanction, or permission, to speak for your agency

          5.   Make it easy for the media representatives to contact you

          6.   Learn the media's time schedules

          7.   Avoid playing favorites among the news media

          8.   Recognize that the media can and do make mistakes

          9.   Don't be disappointed if a story you hoped would appear does not

          10.   Remember that anything you say to the media can, and often does, end up in print

    C.   Contacts with the media

          1.   The media may contact you

          2.   You can call the media yourself and explain that you have what you believe is a newsworthy item

          3.   You may contact the media through a news release

          4.   Highlight 14.2: Example of a News Release

    D.   Media interviews

E.   Other media communications

    1.   Letters to the editor

    2.   Editorials

    3.   Highlight 14.3: Example of a Newspaper Editorial

III.   Using Technology in Your Agency

A.   Understanding computer hardware

B.   Understanding the software

    1.   Database software allows us to maintain extensive records and retrieve that data quickly

    2.   Spreadsheets allow us to calculate and maintain various kinds of financial or numerical information

    3.   Figure 14.1: Information in a Database

    4.   Figure 14.2: A Spreadsheet

C.   Agency software usage

    1.   Management information systems (MIS)—methods for gathering, analyzing, and evaluating data in an agency or organization

    2.   Highlight 14.4: Management Information Systems

D.   Using the Internet

    1.   Increasingly, social workers are using the Internet for many purposes

    2.   Figure 14.3: Other Potential Online Resources

E.   General observations about computers

IV.   Fund-Raising

A.   Highlight 14.5: Fund-Raising

B.   Sources of funds

    1.   Individual donors

        a.   Benefits

        b.   Benefit variations

        c.   Direct solicitation

b. Problems with proposals

    1) The proposal was poorly written

    2) The competence of those who would carry out the proposal was not clearly documented

    3) Inadequate planning was evident in the application

    4) The application itself was not carefully prepared

    5) The proposal was good but needed revisions, and there was insufficient time to modify it

    6) The problem being addressed is not significant

    7) The proposal does not make clear how funds will be used

    8) The means proposed for dealing with a problem don't make sense

    9) Objectives cannot be adequately assessed

    10) The grant seeker has no past record of dealing with the proposed problem

    11) Human subject concerns have not been addressed

3. Kinds of grant and contract proposals

    a. Program proposals—designed to provide a particular service to a particular size system

    b. Research proposals—typically involve studying a particular problem or testing a specific intervention approach

    c. Training proposals—requests for funds to train or educate a specific group

    d. Planning proposals—designed to allow an organization or agency to plan for a new program

    e. Technical assistance proposals—provide for specialized help, allowing organizations or individuals to carry out a program

    f. Contract for services—is simply an agreement between two agencies or organizations for one to provide services to be paid for by the other

4.	Parts of a grant proposal

    a.	Cover page

        1)	Cover page should include information about the agency and persons who are applying for the grant; the subject of the proposal; the starting and ending times for the project and the money requested; and the date of application

        2)	Highlight 14.8: Example of a Cover Page

    b.	Table of contents—a separate page identifying each distinct section of the proposal

    c.	Abstract or summary

        1)	A 200- to 300-word summary makes it easier for the reader to get a quick overview of the proposal

        2)	Complete this portion only after the rest of the document has been finished

        3)	Highlight 14.9: Example of a Summary or Abstract

    d.	Narrative section

        1)	Statement of the problem

            a)	This should not only summarize the issue being addressed but also identify causative factors and past efforts to solve the identified difficulty

            b)	Highlight 14.10: Example of a Problem Statement of a Grant Application

        2)	Goals and objectives

            a)	These are the end products of your grant project

            b)	Highlight 14.11: Example of Goals and Objectives

            c)	Outcome objectives—show what the result will be of our change efforts

            d)	Process objectives—describe the steps you will take to accomplish the outcome objectives

3) Methods

    a) These are the activities you will use to accomplish your objectives

    b) Highlight 14.12: Example of a Description of the Method

4) Evaluation

    a) The evaluation section requires that you think carefully about your ultimate goals and exactly how you will prove that you have been successful

    b) Specify the purpose of the evaluation

    c) Specify the timetable for data collection

    d) Specify what happens when the grant period is over and the money is gone

    e) Highlight 14.13: Example of an Evaluation Section

5) Bibliography

    a) List the references to which you referred in your proposal

    b) Highlight 14.14 Example of a Bibliography

e. Budget section

1) Line-item budget (the most common type for proposals)—identifies personnel costs, operating costs, travel, and capital costs

2) Highlight 14.15: Example of a Line-Item Budget

3) Functional (program) budgets—depict costs based upon specific proposed program elements or functions

4) Highlight 14.16: Example of a Functional or Program Budget for a Peer Counselor and Drug Education Program

5) Highlight 14.17: Example of Allocating Time and Space Costs

6) Highlight 14.18: Example of a Budget Narrative

f. Credentials of staff—describe the credentials of staff members carrying out the activities proposed in the grant

g. Certification of compliance—if required, add a section discussing compliance with civil rights laws and protections for human subjects

h. Cost sharing, matching funds, and indirect costs

    1) Cost sharing—an arrangement whereby both the agency receiving the grant and the organization dispensing the grant contribute to the proposed budget

        a) Indirect costs—often referred to as overhead, they compensate your agency for its expenses in operating the grant activity

        b) Matching funds (cost-sharing grants)—assume that the receiving organization will contribute part of the total project costs

            (1) Hard match—actual cash

            (2) Soft match—allows an agency to provide its share of the costs through contributed services or activities (sometimes referred to as in-kind contributions)

    3) Figure 14.6: Calculating Soft Match

i. Agency or institutional endorsements—includes a signature page for executives of the receiving agency

D. Post-application phase

    1. Positive factors in determining whether an agency receives grant funds or not

        a. Shows a cost-effective operation

        b. Supports other organizations in the community

        c. Reflects cultural sensitivity and diversity

        d. Focuses on primary prevention of the problem

        e. Has a proven track record

        f. Establishes new, innovative programs

        g. Receives funding from other sources

        h. Has a previous relationship with the foundation

        i. Has a reputation that is not too radical

        j. Has a competent and professionally trained staff

2.   When funding is less than requested—generally requires major rethinking about whether the project is workable with the smaller amount

3.   When the grant/contract runs out—you must plan either to continue the program by finding other sources of funds or to terminate it

Experiential Exercises and Classroom Simulations

Exercise 14.1: Working With the Media

A.   Brief Description
Students consider the ways in which the media may be useful or harmful to an agency.

B.   Objectives
Students will:
1.   Recognize the value of the media to an agency.
2.   Examine potential problems from using the media.

C.   Procedure
1.   Divide class into small groups of four to six students.
2.   Ask groups to address the questions shown in the box.
3.   Have each group report their responses to the questions to the entire class.

D.   Instructions for Students
Within small groups respond to the two questions shown in the box below. When requested by the instructor, share your responses with the rest of the class.

Using the Media

1.   Identify at least two ways in which the media can assist your agency in accomplishing its mission.

2.   In a proposed letter to the editor of the newspaper a colleague says he believes that the Mayor is taking money earmarked for your agency and using it to conduct his re-election campaign. What would you advise your colleague about his letter and why?

E.   Commentary
The exercise can be completed with the entire class. It is also possible to construct other scenarios for students to consider.

Exercise 14.2: Agency Technology

A.   Brief Description
Students consider some important considerations in using technology in an agency setting.

B.   Objectives
Students will:
1.   Differentiate among different technological tools used in an agency.
2.   Recognize differences among software programs in use within agencies.

C.   Procedures
       1.   Use this exercise with the entire class rather than with small groups.
       2.   Ask students to jot down the answers to each question as you go through each of them.
             After students have had time to go through each question, open the class to a discussion
             of each item.

Agency Technology

1.   What determines the type of storage system you will need in a computer zip drive, tape
      back-up, etc.?

2.   What is the purpose of a modem?

3.   What is the difference between a spreadsheet program and a database program? How
      might each be used by a social agency?

D.   Instructions for Students
       Not applicable.

E.   Commentary
       Other questions may be added to the list of possible topics to be discussed.

Exercise 14.3: Recognizing Media Coverage

Read your local newspaper for three days, and look for examples of media coverage of human services
organizations/issues. Explain how the articles reflect positively or negatively on the organization/issues

Guidelines for Working with the Media

Obviously, you will be most effective if you have a continuing relationship with media
representatives. Calling a reporter cold without a prior relationship is less effective than contacting
someone with whom you have regularly worked. You can develop this ongoing relationship by
remembering that the media are interested in news. If an event isn't newsworthy, it's not likely to be
reported in print or over the air. Providing story ideas to your media contacts is a good way to build
relationships. Tell them about the opening of a new facility or the launching of a particularly unique
treatment program.

Build contacts with multiple forms of media and a variety of representatives. Perhaps your
newspaper is not interested in a given story, but a television station might be. A call-in radio show could
invite you or a colleague to talk about your program on the air. Each media outlet has its own limitations
and strengths, and a 30-second television news item may lead to more extensive coverage in other media.

Facilitate contacts with members of the media by letting them know how to reach you. Give
them home and office numbers and the names of others who can be of assistance. Remember, reporters
have to have something to report and usually that something comes from other people. Learn the various
schedules under which the media operate. An important piece of news that reaches a given media outlet
after its deadline is useless.

Avoid playing favorites with the media. If the newspaper finds out about something the
television station has already covered, its reporters may wonder why you favored the TV. Unless you are
giving an exclusive interview (a permissible exception), treat all of the media with the same degree of
respect and consideration.

Recognize that the media make mistakes. Asking a newspaper or radio station to publish or air a correction requires great tact and should be used only in the case of major errors. For instance, it's far less important that they misspelled (or mispronounced) your last name than it would be if they garbled the name of your agency. Whenever you can, praise reporters who covered a story, and let them know you appreciated their help.

Realize that your story may never see the light of day. Editors make the final decision on what gets in the paper or on the air. A good man-bites-dog story may preempt your article. Reporters don't like to see this happen any more than you do so just let it go.

Bear in mind that media representatives tend to print or publish what they choose, so if you say something off-the-record, you may see it in print anyway. Reporters operate under a different set of obligations and with a different mission than social workers. Accept this as a cost of doing business.

Never forget your place in the agency. Unless you have been told specifically to speak for your agency, be careful. Talk with your supervisor before agreeing to appear on the 6:00 p.m. news to discuss your agency's manner of dealing with a particular issue. Failure to heed this warning can leave you with serious tooth marks on the rearmost portion of your anatomy.

Exercise 14.4: Interview a Reporter

Set up an appointment to talk with a news reporter for a local radio station, television station, or newspaper. Focus on the following topics:

1.   How are decisions made about what stories to cover?

2.   What can a worker in an agency do to help a reporter cover a story?

3.   What schedule and deadlines does the reporter work under?

4.   What are the primary sources of information used by the reporter in covering a story?

Contacting the Media

There are generally three ways to get in contact with the media.
1.   The media may contact you if they're pursuing a story and think you might be of assistance.
2.   You can contact the media yourself if you have a newsworthy item. In this case, it helps to have some familiarity with local reporters for the various media, but if you haven't established such relationships, you'll have to start from scratch. If you are right in your appraisal of the information's importance, reporters will readily agree to talk with you.
3.   You can issue a news release—a written communication designed to solicit media interest in a story connected with your agency or organization. A sample news release is shown below.

Fremont Street Neighborhood Association
1234 Fremont Street
South Swampland, Missouri 65803
417 863-1000

For Immediate Release:
  Neighborhood Association Pushes City for Action
  South Swampland, MO—August 1, 2005
    The Fremont Street Neighborhood Association has filed suit against the City
    of South Swampland for failing to protect adequately children walking to
    school along East Doyle Avenue. Association president Diane Chambers
    said that two children were hurt in drive-by shootings during the past four
    weeks while the city does nothing about the problem. The Neighborhood
    Association Board of Directors voted yesterday to sue in Circuit Court,
    charging the Mayor and Police Chief with discrimination against the
    predominantly African-American neighborhood along Fremont Street. The
    association is calling for increased police patrols and arrests of the gang
    members who frequent the area brandishing weapons and selling drugs to
    children. They also demand the city close the south end of Fremont Street
    to prevent drivers from racing down the street. "The city's failure to take
    action to alleviate the problem left us with no choice" said Chambers. "We
    are also considering filing a discrimination complaint with the state office of
    civil rights" she said. Chambers said a rally is scheduled for 10:00 A.M.
    Monday to draw attention to the problem. Following the rally, former
    Fremont Street resident and professional ballplayer Sam Malone will hold a
    news conference along with Association officers.

  For further information contact Diane Chambers 863-1000 or 883-5060.
                                 ###

News releases should always be typed and double spaced, with margins of at least one and one-half
inches all around. It is recommended that they not exceed one page in length.

Exercise 14.5: Writing a News Release

One of your new tasks is assisting the agency director in working with the media. She asks you to
prepare a hypothetical news release to test your media savvy. This news release will announce the
opening of a new homeless shelter providing educational services for both adults (job readiness skills)
and children (elementary and high school subjects). The director tells you to use your imagination in
writing the release. Use the example in highlight 14.1 as an example, and pay attention to the
requirements for typing, spacing, margins, and length.

Media Interviews

  Being interviewed by the media can be fun. You're in the spotlight for a while and it feels good—but
don't forget the purpose of the interview. You have something newsworthy to say and reporters want to
capture it in a fashion that meets their organization's needs. Prepare for the interview by recalling the
different needs of print and air media. Interviews with a print reporter can last as long as an hour, but
covering the same topic with a television reporter may take no more than 10 minutes—and only about 30
seconds will be aired. Prepare yourself for this by thinking about how best to convey the important

information you have to share. For television interviews, consider "sound bites," short succinct points that the media are likely to use on the air.

Recognize that reporters are paid to probe and ask tough questions. Don't get defensive and don't be afraid to say you don't have an answer. Offer to get further information if appropriate. Be cooperative, credible, and helpful, and you'll be developing contacts you can talk to in the future.

Exercise 14.6: Preparing Sound Bites

A local television reporter has decided to interview you further about the news release you prepared above. Remember that the broadcast media tend to prefer comments that are short and to the point. Write two sound bites that take no more than 15 seconds to say and that convey key ideas about the program described in your news release.

1.

2.

Letters to the Editor

Print media normally have a letters-to-the-editor section in which individuals can express opinions or inform the public, as the paper itself does in its editorials. Use this method whenever necessary but always pay attention to the limitations and guidelines established by the publication, including spacing, length of letter, anonymity rules, and possible editing. Short letters are more likely to be published without editing. Expect long letters to be edited.

Don't libel anyone by making defamatory statements. Neither you nor the paper wants to be sued. If you're expressing an opinion, state it as such.

Generally, letters to the editor should be related to something that has appeared in the paper. You may be able to get the editors to write an editorial supporting your plan or program. You'll have to approach the editor or editorial board directly about this, but it's worth the effort because the newspaper's opinion on a topic probably carries some weight with the public.

Exercise 14.7: Draft a Letter to the Editor

Prepare a letter to be sent to the editorial page of your local newspaper. Express your opinion on a topic that was covered in the paper during the last week. Turn in your letter and the original article or news item to which your letter relates.

Agency Technology

A variety of technological inventions are used in the average social agency. These range from fax machines to voice mail, dictation equipment, and computers. Each is a tool designed to assist us in doing our job. Of all of them however, the computer has perhaps had the greatest impact on everyday operations. In the following section we will discuss computer hardware and software, and their use in the typical agency.

Computer Hardware

Most of us know something about computers. Although our VCR at home may still blink "12:00," we probably understand something about computers because of experiences in high school and/or college. The personal computer found in most agencies has three to four main electronic components.

The central processing unit (CPU) is the internal storage and processing/control system for the computer—the "box" containing the memory chips used to store data. Two primary operating systems-- IBM-compatible or DOS machines, and the less common Apple computers—are found in most personal computers today. Because they have far more business users, we will focus most of our attention in this section on DOS machines.

A number of characteristics affect the performance of the computer's CPU, including the main operating chip and the speed at which it operates. Most computers for sale in the late 1990s contain a CPU using what is known as a Pentium chip. The speed of the operating system is usually measured in megahertz with newer machines running at 90 megahertz or more.

Another factor affecting performance is the random access—or short-term—memory (RAM) of the unit. It is common today to see computers with 16 megabytes of RAM, and even those newer machines will be out of date very soon.

Each computer has one or more data-storage devices including a hard drive. The hard drive allows permanent storage of data, and its capacity is measured in megabytes or gigabytes. A byte equals a character, a megabyte a million characters, and a gigabyte a billion characters. For comparison purposes, one megabyte equals about 775 pages of double-spaced text. The hard drive is a small disk similar to a compact disk. Typical machines also have a floppy drive that can be used to store data on disks. The most recent floppy disks are about 3 inches square and hold about 1.44 megabytes of data. Like the hard disk, the floppy disk retains its memory after the machine is turned off.

To display data, each computer uses a monitor, a small television-like screen. These screens, like TV sets, come in different sizes, usually 14-17 inches. Color monitors are common, but monochrome monitors are still in use.

Each computer also has a keyboard from which to operate the CPU. The keyboard typically resembles a typewriter although more recent designs vary the layout somewhat. In addition to the standard typewriter keys, keyboards have special function keys—usually at the top of the keyboard—that operate certain software programs. A separate number pad similar to a calculator is located on the right-hand side of the keyboard.

Getting data out of the computer is simple if the machine is hooked to a printer. Printers allow the user to print whatever is on the computer screen and in its memory. Printers come in various types from dot matrix machines to laser and ink-jet units. Each type of printer offers a variety of options and speeds.

Many machines today are equipped with modems, devices used to exchange data with other computers. "Surfing the Internet" from your computer is not possible without a modem. The speed of a modem determines how fast data can be transferred from one computer to another.

Exercise 14.8: Understand the Hardware

If you have a computer at home, describe its hardware in detail, including the characteristics of the CPU, monitor, keyboard, modem, and other devices. If you do not have your own equipment, go to the computer laboratory of your college or university. Interview the lab monitor/director to learn about the equipment in the lab, and use the lab information to complete this exercise.

Computer Software

Without software, the computer makes a great boat anchor or doorstop. It is the software that allows us to do word processing, create data bases, and keep financial records. Software can serve one or multiple purposes. Integrated software packages, for example, might include word processing, spreadsheets for financial records, and a database for keeping track of names, address, and the like. Databases are particularly useful for maintaining large accumulations of information, for instance, all clients seen by an agency, their addresses, demographic information, records of worker-client contacts, and more. Look at the sample database below.

Last Name	First Name	Birthday	Spouse	Number of Children
Batchelor	Stephanie	06/12/1950	Bryan	1
Blucher	Sahid	11/07/1949		
Clark	Raymond	08/09/1965		2
Delta	Alexis	09/08/1956	Max	3
Forrest	Richard	10/08/1943	Margaret	
Hobart	Corey	02/06/1970	Lee	
Layton	Leland	12/05/1962		1
Mansard	Rachel	03/10/1965	Leon	4
Martino	Kair	04/06/1939		
Rutondo	Lupe	04/01/1945		
Smith	Fred	05/01/1967		
Trump	Laurie	02/22/1969	Mort	
Wolk	Frank	06/08/1956	Kate	5
Zorro	Ivana	01/07/1960	Niklaus	2

Spreadsheets are used primarily for accounting purposes. Each spreadsheet is a sort of electronic ledger which allows us to keep track of expenditures by category. For example, an agency director might want to know how much was paid for electricity in the agency as a prelude to considering more energy-efficient lighting. A small spreadsheet is displayed below.

Date	Item	Cost	Category
1-3-98	Postage	14.56	O1
1-5-98	Desk	456.00	E3
1-5-98	Chair	134.00	E3
1-7-98	Paper	95.66	S2
Total		**700.22**	

Spreadsheets can have many more columns and rows depending on what financial information you are keeping track of. Spreadsheets allow you to build formulas and automatically recalculate totals. The categories are simply shorthand ways of identifying expenditures by type.

Agencies use many types of software. For example, there are software packages that allow clients to input their social histories or to take certain psychological tests. Other software is used by workers to maintain case notes. Computer software programs can even identify likely agencies to which a client might be referred or discover whether a client qualifies for a particular public assistance program.

Agencies use computers as part of their management information system (MIS) which gathers, organizes, and evaluates data such as demographic characteristics of clients served, primary problems for which clients sought help, and the average number of service hours provided by workers. The MIS can also be used to maintain records on agency personnel and identify gaps in the training or experience of current personnel. Frequently, computers in an agency are networked so that information can be shared by various departments. Thus, a secretary typing a letter, the bookkeeper preparing a bill, and the worker entering case notes may all simultaneously have access to a client's record. Networked computers allow electronic mail (e-mail) to be sent within the agency.

Of course, computers can be used in macro practice outside agencies. Software can track donations for a political candidate or a new domestic abuse shelter. Computers can maintain a database of all neighborhood residents involved in the neighborhood watch program. More sophisticated software can identity pockets of poverty in a community by compiling data on home addresses of children receiving free school lunches. Criminal victimization information can be computerized to pinpoint neighborhoods with high crime rates.

Desktop publishing software can produce brochures and flyers about a program, advertise a new service or a public meeting, or produce other communications. This software rivals in quality anything produced by professional print shops, so anyone with a computer can create a variety of impressive documents.

On the other hand, computers cause a variety of headaches—as anyone knows who's life has been snarled in a computerized error. Computer problems are difficult to correct because the machines do exactly what you tell them to do. If you make a mistake entering data, the machine doesn't know that. Learning how to effectively use a computer is not difficult, but it is time consuming. Classes are available at every level from post-technical school to university. Most common programs have workbooks and other aids available for purchase at any bookstore. Learning to use a computer can enhance your skill as a social worker. It can also teach you humility.

Exercise 14.9: What Software Is Used?

Interview the administrative assistant or other official who oversees computer use in a local human services agency. If you are currently in field placement, use your own agency. If not, make a telephone appointment to talk about computer use in another agency of your choosing. Describe what kinds of software programs are employed and for what purposes. Be specific in asking about brands and other details.

Fundraising

Both public and private (for-profit and not-for-profit) agencies are deeply involved in fundraising. The need for funds to maintain existing programs, develop new initiatives, and serve different clienteles, places a continuing burden on social agencies. Yet few social workers begin their careers with the goal of becoming fund-raisers. We may not perceive it as a social work function, may lack confidence in our ability to raise money, or may lack the training or experience for this task. In addition to fees paid by clients, there are at least four major sources of funding used in human services:

- The first is public or tax dollars. These funds go to public agencies and, indirectly, to private agencies which have contracts with the public agency. The contracts usually stipulate that the private agency will provide a service the public agency can't or prefers not to offer.
- These contracts represent a second major source of funding for many agencies.
- Grants are a third source. Unlike contracts—which are essentially agreements between two agencies—grants may be considered "free" money, usually to be used for one-time projects. This money supply ends once the project is completed or the program established.
- The fourth source of money is donations and gifts, which often come with fewer restrictions than grants and contracts. Donations and gifts may be received from foundations, individual or corporate donors, benefits, and dues from organizational members. Donations from individuals can be gathered in various ways. Some agencies hold raffles using donated prizes or gifts. Others sponsor events such as concerts, carnivals, or dinners to raise money. Some solicit donors directly for gifts or invite them to benefits. Benefits are events held for the specific purpose of raising money for a particular cause. Musicians and performers, for example, have held benefits to help farmers, children, and others. A sporting event may be held with proceeds going to a given charity. Benefits can include a giant garage sale, an auction, or a pancake dinner, among other possibilities. Benefits work best when the event is attractive enough to draw people and the cost-benefit ratio is high. Some benefits become annual affairs and provide a substantial amount of money for an agency or organization. One family service agency conducts a celebrity auction each year, auctioning items signed or donated by famous athletes, movie stars, and other public figures.

Preparing for benefits takes careful planning. Poor attendance, cost overruns, or bad weather can end up *costing* the agency money. Benefit organizers must advertise the event, sell tickets, arrange actual activities (dance, auction, golf tournament), and estimate costs and revenues. Anyone who contributed money or time to the benefit must be acknowledged.

The amount of money to be raised from a benefit is generally limited. It is usually not possible to raise the hundreds of thousands of dollars needed to operate an agency year round. Regardless of how much is raised, however, the funds must be accounted for. A local service organization contracted with a professional fundraising firm to operate its carnival benefit. When it was all over, the vast majority of the $80,000-90,000 raised ended up in the pocket of the fundraising firm, which charged for its consultative services and expenses.

Direct solicitation of money is another option. Private individuals can be asked to give money for agency operating funds or to pay for a special project. The amount you ask for depends a great deal on the resources of the donor. If you can identify larger donors, you can amass the same amount of money and approach fewer people. For example, you could ask 200 people to give $10 each, or ask four people to give $500 each.

Potential donors can be gleaned from newspapers, membership lists of professional or business organizations, newsletters of colleges and universities, from other supporters, and from other organizations. Once you identify a potential donor, make an appointment, prepare your pitch, and show up on time. Explain why this donor should want to support your organization or project. Connect the donor's interests with those of your project. Be certain to accept and collect any donation immediately. Promises to give at a later date are often forgotten.

Individuals are not the only source of donations. Corporations routinely donate money, services, and goods to charities. For example, a fast food restaurant may donate a portion of a given day's revenue to a daycare center. Other corporations might donate vehicles, office furniture, computers, and/or cash. Another source of potential gift giving is community groups, organizations, and associations, including social, fraternal, and professional groups—Rotary, Kiwanis, Junior League, etc. A list of these groups is usually available at the public library or from the local Chamber of Commerce. Offer to speak about your agency at one of the group's meetings. Prepare a written request for assistance to give to the group's board of directors or finance committee. Explain the importance of the project to be supported and ask for their help. If money is not needed, ask for their help on a specific project such as constructing a playground for an inner city neighborhood. Donations of labor can be very helpful and give people a sense of involvement in the agency's work.

You can also raise funds by establishing an organization to which members pay dues. The Society of Balding Middle Aged Men may be just the ticket. Once such an organization is created, it can devote itself to bettering the life in your community. Dues paid by members can be spent on such improvements as removal of mirrors from public washrooms (The mirrors just remind us about Mother Nature's ravages.) Americans are "joiners." Most of us belong to multiple groups or organizations, so establishing an organization is not a farfetched idea, but the decision to start a group usually arises from a clearly identified goal. Thus, the Southlake Refuse Group was formed to oppose creation of a landfill in the neighborhood. Money raised from member dues was used to oppose landfill legislation aimed at Southlake. Sometimes it is easier to ask people to join a group whose purpose they agree with than it is to ask them to donate money. Belonging to a group is a way of feeling connected and the dues raised are less restricted than other kinds of donations. Dues can be spent on anything the organization's leadership and members think is appropriate. The group is usually not accountable to others. Realistically, the amount of money that can be raised through membership groups is limited unless you have a national organization with hundreds of thousands or millions of members.

Money can also be raised through mailings and telephone solicitations, but this is difficult because you are often calling or contacting people with no predisposition to contribute to your cause. It's easier if such solicitations are directed at people with some connection to your group. Obviously, it's much easier for a college to raise funds with phone calls or letters to alumni than with calls to people unaffiliated with the school. Both written and verbal solicitations must be professionally done, well rehearsed, and free of errors in grammar and usage. Nothing loses a donor faster than a poorly prepared pitch or an error-filled letter or brochure.

Using the same agency you used above—or a different one if you prefer—interview the director, deputy director, or other supervisor about the various fundraising approaches the agency employs. (This interview can be conducted in person or over the phone.) Explain that this is a class assignment. Among the questions you will need to ask are:

1.   Does the agency receive tax dollars either directly or indirectly?

2.   Does the agency have any contracts for services with other agencies?

3.   Is the agency currently receiving any grant monies and for what purposes?

4.   Has the agency held or participated in any benefits designed to raise funds?

5.   Has the agency received any donations of money, goods, or services from individuals, groups, or businesses?

6.   Does the agency charge fees for providing services to clients?

Grants and Contracts

We have already mentioned grants and contracts as important sources of funding for human services programs. Grants and contracts are somewhat similar in that both are transfers of assets from one body to another, and both usually require the submission of a written proposal outlining what is to be done with the money. A reviewing agency can approve the grant or contract as written, require modifications in the proposal, and/or supply only a portion of the funds requested. In addition, the granting/contracting agency can simply say no to the request for financial assistance.

Finding Grants

There are several primary sources of grants and/or contracts.
1.   Every level of government from local to national provides grants and contracts.
2.   Many foundations and private organizations are established especially for such purposes. The foundation's money often comes directly or indirectly from a business or other commercial interest.
3.   Some grant money comes directly from companies.

Each of these sources offers both advantages and disadvantages. Government grants and contracts are more restrictive because this is taxpayers' money. Foundations and businesses may be more willing to fund untested but promising ideas. Lists of non-governmental grant sources can be found in such library documents as *The Foundation Directory* and the *Annual Register of Grant Support*. Both publications contain substantial information for anyone seeking information about types of programs funded, typical size of grants, and deadlines for submitting proposals. Other periodicals such as the *Foundation News* and the *Foundation Center Information Quarterly* offer additional help.

Carefully review the interests of a particular foundation to be sure you're not wasting your time by writing them. Writing to a foundation that primarily supports research on the octopus is unlikely to be productive unless you're testing new ways to hug children.

Foundation grants vary in size depending upon the assets of the particular foundation. Some fund new programs, and others only established ones. Some will pay for capital items such as computers, furniture, or a building, but most do not wish to spend money on such items. A given foundation may provide grants on a national basis while another organization may fund only projects in a given state or region. If grant writing becomes a major portion of your job, consider subscribing to such services as the Taft Information System or the Foundation Research Service. Government grants are often identified in the *Federal Register* and the Catalog *of Domestic Assistance*. For state-level grants, check *The State Contract Register*. These sources describe a very large array of possible grantors and announce Requests for Proposals (RFP). The RFP lists the programs a given governmental unit supports, describes the dollar amount, and specifies the appropriate deadline for submission of an application.

Grants from businesses or corporations are usually, but not always, given through a specific charitable division, typically to not-for-profit agencies. Their proposal review process is not much different from that of other potential sources. As might be expected, many businesses provide grants in areas directly related to their own industry or area of commerce. There is always some risk in accepting funding from an organization with a particular agenda, because the money may come with subtle or not-so-subtle pressure to reflect favorably on the granting agency.

Exercise 14.11: Look It Up

Consult one or more of the directories/resources mentioned above. These will probably be found in your college or university library. Locate one granting agency with which you share an interest, maybe an agency that funds human services programs or one that supports some highly specialized cause.

1.   Provide the agency's name and address and identify the kinds of programs/ideas it supports.

2.   What information, if any, is available about grant application deadlines?

3.   List any other information you might need to prepare a grant request to this agency.

Thinking about a Grant?

If you have a particular idea you'd like to explore, send a letter of intent to the agency or organization from which you seek assistance. Most funding organizations will at least respond to your idea, and some may even ask to talk with you further about your ideas. Obviously, the larger the foundation, the greater the likelihood that it can provide some assistance and early feedback. As part of the review process for a grant application, some private foundations and corporations will expect to make a site visit to your agency. This may seem odd, but it beats the heck out of writing a hundred-page proposal when ten pages and a site visit will suffice.

Applying for a Grant

There are generally three steps in the grant application process. In the pre-application phase, you identify potential grantors. Use one or more of the reference documents mentioned earlier, and at the same time keep your eyes and ears open for possible funding sources. Discard those possibilities that offer remote or nonexistent chances of funding your project or whose restrictions are not acceptable. You will have made preliminary contact with the likely grantors, discussed deadlines, and reviewed the funding body's expectations and interests, thereby obtaining an appreciation for the kind of proposal the body seeks, its length, and any other significant information.

In the application phase, you prepare a draft of your proposal containing a statement of intent, an explanation of why the project is worthy of funding, a presentation of the problem it addresses, and specifics about who will do what, when, and why. The potential recipient of the grant will probably be your agency, since grants are rarely given to individuals. This means that you will need to fully discuss the proposal with your supervisor and probably with someone higher in the organization. A grant application (or at least the agreement to accept a grant) probably requires permission from the agency's board of directors. The proposal will describe who will administer the grant and outline that person's experience in such endeavors. It will indicate the facilities and staff required to carry out the project. Any contributions and assistance to be provided by your own agency will be listed. Grantors rarely like to fund projects unless the receiving agency provides a significant contribution to the overall effort. This contribution may be in the form of cash, services (such as typing and computer data entry), supervision of workers, and equipment. A grant proposal may also require evidence that no one will be hurt by participating in the project. Human subjects must be protected from harm, records from the project may need to be kept for a number of years to protect the identity of participants, and the proposal should indicate how these steps will be accomplished.

The greater the attention you give to this step, the less likely you are to stumble later on. Details worked out in advance will not slow the project down once money is available.

Writing the Proposal

Writing the actual proposal (in the application phase) means attending to several factors. Your proposal should reflect "a good idea" that the funding agency can support. The problem addressed by the proposal must be important enough to justify spending scarce resources. The soundness of the idea is perhaps the most important consideration. Of course, the proposal must be well written with no grammar or other English usage problems. The track record—or at least a clear indication of professional competence—of those who will carry out the project must be evident. Include all sections of the proposal, including evaluation. Identify measurable objectives. Describe the actual services to be provided. The budget must be clearly indicated and accompanied by an appropriate narrative describing any unusual expenses in detail. Consider whether the objectives of your proposal justify the amount of money you have requested. The length of your proposal can vary depending upon the granting agency's expectations. Some want long detailed proposals while others prefer that you keep to just a few pages. Deadlines must be observed. Granting agencies are not impressed when your proposal arrives a week late.

Kinds of Proposals

There are several typical kinds of grant proposals.

- Program proposals suggest a particular service to a specific group, such as the unemployed. A new job training program for public assistance clients would be an example.
- Research proposals seek funding to study a given problem or to test a new intervention, such as a study of the educational problems of homeless children.
- Training proposals are requests for funds to train or educate a given population—perhaps to train all agency staff to better serve Hispanic clients.
- Planning proposals request funds for planning new services or programs. (Planning proposals may be followed by a program proposal after the planning phase is completed.)
- A proposal for technical assistance seeks specialized help to assist an agency that needs skills or information not ordinarily available. An agency might seek a technical assistance grant to hire a specialist who could design an intensive in-home child abuse prevention program. Such specialized assistance is sought because the agency has no regular staff with that capability.
- A contract for service—although not exactly a grant proposal—is a written agreement between two or more organizations specifying that one will provide a given service and that the other will pay for that service.

Contents of a Grant Proposal

The several standard components of a grant proposal are identified below:

1. A cover page or a letter should accompany each proposal. Often the granting agency will provide a cover sheet for you to fill in with the appropriate data. If none is provided, your cover sheet should briefly state the title of the proposal and the names, addresses, and phone numbers of both the prospective granting agency and your agency. The subject of the proposal should also be listed, along with the starting and ending dates of the project and the amount of money requested.
2. A table of contents helps readers locate information easily.
3. An abstract or summary of the proposal should state in 200-300 words the objectives, methods, results, and value of your proposal. The abstract is very important. In fact, some granting agencies make their decisions based largely on the quality of this document.

4.	The narrative section of the grant describes the problem and your proposed solution. Goals and objectives should be included here, along with the methods to be employed and an evaluation component. A grantor wants to know that you fully understand the problem and expects to see statistics, demographic data, and other references indicating your knowledge of the territory. Your goals and objectives should be clear, reasonable, measurable, and worthwhile. Objectives may include outcome-oriented items such as a decrease in cases of reported child abuse or process objectives that indicate the steps you will take to achieve your outcome objectives. The methods section of the narrative will detail how you and your agency intend to accomplish the objectives. Will you begin a new program, expand an existing one, or undertake a time-limited project? Will new staff be needed, job descriptions created or revised, or existing staff trained in new procedures? Carefully consider the evaluation portion of the narrative. Are your objectives measurable? Who will conduct the evaluation—an internal person or an external evaluator? Will you assess outcome objectives, process objectives, or both? Lacking the expertise and time to conduct a thorough evaluation, some grant writers indicate that this portion of the project will be conducted by an outside group. Finally, the narrative should describe your plans after the grant runs out. Will some other body continue funding if the proposal proves successful? Willingness of the receiving agency to pick up the costs for the program after the grant ends increases the likelihood of funding.

5.	A bibliography section should contain the references cited in the proposal.

6.	The budget gives explicit detail, usually in a line-by-line format. That is, each item to be purchased is categorized into such areas as personnel, equipment, supplies and expenses, travel, and evaluation. Many granting agencies have their own forms for listing this information and you should use these. If none is provided, develop your own. The budget should describe what expenses the grant recipient is covering and what funds are being requested from the grantor. You may have to apportion these items to show, for example, that your agency is contributing 10 percent of a supervisor's time and salary. At the same time, 100 percent of a worker's salary will be requested from the grantor. You may even have to apportion such things as space: Maybe 10 percent of the rental costs and utility expenses for that supervisor's office are listed as agency contributions. Often the granting agency requires a contribution from your agency (this contribution is called cost sharing or matching funds) to ensure that your agency is truly committed to the proposal. Cost sharing can allow your agency to contribute hard match (money) or soft match (in-kind contributions). An agency that donates a portion of a supervisor's time to a project is making an in-kind contribution. Budgets should be realistic and understandable. Confusing items or amounts may lead the grantor to conclude that you are not sufficiently honest or competent to be trusted with their money. Remember to include indirect costs—such items as clerical support, operation and maintenance of a building, computer time, and other administrative expenditures. This represents an estimate of the actual time and effort the receiving agency will expend on the grant. Many receiving agencies build indirect costs into a proposal so that a proposal for a $100,000 project may increase to $130,000 when the agency adds its indirect costs. That additional $30,000 will be added to the amount requested from the grantor. The actual percentage of indirect costs charged by the grant recipient or allowed by the grantor can vary widely.

7.	The final portion of the grant application is agency or institutional endorsements, the signatures of appropriate agency executives or others who are accepting responsibility for the grant. Letters of support from other agencies can also accompany the proposal and be included in this section.

Post-Application Phase

Once received, grant applications are reviewed by an individual or a committee empowered to fund the proposal as is, reduce the amount of money given to your agency, or reject the project outright. Once the money runs out, your agency will have to decide whether to continue funding the project at full or reduced amounts, expand the program, or end it. Ideally, the program will have demonstrated its effectiveness and become an ongoing part of the agency.

Staff credentials may need to be included in a separate section if they are not detailed in the narrative. The same is true of information about how the agency will deal with such things as rules governing protection of human subjects, civil rights laws, and similar concerns.

Exercise 14.12: Check It Out

Get your hands on a grant application prepared by an agency, organization, or other group. This could be your placement agency if you are currently in the field, another agency with which you are familiar, or your college or university grants office. It doesn't matter whether the grant application was successful or not, because your purpose is simply to compare the actual grant to the guidelines described in this book. For purposes of the assignment, determine the following:

1. What kind of proposal was this—program, research, training, planning, technical assistance, or contract for service? Explain the reasons for your choice.

2. Which if any of the following sections were included in the proposal: cover page, table of contents, abstract or summary, narrative, budget, budget narrative, bibliography, agency or institutional endorsements?

3. What indirect costs were included in the proposal?

4. How much money was the receiving organization proposing to spend as its portion of the grant (their match)?

5. Was the match in-kind or cash?

6. Are credentials of the staff described in the application?

7. What mention, if any, does the proposal make about protections for human subjects (if such protections would apply)?

8. To what extent are the objectives contained in the proposal clear and measurable?